THE PIRATE KING

The
PIRATE
KING

The Strange Adventures of Henry Avery
and the Birth of the Golden Age of Piracy

SEAN KINGSLEY
and REX COWAN

PEGASUS BOOKS

NEW YORK LONDON

THE PIRATE KING

Pegasus Books, Ltd.
148 West 37th Street, 13th Floor
New York, NY 10018

First Pegasus Books cloth edition April 2024

Interior design by Maria Fernandez

Library of Congress Cataloging-in-Publication Data is available.

ISBN: 978-1-63936-595-1

10 9 8 7 6 5 4 3 2 1

Printed in the United States of America
Distributed by Simon & Schuster
www.pegasusbooks.com

CONTENTS

PART THREE

*If you can finde out a key whereby to picke this locke,
you are able to reade any thinge.*

—Letter from Richard Lawrence to
code breaker John Wallis, 1657

Timeline

1660: Henry Avery—sailor, trader, and pirate king—is born around Bideford and Plymouth, Devon.

1660: Daniel Foe, tradesman and author, is born in the parish of St Giles, Cripplegate, London.

December 1684: Dr. Thomas Tenison, the future archbishop of Canterbury, opens London's first public library (and secret spy factory) in St Martin-in-the-Fields.

July 6, 1685: Defeat of James Scott, the Duke of Monmouth, in the Battle of Sedgemoor, Somerset, while attacking King James II. Daniel Foe, one of his fighters, flees into exile.

April 11, 1689: Dutchman William of Orange and Mary (eldest daughter of King James II) are crowned king and queen of England.

1692: Daniel Foe hunts off the Lizard, Cornwall, for sunken treasure with Joseph Williams, inventor of a diving engine.

1692: Daniel Foe starts working in intelligence for King William III of England.

Summer 1693: Henry Avery signs onto the Spanish Shipping Expedition to fish wrecked treasure in the Americas and sails into La Coruna, northern Spain, as chief mate of the *Dove*.

May 7, 1694: Henry Avery seizes the *Charles II* English frigate in La Coruna, renames it the *Fancy*, and turns to piracy.

August 1694: Nicholas Trott is appointed governor of New Providence, the Bahamas.

1694: *A Copy of Verses Composed by Captain Henry Every, Lately Gone to Sea to Seek His Fortune* is published, supposedly written by the pirate king.

1695: Daniel Foe changes his surname to the fancier-sounding Defoe.

Summer 1695: The *Fancy* takes on supplies at Madagascar; the ship's hull is cleaned of barnacles.

September 1695: In the Indian Ocean, Henry Avery captures the *Fateh Muhammed*, owned by Abdul Ghafur of Surat, India's wealthiest merchant.

September 8, 1695: In the Indian Ocean, Henry Avery seizes the Mughal emperor's *Ganj-i Sawai* (*Gunsway* in English), the greatest pirate treasure ever taken.

September 1695: Samuel Annesley, president of the East India Company's council in Surat, India, and his workers are locked into their factory in revenge for the English plundering the *Gunsway*.

February 1696: English spies foil a plot to assassinate King William III on the outskirts of London when returning from hunting.

April 1, 1696: The *Fancy* pirate ship arrives off New Providence, the Bahamas; Henry Avery changes his name to Henry Bridgeman.

June 1696: Two sloops, with part of the *Fancy*'s pirate crew, land in Dunfanaghy, northern Ireland, and Westport in western Ireland.

July 17, 1696: King William III issues a *Proclamation for Apprehending Pirate Every*.

July 22, 1696: The East India Company publishes *The Companyes Declaration for Apprehending Every & His Ship*.

September 1696: William Kidd arrives in the Americas on the *Adventure Galley* to hunt pirates, only to turn pirate himself.

October 1696: Trial of six of Henry Avery's pirate crew at the Old Bailey, London.

November 25, 1696: Five men from the *Fancy*'s pirate crew are hanged at Execution Dock, Wapping.

Late 1696: Publication of the ballad *Villany Rewarded; or, the Pirates Last Farewel to the World*.

February 1697: John Tyzack gets permission from the Lord Commissioners of the Treasury to search Cornwall for Henry Avery and his pirates' buried treasure.

February 1697: The Lords of the Admiralty send warships to the East Indies and Madagascar in search of the pirate king.

December 1698: A royal pardon is offered to all pirates of the Caribbean—except for Henry Avery.

1700: Robert Davis, Defoe's brother-in-law, invents a new dive engine. Off Bumble Rock, Cornwall, they salvage silver bars from a sunken wreck.

December 27, 1700: "Avery the Pirate" writes a letter from Falmouth, Cornwall, in secret code to the Reverend James Richardson at the library on Orange Street, St Martin-in-the-Fields, London.

February 21, 1702: King William III falls off his horse at Hampton Court and dies.

1702: Cornelius Ffurssen searches for the pirate treasure of the *Fancy* in Cornwall.

March 8, 1702: Queen Anne becomes ruler of England.

December 1702: Daniel Defoe publishes *The Shortest Way with the Dissenters* and is accused of seditious libel. At the Old Bailey, he is fined and sentenced to three days in the stocks.

Late 1703: Daniel Defoe starts spying for Secretary of State Robert Harley and Queen Anne.

September 1706: Defoe and his spies head to Edinburgh to stop Scotland breaking away from the union with England.

May 1, 1707: The Act of Union becomes law. Scotland and England are "United into One Kingdom by the Name of Great Britain."

1708: *Some Memoirs Concerning That Famous Pyrate Capt. Avery* are published.

1709: Adrian van Broeck publishes *The Life and Adventures of Capt. John Avery.*

November 1712: Charles Johnson's play about the pirate king Henry Avery, *The Successful Pyrate*, opens at the Theatre Royal, Drury Lane, London.

July 1713: Queen Anne's War ends after eleven years. Thousands of out-of-work sailors and privateers turn to piracy in the Americas. New Providence, the Bahamas, becomes a notorious pirates republic.

January 1717–November 1718: A "Mr. Ivery" (Avery?) turns up spying in Dunkirk, northern France.

July 1718: Woodes Rogers arrives in New Providence, the Bahamas, to crush the pirates.

1719: John Avery's supposed autobiographical *The King of Pirates: Being an Account of the Famous Enterprises of Captain Avery, the Mock King of Madagascar* is published.

1720: Daniel Defoe publishes *The Life, Adventures and Piracies of the Famous Captain Singleton*, based on the life of Henry Avery.

1724: *A General History of the Pyrates* by Captain Charles Johnson is published, the first pirate bestseller.

April 26, 1731: Daniel Defoe dies in London while hiding from debt collectors.

1779: John Knill, mayor of St Ives in Cornwall, hunts for Henry Avery's lost pirate treasure.

1978: Zélide Cowan discovers the "Avery the Pirate" letter in the Scottish Record Office in Edinburgh.

2021: Metal detectorists in Rhode Island discover silver coins from Yemen and claim they come from Henry Avery's raid on the *Gunsway*.

Preface

Mayhem, mavericks, rollicking humor. Everyone loves pirates, those rogues who gave us Captain Hook in *Peter Pan*, Long John Silver in *Treasure Island*, the *Princess Bride*'s Dread Pirate Roberts, and, the biggest star of all, Captain Jack Sparrow. The $4.5 billion *Pirates of the Caribbean* franchise is an entertainment industry in its own right, from much-cherished movies to rides and spectacles at Disneyland.

Ask almost anyone and they'll tell you it all began with Edward "Blackbeard" Thatch, "Calico" Jack Rackham, "Black Sam" Bellamy, and pals in the Caribbean. Many people are even familiar with their sinful lair, the pirates' republic on the island of New Providence in the Bahamas. There, so the most common take goes, the golden age of piracy began in August 1715 when ships full of desperadoes—mostly bitter Englishmen who lost their jobs as sailors at the end of Queen Anne's War (1702–1713)—started looting the Spanish treasure fleet, and its fourteen million pieces of eight, sunk in a hurricane off eastern Florida. Flush with success and the taste of easy cash, the pirates of the Caribbean were born.[1]

It's a terrific story, and those colorful characters from Blackbeard to Mary Read really did bring mayhem to the high seas. Yet none of it actually began with this cast in 1715. Twenty years earlier, it was another man who lit the fuse and hurled the hand grenade that kick-started the golden age of piracy. Henry Avery was an angry young man who had been messed with one too many times.[2] In May 1694 he stole an English frigate in the port of La Coruna in northern Spain, renamed it the *Fancy*, and headed east.

Not to the Americas. As glittering as they were, the richest plunder in the world was not stowed on Spanish galleons but in the holds of Mughal ships trading between the western Indian port of Surat and Jeddah and Mocha on the Red Sea shores of Saudi Arabia and Yemen. Avery knew what he was doing: Aurangzeb, the emperor of India, was the richest man in the world, his country the wealthiest on earth.

In the fall of 1695, Avery waited at the southern foot of the Red Sea for the Indies' fleet to pass and drop into his clutches. That September he attacked the *Ganj-i-Sawai* (*Gunsway* in English, meaning "exceeding treasure") and helped himself to anywhere between £325,000 and a cool £600,000 of treasure worth a high of $149 million today.[3] The most accurate figure of "fifty-two lakhs of rupees in silver and gold" rounds out to about $108 million.[4] Overnight, Avery was celebrated as the arch-pirate and, most famously, the pirate king. After dividing his spoils among his crew and scattering from the island of New Providence, Avery vanished into thin air to enjoy his ill-gotten loot with his head intact.

The romance surrounding Henry Avery is the mother of all pirate mysteries. What really happened to him? More ballads, pamphlets, and books were written about Avery than any other pirate of the golden age. Some swore he went to ground on the island of Madagascar in East Africa, where he founded a democratic colony for misfits and outsiders, called Libertalia—the original land of the free—that became the political template for the Enlightenment in Europe.[5] Others reckoned he laid low in the hills above southern France, knocking back fine wine. Or maybe he ran off to Dublin, Plymouth, London (in search of his wife), or Scotland (with his quartermaster's wife), or was cheated out of his riches in Bristol?

Only one thing is certain. In the summer of 1696, the pirate king became a ghost. "Avery was never heard from again,"[6] Colin Woodard wrote. "Henry Every, the Arch-Pirate, had disappeared behind the smokescreen of false leads that he had fed his gullible men. He was never seen or heard from again," Frank Sherry agreed.[7] Or so Steven Johnson concluded, "The fog around the birth of that Devonshire sailor is almost as thick as the one that surrounds his death . . . he became a ghost."[8] The missing case of Henry Avery the pirate king has been the most puzzling cold case in pirate history for 327 years. Until now.

On a cold day in 1978, the historian Zélide Cowan was scouring an archive in Scotland for nuggets of information about a Swedish East Indiaman sunk off a tiny island in Orkney. The trawl was not going well when she stumbled across an old letter. It had been misfiled. It shouldn't have been there. As soon as she read its title, penned by "Avery the Pirate" in December 1700, Zélide knew she had stumbled across a once-in-a-lifetime historical treasure. The four pages were written four years after Henry Avery supposedly disappeared. In one stunning document, the pirate king was back from the dead.

For the next decade, Zélide and her wreck-hunting husband, Rex Cowan, tried to make sense of the letter. They visited archive after archive and sent letters to experts. Who wrote the letter, in which town, and where it was heading were clear as day. The great mystery was the content. Why were the lines written in a numeric code? What did they say?

Soon, the next big shipwreck discovery came along needing their total attention. Life left Avery languishing in a dusty file until December 2020, when Sean Kingsley visited Rex in London. Sean was working on a special issue of *Wreckwatch* magazine about pirates. Did Rex know anything about those lovable sea rogues? he innocently asked. Rex, a walking encyclopedia, did and he remembered the excitement of the mysterious letter discovered all those years ago. One chance meeting rolled back the years. Cowan and Kingsley resolved to crack the enigma of the "Avery the Pirate" letter once and for all.

The amazing history that we can now reveal in *The Pirate King* in many ways beggars belief. The web of coincidences is incredible. The letter from 1700 links three of the greatest characters of the age in England by tying Henry Avery to Daniel Defoe, author of *Robinson Crusoe,* and Dr. Thomas Tenison, the archbishop of Canterbury. The following pages are the tale of a lifelong friendship between the man who wrote the first novel, the greatest pirate of them all, the highest churchman in the land, and their unholy alliance to do whatever it took to protect their country from conspiracies and invasions.

You could not make it up. Sometimes truth is stranger than fiction. Take Defoe. To most he is a great author, pure and simple. But writing was just a way to make money. His life's work was much more serious and darker. What you saw with Defoe was a carefully crafted smoke screen. Daniel published *The Life and Strange Surprising Adventures of Robinson Crusoe* as a "true story," as autobiography. It was no such thing—it was a literary hoax. Yet among its exciting pages lurks more than a kernel of truth. The character of Robinson Crusoe was based on the life of Scotsman Alexander Selkirk, who robbed Spanish ships with privateers—legalized pirates—off South America before being castaway on a desert island in the eastern Pacific Ocean after mutinying.[9]

Four and half years later, Selkirk was saved by a ship piloted by William Dampier and captained by Woodes Rogers. In a remarkable web of coincidence and fate, in real life Dampier was a crew member of the same Spanish Shipping Expedition as Avery when he turned pirate in Spain in 1694;[10] Defoe was a lifelong friend of Avery, the Robin Hood of the sea who would become the pirate king; and Rogers ended up the pirate hunter who crushed the golden age of piracy as the governor of New Providence in the Bahamas.

Today, Defoe's *Robinson Crusoe* is appreciated for the real history underpinning it. In his association with Henry Avery the pirate king, so we have discovered, Defoe had extremely good cause—even a necessity—to cover his tracks and hide his actions. "Lie Like the truth," the brilliant author once wrote. *The Pirate King* could equally be subtitled, taking a leaf out of *Robinson Crusoe,* as *The Strange Surprising Adventures of Henry Avery.* Both characters made an art of lying and subverting. As needs be, Henry Avery would call himself Captain John, Henry Bridgman, Long Ben, and Johnson. Defoe, who was actually born plain Foe, used even more aliases, most frequently Claude Guilot and Alexander Goldsmith.[11]

As well as revealing the sequel of how Avery survived and what he did next after pulling off the richest heist on the high seas, *The Pirate King* digs into his psyche, as well as Defoe's. The pirate king has been misunderstood for centuries. He was not the brainless thug, an "overgrown Thief" and "Royal Out-law"[12] who stole the *Charles II* to become a pirate out of crazed greed. He was not just a man with a "Temper on Fire"[13] with a "mortal hatred"[14] against his whole nation, bent on breeding "Faction in Hell."[15] The pirate king who emerges from this book is a highly complicated human whose "good Genius" was "superior to his evil."[16] The human reasons behind his piracy can be tracked back to the unforgettable trauma of his youth.

"How strange a checker-work of Providence is the life of man!" Daniel Defoe wrote in *Robinson Crusoe*.[17] *The Pirate King* mixes historical reality with best-fit literary reconstructions, using quotes said to have been spouted or written by the main characters, to expose three strange lives breathed in fascinatingly changing times when the world was opening up and becoming modern.

—Sean Kingsley, Virginia Water,
and Rex Cowan, London

THE PIRATE KING

PART ONE

Dusty Treasure

The house lay in chaos. Boxes were stacked against every wall, nook, and cranny. Rex Cowan was downsizing. Zélide and Rex had lived in the leafy Hampstead suburb of north London for over fifty years. There they brought up three children and circled the world in search of lost ships and treasured cargoes. It was not just brick and mortar. The home held a lifetime of memories.

Early in his career, Rex, a lawyer by training, had cashed in his Mercedes for a rickety research boat and turned wreck hunter. Zélide did the historical research; Rex searched the high seas. Together they were a slick team that successfully tracked down some of the world's most iconic sunken Dutch East India Company traders. The Netherlands knighted Rex for his services to underwater exploration. Now it was all ending. The books, research files, and articles Rex had religiously kept and curated in the pre-internet age had to go.

Sean Kingsley was standing on creaking floorboards on the second floor of Rex's town house. Sean and Rex went way back. Both were wreck hunters who could talk rotten wood, coins, and pottery till the cows came home. Kingsley was in his early fifties, Cowan coming up to the ripe old age of ninety-four. In many ways they were cut from the same cloth. Both Londoners, a son and a grandson of Jewish parents and grandparents who fought to give their families a new start in England after Adolf Hitler ransacked Europe.

Sean scratched his stubble and sighed. It was December 2020, and he had promised to store and save some of Zélide's stardust research. Somewhere in hundreds of cardboard boxes was her masterpiece, a finished manuscript on the history of early divers. Rex had narrowed the hunt down to fourteen boxes. Sean had promised to scour them for Zélide's magnum opus and see it published under her name.

After piling his Jeep high with Rex's paper treasure and taking it home after his last trip to town, Sean brought bad news. The boxes were full of fascinating nuggets of ships and cargoes lost off Cape Verde, the Florida Keys, and beyond, and letters written to and from the pioneers of deep-sea exploration. Inspiring stuff. But no diving manuscript.

"Well, where the bloody hell is it?" Rex had mused.

While Rex mumbled and grumbled, Sean's mind drifted far off to the Caribbean. As the editor-in-chief of *Wreckwatch* magazine, he was deep into preparing a special issue on pirates—Captain Kidd, Blackbeard, and their life and times. Rex was a walking encyclopedia. It was worth a punt. Sean steered the conversation in a new direction.

"Tell me, Rex, I don't expect you know anything about pirates, do you?" he had innocently asked.

Rex's crestfallen face lit up. His eyes sparkled and a mischievous grin spread across his lips. "Pirates—and how. Wait here. Don't move a muscle," he ordered.

And he was off, rolling back the years as he hurtled upstairs. After a few minutes of crashing and banging, a dust-covered Rex returned beaming. Three thick, faded brown folders were tucked under his arm.

"Here, take them," he insisted.

Over tomato soup, Rex broke bread and began sharing an astonishing tale. A tale of discovery, danger, and strange surprises that he had not spoken about for thirty-two long years.

☠

On a windy day in the summer of 1978 in the Scottish Record Office in Edinburgh, Zélide Cowan had come across the most curious document she had ever seen. And she had seen it all. Few languages foiled her all-seeing eye. Apart from the lines spread out in front of her.

The problem was not the script, which was as clear as the day the letter was drafted. The letter's title said it all: "Copy. Letter from Avery the Pirate. 27:/ Dec.r 10.1700."[1] Zélide, an expert in maritime history, knew that Henry Avery, the greatest pirate of the golden age, vanished in 1696 and was never seen again. It was pirate history's longest cold case. Avery, the man who lit the fuse and flung the grenade that started the golden age of piracy. He was the enemy of all mankind who seized the richest loot on the high seas off India and escaped with the Mughal emperor's treasures. And then disappeared into thin air.

The letter lying flat in front of Zélide changed everything. If their contents were true, the pirate was not just alive and kicking four years after disappearing, he had swapped one undercover lifestyle for another.

The problem Zélide had reading the Avery the Pirate letter was that it was written in code. Avery was replying to an earlier letter he received on December 10, 1700, and confirming that he was setting off on a mission. He awaited instructions and would report back imminently. Avery signed off with the alias "Whilest 2." Two lines written lengthwise down the left side of the first page signposted where a reply should be addressed: "Direct for me to be left at the posthouse in Falmouth," a coastal town in Cornwall. The most peculiar of historic letters was addressed to "The Reverend Mr. James Richardson att the Liberary over against Orenge Street, St. Martins in ye. Fields, London."

To the Avery letter's tantalizing lines, whoever had made this copy added a note once annexed to the original: a list of gleaming treasure that the pirate king dragged home as his slice of the loot seized from the Mughal emperor's ship the *Ganj-i-Sawai* (*Gunsway* in English).

Ganj-i-Sawai meant "exceeding treasure," and the plunder beggared belief—a chest full of rubies, sapphires, emeralds, diamonds and, in a second crate, 120 gold ingots.

Zélide's brain was scrambled as she headed out of the archive that day. She needed a good few gin and tonics to settle her nerves. She had traveled to Edinburgh in search of historical nuggets about a sunken Swedish shipwreck, the *Svecia*, that she and Rex had found off the coast of Scotland. The armed merchant ship hit the rocks between the Orkneys and Fair Isle in the summer of 1740, returning from Bengal laden with dyewood, saltpeter, silk, and a supposed £250,000 in treasure. Instead of cracking the *Svecia*'s backstory, Zélide was heading home to London having discovered a completely different dusty treasure.

When they were not digging up sunken wonders, Rex and Zélide spent the next decade chasing shadows. They delved into archives from Cornwall to London. Old maps confirmed that the capital's first public lending library was opened on Orange Street in 1684, where the Avery letter was addressed to. More documents proved that a Mr. James Richardson truly was its librarian as well the head teacher at the annexed Archbishop Tenison's Grammar School.

Rex lost many nights' sleep trying to slot the elusive pieces of the puzzle together. This much he knew: Henry Avery the pirate king was alive and kicking in December 1700. He seemed to be in hiding, writing in code. The library on Orange Street in London, set up by Dr. Thomas Tenison, the future archbishop of Canterbury, was the real deal. The letter's contents stacked up.

In 2020 Rex's hunger to unravel the truth behind the letter burnt as brightly as in 1978. For himself. For the memory of Zélide, now sadly departed. For history. Rex hoarded his research. It was priceless to him. He had curated the pirate king archive for over forty years. It was time to pass his dusty treasure down the line.

Now the mystery was Sean's problem.

☠

In December 2020 the world was locked down. The biblical scourge of COVID-19 gripped the planet. Travel was banned in England. Christmas was cancelled. No matter. Sean Kingsley had his own special present. Instead of family cheer, hearty turkey, and cheesy cracker jokes, he retreated to his study on the edge of Windsor Great Park and started a forensic examination of the Avery files Rex Cowan had entrusted him with.

First things first. Was the eyebrow-raising letter true pirate gold or forged? Past scammers went to great lengths to fake and sell documents, especially when it came to inventing treasure hunts and selling them to starry-eyed romantics to make a fast buck. The dusty files showed how between 1978 and 1987 Rex and Zélide had made a deep dive into a web of archives. They ended up convinced of the letter's authenticity.

Sean felt pulled in two directions. The master letter had all the hallmarks of being authentic. No average person knew how to write in code, whose dark mysteries were familiar only to a select group. But the list of treasure tacked to a second sheet of paper felt somehow like a Disney caricature, too good to be true.

As Sean worked his way through a decade of research scribbled down in pen and pencil over forty years ago, thrill replaced skepticism. In the British Library, Rex and Zélide had dug up a manuscript that confirmed Tenison really did sponsor a school with a fine library attached off Orange Street. The library was so obscure that no scammer would know to address a bogus letter there.

Then there was the question of how the letter found its way into the Scottish archives and the mystery of who made the copy and why. Sean's discussions with the National Records of Scotland found out that the letter was part of an archive ranging in date from 1497 to 1897 donated by Scotland's Hamilton-Bruce family of Grange Hill and Falkland. Sean was working on the Avery letter from a photocopy taken by Zélide in 1978. A closer look at the original spotted a watermark in the margin reading

"C. Ansell 1806." So, the mystery of when the letter was copied was solved. But who made the copy?

One family member of the Hamilton-Bruces jumped out as an obvious candidate who had all the right reasons to copy the Avery the Pirate letter. Professor John Bruce, born in 1745, was a serious man. The professor of logic in Edinburgh from 1778 was also a founding member of the Royal Society of Edinburgh.[2] His only happy place, though, so colleagues joked, was "buried in old records."[3] Bruce got his wish, being appointed keeper of the state papers held in the Palace of Whitehall as well as becoming the official historian to the East India Company from 1793 to 1817.[4] The dates when the pirate letter was copied and Bruce's dream job added up perfectly.

Bruce would never have been duped into copying, filing, and carefully keeping a faked document. He had access to unseen archival material, much of which he kept private, and every likelihood of stumbling across the Avery letter. And the good professor had a vested interest in the pirate king as well. Bruce was a strong supporter of justifying England and the East India Company's trading monopoly in India. He knew all about Henry Avery and the damage he caused East-West commerce. In his three-volume *Annals of the East India Company*, Bruce regretted that "notwithstanding the most diligent search, Captain Avery has not yet been discovered."[5] The scholar had done his darndest to track down the pirate and had failed.

All the evidence convinced Sean, like Rex and Zélide, that the Avery letter was genuine. Big mysteries remained, however. What was Avery doing in Cornwall in December 1700? Who was he meeting? Why was he writing in code? And what business did Archbishop Tenison and London librarian James Richardson have being caught in the middle of secret communications? To answer these mysteries, Sean and Rex would have to rewind time to where it all started, in the second half of the seventeenth century, then build up a forensic picture, block by block, of how the legend of the pirate king was born and set the world alight.

Disinherited

he sea was in young Henry Avery's blood. He was brought up around the docks and decks of wooden ships in the ports of Bideford and Plymouth in Devon.[1] After breaking his back for several years in the service of the Crown, his father struck out on his own as a merchant and earned a reputation as a highly able seaman.

As the coin started to roll in, the Averys moved to a smart estate at Cattedown in Plymouth, a "Sort of an Eminence over-Looking an Arm of the Sea."[2] There, young Henry lived a short burst of life of great privilege. He had every reason to believe this was his natural station in society. Henry, watching intently his father's way of dealing with people, had a short temper and little patience suffering fools. Even at school, "he gave Indications of such a daring and commanding Genius, as made some of his little School-Fellows very uneasy, and give in many Complaints against him, for his tyrannical Treatment."[3] Little could he know these were his golden years before a fall.

The boy spent his spare time traipsing around Plymouth's cobbled lanes and exploring docks, breathing in deeply the stench of tar, sweat, and hops, oil, and fruit from dropped shipping crates. Weaving and the leather industry brought good livelihoods to many families, as did brewing beer for thirsty sailors, while fishing enjoyed a constant market.

Henry watched enthralled merchants and heavily laden trading ships come and go between the West Indies, the American colonies, and the Mediterranean. He talked freely with old salts fixing sails and dockers rolling wooden barrels into warehouses.

Young Henry loved nothing more than hearing tales of old Plymouth in the happy times when his father was home between voyages. The town may have been small but, as England's leading port, it had a big reputation. As Henry skipped to keep up with his father's long strides, passed the steep rocky slope where the wrestling giants Corinaeus and Gogmagog were carved into the hillside hundreds of years before,[4] Avery Senior pointed out the town's highlights. There were the caves where humankind was born, full of ancient human bones said to be tens of thousands of years old.[5]

Young Henry peered starry-eyed at the slippery, brown seaweed-covered quay where Thomas Stukeley sailed to Florida and Sir Walter Raleigh left for Guyana. On the Hoe the legendary Sir Francis Drake, who had already navigated the known world, calmly finished a game of bowls before giving a bloody nose in 1588 to the biggest Spanish Armada to ever invade England—73 ships armed with 2,431 guns.[6]

Henry's father shared with his son tales about how in 1606 King James I granted the Plymouth Company royal charters to settle on the North American coast known as "Virginia."[7] Henry eavesdropped when merchants whispered about the best way to embezzle cargo from enemy naval prizes towed into port. Crime—legal piracy—could pay big, he learned. Plymouth was a city for adventurers, and young Henry was desperate to join its ranks, to make his mark on the world.

Only fate had no intention of handing Henry Avery an easy ride. As the years passed, his dreams, his stability, were dashed. His mother died when he was six years old, his father when he was just eleven.[8] Being orphaned and abandoned without the bosom of a family, love, and guidance was a sorry start to life that was about to get worse. Henry learned about the evil wiles of man before his voice broke.

With his father having passed over the bar, Henry's welfare fell on the shoulders of Aunt Norris and Bartholomew Knowles, a merchant friend of the family. When the boy's aunt died four years later, Avery, alone in the world, inherited a "competent Estate" worth £500 and with it "Grandeur and Wealth."[9] The sixteen-year-old boy was rich, but no gentleman. Bred to the waves, he went to sea as a cabin boy and swiftly rose up the ranks, showing an "uncommon Readiness in the Practice of Maritime Affairs."[10] Knowles, now his governor, watched the lad's ease at sea and encouraged him to join the man-of-war the *Resolution* and its fleet headed to Algiers in North Africa to wipe out a pirates' lair.[11]

Henry Avery had lots to learn. Blessed with "Extraordinary Vigor and Sprightliness," he next signed onto the warship *Nonsuch* sent to the West Indies to protect English plantations from attacks by Spanish coastguards. These daring adventures "flush'd him with expectation of success in his Future Encounters and gave Additions to a Courage."[12]

While Henry Avery was trying to be a hero, fighting enemies in foreign lands, Bartholomew Knowles sniffed a windfall and set in place "long projected evil designs."[13] New deeds to the Avery estate of Cattedown in Plymouth were forged thanks to an equally corrupt attorney while its master was away at sea. The schemer helped himself to the youth's inheritance. By the time Henry Avery returned to Plymouth with great expectations, Knowles was dead, and his birthright vanished. Avery spent the last of his ship's pay taking Knowles's family to court and losing.[14] He angrily accused "both Judge and Jury, and laid Partiality and Bribery to their Charge."[15] Young Henry could not even fall into the arms of his betrothed for comfort. The farmer's daughter he fell in love with had run off with an innkeeper while he was attacking Algiers for king and country.[16]

Something snapped. Henry Avery, treated in a "scandalous and unjust Manner,"[17] became a bubbling cauldron of fury with a "Temper on Fire."[18] He packed up his worldly goods and, "being bred to the Sea" from a youth,[19] fled to London. Yet this nobody would always love his king and country. As for the corrupt and abusive people in positions of power and privilege, "he conceived a mortal hatred against the whole Nation, for the suppos'd injury of a few Persons."[20] The only escape, the only place he felt truly free to breathe, was on the high seas. Henry Avery would make something of his sorry life. The orphan and ruined estate lord swore that when the chance arose, he would "avenge himself upon his Country's Enemies."[21]

Avery would not be heard of for a few years. Reckless, carefree, and full of "Extraordinary Vigor and Sprightliness,"[22] he commanded a fire ship in the Dutch War with dashing heroics and what sounds like a death wish.[23] A fellow sailor remembered seeing him in battle, "all in Flames grapple the tall stour Hollander [Dutch ship] . . . the Showers of fatal Hail flew thick, and pierc'd our burning Canvas—Board and Board we lay, he was the first and last in Danger—We saw 'em both blow up, the dreadful Shock in a tumultuous Eddy whirl'd the Waves."[24]

All the while, Avery bided his time with a leaden heart. He had "declared War upon Mankind, renounc'd the Rights he was born to as a Member of Society."[25] When he made his move to "breed Faction in Hell,"[26] vengeance would be sweet.

The Outsider

O ld England had little tolerance for anyone who was culturally or religiously different, "others," whether that meant the color of one's skin or god of choice. Long before he wrote *Robinson Crusoe*, became the world's first great novelist, and had a hand in the eighteenth-century blockbuster *A General History of the Pyrates*,[1] Daniel Defoe—or Foe, as he was born—spent most of his life a bag of nerves, hiding under a rock. The Foes came from a minority faith of old Puritans known as Dissenters.[2] They were Protestants who refused to bow down to the beliefs of the Church of England. Snubbing the majority line put a target on Daniel Foe's back, whether walking the streets, seeking an education, or looking for a job. The chip on his shoulder made him even more of an outsider than Henry Avery.

Daniel Foe was born in the bustling London parish of St Giles, Cripplegate, outside the northern city walls. He felt locked out all his life. The times were chaotic, unstable. In the year Foe was born, 1660,[3] the Stuart monarchy was restored to the throne. The Puritans, Daniel's family faith, were all washed up. A backlash was heading their way. These days of horrors that were unimaginable for an adult, let alone a small lad, felt like the end of the world was nigh. In 1665 the bubonic plague rode into town and killed more than seventy thousand Londoners. Almost eight thousand of Cripplegate's population of twenty thousand were put in the ground. The city had not had the chance to catch its breath when in September 1666 the Great Fire burnt down two thirds of London and wiped the medieval city of wooden homes, shops, and warehouses off the map.[4]

Then, in June 1667, during the Second Anglo-Dutch War, panic and national humiliation swept the city. Dutch ships sailed up the River Medway, sank and captured several English warships, and escaped untouched.[5] The gunfire crackled as far north as London. The heart of England was at risk of being pierced. Foe was seven years old and felt the cold sweat and fear enveloping London.

Daniel Foe was around ten years old when the one stable rock the boy relied on,[6] the family fold, collapsed. The death of his mother, Alice, cast him adrift in a precarious world. With his father, James, away on business more often than not, Daniel was left to look after himself—sink or swim.

Life for Dissenters made escaping trouble impossible. The Foes had backed their pastor, Dr. Samuel Annesley, when he refused to obey the Church of England Act of Uniformity in 1662 and use the new Book of Common Prayer in church services. Two years later, more than five people were banned from worshipping together if they refused to use the official prayer book. The screws of terror and persecution against dissenting Protestants tightened in 1672. More than three thousand ministers left the church rather than accept the Act of Uniformity.[7] Another eight thousand imprisoned Protestant Dissenters died in jail during the reign of King Charles II.[8]

Young Daniel spent his life peering over his shoulder at popery, the threat of Catholics seizing power. A Catholic king invading Britain from France or taking the throne by stealth, as James, the Duke of York and brother of King Charles II, threatened, petrified Dissenters. The minority into which Daniel Foe was born were a desperate people, harassed by severe laws and at the mercy of bullies and informers. When London's bells called the faithful to Sabbath prayer, they did not ring for the youngster.

Because of their religious faith, the persecuted Foes were excluded from public life. One line of work that promised unchained opportunities was commerce, as Britain's global ambitions raced forward to the backdrop of the brave new London emerging from the rubble left behind by the Great Fire and the Great Plague. Daniel Foe was born and bred the son of a well-to-do candlemaker who seized these opportunities to branch out into overseas trade and become a successful player in the capital's business community.

Daniel spent many happy hours in his youth with his uncle Henry at Aldgate in the east end of the city. Henry had done well as a saddler and was master of a large house with six hearths, flanked by warehouses.[9] In the workshop filled with the smell of fresh leather, Foe listened wide-eyed to stories of his uncle's merchant business, trading with the British colonies in America, which were starting to open up. Chatter about great profits across the ocean fired Daniel's imagination. Like Robinson Crusoe, a "wandring disposition" began to grow inside that would inspire his career. It was no coincidence that Defoe's writing was obsessed with isolated and marginal individuals who found a new identity, self-consciousness, and status. His words were the stuff of his own dreams.

James Foe, a serious and Puritanical man who disapproved of the scandalous happenings at court, pointless plays, gaming tables, public-dancing rooms, and music houses that flourished in fashionable London, worked day and night to set his son up for life. From a "tallowchandler," Foe clawed his way to being a "generosus" gentleman by 1671.[10] His son would have the education such position demanded.

From the age of sixteen, Daniel attended Charles Morton's academy at Newington Green in north London, the next best option for the sons of prosperous Dissenters barred from Oxford and Cambridge.[11] Even though teacher-priests like Morton walked on eggshells in fear of the thought police, Foe got a first-class education. Morton, a distinguished scholar and a former fellow of Oxford before the bad times, later emigrated to America, where anything was possible, and was appointed the first vice president of Harvard College.[12]

In his years at Morton's academy from 1676–1680, a lingering anger against the ruling elite began to invade Daniel Foe's soul. The teenager became defensive. Whatever he achieved, to much of England's good and great, he would never belong. When Foe started making a name for himself in writing, critics took cheap shots by poking fun at his poor Latin grammar. The satirical journalist and political essay writer Jonathan Swift called Daniel "illiterate." Foe quipped back he would rather be a man of the world than a "Learned Fool." The chip on Daniel's shoulder weighed heavily. He dreamt of becoming a hero, a saint, or the right-hand man of a great figure.

From these experiences, and Morton's poorly stocked academy library, which left a lot to be desired—unlike at Oxford and Cambridge—Foe became a lover of libraries, a voracious reader of books and, later, a hungry buyer. Daniel shunned Puritan religious literature. Oliver Cromwell and the poet John Milton did not impress him. Foe's heroes were the explorer Sir Francis Raleigh and Gustavus Adolphus the Great, the king of Sweden who transformed his nation into a European superpower.[13] The youngster read deeply about travel and claimed to have studied every history published in English. Libraries would play a major role in the author's secret future life.

If his father had his way, after training to be a priest, young Daniel would have gone into the clergy. A crisis of faith crushed those hopes. Momentous history inspired Foe to change direction. On holiday from the academy, Daniel felt the thrill of the cut and thrust of world currents with the Popish Plot, a fictitious scheme that alleged Jesuits were planning to murder King Charles II in 1678 and put his Catholic brother James on the throne.[14] In 1681 King Charles II dissolved Parliament to try and exclude James from the Crown. For Daniel Foe, real-world adventure trumped the sleepy life of the clergy.

Foe started to toughen up and get streetwise. He took up boxing to defend himself. The writer who, first and foremost, would work as a trader that imported wine and brandy, began hanging out in taverns, developing a fine palate, and watching plays at the theater. What Daniel called "legions of strong lusts within" increased his feeling that the church was not his calling. Foe later described how in his sleep, "the Devil so haunted [him] with women, fine beautiful ladies in bed with him, and ladies of his acquaintance too, offering their favours to him" and "being a man of virtuous life and good morals, it was the greatest surprise to him imaginable." Daniel never forgot these awakenings, "Fatall and Accurst Desyres, That burst from Thence with too Uncertain Fires."[15]

A few weeks before his nineteenth birthday, and still studying at Morton's academy, Daniel Foe seems to have given in to the hunger to wander. Without his father's approval, and perhaps supported by a wealthy college friend, Daniel embarked on a footloose grand tour of Europe. As his writings later put it, "A gentleman ought always to see something of the world, before he confines himself to any particular part of it."[16]

By the winter of 1679–1680, his three-year college education was over. A Dissenter and outsider who wanted to prove the world wrong, and too smart for his own good, Daniel Foe now had to carve out a living. As much as he played the superior brain of a detached, critical, and amused observer of society, he was all too aware that the Foes were no gentlemen. Daniel was inbred to hate "idolators who worship escutcheons and trophyes, and rate men by the blazonry of their houses,"[17] especially since this was exactly what he secretly felt should be his true lot in life.

The embattled young man's lingering, yet starstruck, resentment of the ruling elite followed him into the start of a glittering and unexpected career. But it would start with hard graft. Inevitably, like his father and uncle, Daniel Foe the dreamer was about to become a true-bred merchant. Adventures and danger would have to wait.

On the Pirate Account

After making the sea his home, Henry Avery went in search of adventure. Such was his love of danger that friends worried he had a death wish. His behavior was loose, bold, and wicked. In these early years, according to Avery's own later memories, he was:

> perfectly unfit to be trusted with liberty, for I was as ripe for any villainy as a young fellow that had no solid thought ever placed in his mind could be supposed to be. Education, as you have heard, I had none; and all the little scenes of life I had passed through had been full of dangers and desperate circumstances; but I was either so young or so stupid, that I escaped the grief and anxiety of them, for want of having a sense of their tendency and consequences.[1]

After working on the sixty-four-gun warship the *Rupert* and the ninety-gun *Albemarle*, and perhaps the Royal Navy's *Resolution* and *Edgar*, Avery headed to the West Indies on HMS *Nonsuch* to guard English plantations from Spanish attacks.[2] In the pirates' lair of Port Royal, Jamaica, the angry young man's head was turned by the wickedest city on earth. An impatient Avery jumped ship onto a buccaneering boat in "Quest of Plunder."[3] The Spanish gold and silver ingots he returned to port with convinced him to chance his hand on the account, to turn pirate.

A rare description of what Henry Avery looked like was written in these years. He was said to be "fat, and of a gay jolly Complexion," extremely gifted at mathematics and the art of navigation. In his everyday life, he held "many principles of Morality." Avery showed a "strong natural judgement" and "the art of gaining the Affection of the Mariners." As for temperament, Henry was usually "daring and good humour'd, if not provok'd, but insolent, uneasy and unforgiving to the last Degree, if at any time impos'd upon."[4] Avery was not a man to cross.

And so a "wandring Life" began. In the Bay of Campeche in Mexico, Avery started plotting how to get his hands on a fine ship and command his own fortune. So far, he had strictly attacked Spanish shipping—foreigners. Never his fellow English or Dutch allies. All that changed when Avery took passage on an English ship that turned out to be "in the Service of the Devil." Avery was forced to join their lot in a "War with all Mankind."[5]

Home was a sixteen-gun pirate ship run by Captain Redhand, so-called for the blood his fists joyfully shed, and manned by "one hundred and sixty stout Fellows, as bold and as case-harden'd for the Work as ever I met with upon any Occasion whatever."[6] From Cuba to the Leeward Islands, Santo Domingo in the Dominican Republic, Florida and Brazil, the adventurers ate whatever came their way, whether penguins, seals, or goats, and shared in the spoils of prize after prize—rum, indigo, sugar, beef, beer, and cash. Avery cut his teeth on the pirate's account for four years, took to raiding enthusiastically, and "in a little Time the Novelty of the Crime wore off, and we grew harden'd to it, like the rest."[7] Redhand liked and trusted Avery and asked his opinion in times of crisis.

Near Santo Domingo in the Dominican Republic, the pirates seized a Spanish prize with "65,000 Pieces of Eight in Silver, some Gold, and two

Boxes of Pearl of a good Value." Off the Juan Fernández Islands in Chile they took a trader to the "Value of 160000 Pieces of Eight in Gold . . . as good as any in the World: It was a glittering Sight, and enough to dazzle the Eyes of those that look'd on it." Eventually, Redhand, the "barbarous Dog," ran out of rope chasing two ships carrying the revenue of the kingdom of Chile and silver heading for Lima, Peru. In the skirmish that followed, a Spanish broadside blew off Redhand's head. Avery, now appointed captain by the crew, reaped a cut of a windfall of "116 Chests of Pieces of Eight in Specie, 72 Bars of Silver, 15 Bags of wrought Plate," supposed to be donated to the Blessed Virgin in a church, and "about 60000 Ounces of Gold, some in little Wedges, some in Dust."[8]

☠

In the late summer of 1693, four ships slipped into the bay of La Coruna. The journey was a thousand-mile sail across the English Channel and south to the coast of northern Spain. The sailors rubbernecking to get a first glimpse of the picture-perfect saucepan-shaped port city had mixed feelings. They had freely signed up for adventure, other than a sorry group of sick and wounded seamen press-ganged out of prison.[9] La Coruna had been home to England's mortal enemy, Spain, in so many wars. Now the two powers were on the same side in an adventure of a lifetime. The men knew the city would be just as resentful of their arrival as they felt in arriving. The distrust was mutual. The sooner the fleet could get their paperwork sorted out, turn about, and ship out to the Americas, the better.

Little about the Spanish Shipping Expedition and the scandals that engulfed it was normal. Getting the deal over the line—in the making since 1688—had been a political nightmare to test the greatest of minds. The scheme was the brainchild of Arturo O'Bruin, a Catholic "wild goose" Irishman forced to go into exile in Spain by his island's furious Protestants. O'Bruin had no plans to go quietly, and by 1688 had clawed his way up the greasy pole to the position of lieutenant field marshal in Spain's Atlantic fleet.[10]

Over the dinner table, Madrid's power brokers had shared their pain at how many Spanish treasure ships ended up wrecked in local waters and off the Americas. If only they could salvage the loot, the royal coffers would overflow. The Spain of the late seventeenth century was a very different place to the early century. The golden age was over. For now, Britain and Spain shared a desperate goal to "destroy those permanent dens of thievery" in the Indies by cleaning the seas of buccaneers.[11] The Spanish Shipping Expedition would tackle both conundrums.

Most of these thieves were English pirates who merrily sailed in and out of the British Isles without worrying about being collared for their crimes. Late in his reign, though, King Charles II confessed to the Spanish ambassador to England, Don Pedro Ronquillo Briceño, that Jamaica's harboring of pirates was "a difficult contagion to cure."[12] After Charles's death, King James II ordered his colonial governors to prosecute the pirates. Warrants and hot air made little difference. A heavily armed force was needed to rid the Americas of the menace. Who would pay for it, though?

Then inspiration struck. Ronquillo was captivated when William Phips returned to London in 1687 to a hero's welcome after salvaging the Spanish galleon the *Concepción* off Hispaniola in the Dominican Republic. Gold fever swept the land as get-rich-quick schemers made deal after deal to harvest the seas. London speculators were "laughing their way to the bank," Ronquillo wrote.[13]

If Madrid promised to give O'Bruin a split of any treasure salvaged from any Spanish wrecks, his investors could be persuaded to back for free a foreign squadron to take on the pirates and smugglers. Spain would not have to pay a piece of eight. The timing felt right. King William III had signed an alliance with Spain against Louis XIV of France and were now allies in the Nine Years' War (1688–1697). "Galloping Francophobia" was the common enemy. The scheme planned "to pass into the Americas to dive on wrecks and arm a squadron of five ships as privateers to cleanse those seas of enemies, pirates, and illicit commerce, as well as to dislodge enemies from any of Your Majesty's lands which they occupy."[14]

O'Bruin, now promoted to an admiral, got his eight-year deal on October 30, 1690. The terms were reasonable enough: one third of all treasure salvaged would go to the king of Spain, plus all artillery from Spanish navy vessels discovered underwater, and one third from non-naval ones. Everyone's salaries, including O'Bruin's, were to be paid out of the expedition's profits. Spain was after a free windfall.[15]

It was the small print that would eventually scupper the scheme and persuade Henry Avery to take extreme action. In May 1691 Admiral O'Bruin agreed in writing that two thirds of the one thousand men hired for service must be Spanish and the rest strictly Roman Catholic.[16] O'Bruin kept this not-so-little detail under his hat and conveniently ignored it. The point would blow up in his face.

The unusual deal called for O'Bruin to assemble a fleet of five frigates out of his own pocket, the largest to be at least 600 tons, armed with over 50 guns, and manned by 250 sailors and 100 soldiers. To sweeten the pill, the king of Spain's take was later diluted from one third to one fifth of any recoveries. But where the admiral could raise the funds got even tougher: investors had to be "Spaniards or vassals of His Majesty or married Irishmen residing in Castile."[17] The terms were mission impossible.

Still, desperate to make the deal, O'Bruin signed on the dotted lines and swiftly ignored his pledge. To improve his chances of success, O'Bruin hired John Strong in 1692, the diving expert who made Phips's wreck salvage a runaway success. Next, he caught the ear of a powerful merchant and founding director of the Bank of England, Sir James Houblon. With the £40,000 backing of Sir James and other considerable merchants of the City of London,[18] the admiral was able finally to hire crews to man the fifty-gun *Charles II*, the forty-four-gun *Santiago* (*James*), the twenty-four-gun *Espiritu Santo* (*Dove*), and the *Seventh Son* as a small scout ship. His flagship would be the *Nuestra Señora de la Concepción*, armed with fifty-four cannon. After successfully testing Strong's diving equipment in the River Thames, O'Bruin's fleet prepared to sail from England in the late summer of 1693.[19]

When the fleet left for La Coruna, Henry Avery sniffed the opportunity of treasure and signed up as chief mate of the *Dove*. He was told the crew needed to stop briefly in northern Spain to pick up passes and instructions for the Americas before a quick turnaround. Only none arrived. The weeks passed. The sailors were poorly fed, fearful of going ashore or mixing with the pestering beggars and bare-legged girls mocking the foreigners. The crew spent an unhealthy amount of time belowdecks, crammed in its airless and foul-smelling wooden walls.

La Coruna had its own uneasy reputation among English mariners as the port where the invincible armada left to invade the British Isles in 1588 with 131 ships and over 25,000 sailors, soldiers, and officers.[20] As a Plymouth man who spent his childhood in the town where Sir Francis Drake prepared to engage the armada in battle, Henry Avery had no love for La Coruna or its people.

After eight months at sea and in port, and no sign of the six months' pay owed, the men were on edge. When a few of the crew demanded what they were rightfully owed, they were thrown in jail. King Charles II of Spain may "pay them or hang them if he please," the agitators were told. The Spanish treated the English crews like "contrabandists," "smugglers," and "pirates."[21]

Avery smelled a rat. He was not alone. A fault line had developed between Irish Catholic and English Protestants. One Popish crew member ranted openly that King William III of England was a criminal. "God damn the King, fuck him to the pit of Hell," he slurred over too much beer. The Protestants, on their side of the deck, moaned about "infestive false hearted Spaniards."[22]

After gathering a bit of intelligence and keeping his ear to the ground, the scales dropped from Avery's eyes. The expedition was a giant deception, he learned too late. In the law courts, a sea captain from Andalusia with a local dive-salvaging contract, Antonio Verde, was blocking O'Bruin from working the wealthy wrecks off Cadiz. And the dream of West Indies treasure was over. The fleet, it turned out, was not just carrying dive equipment. Houblon had hedged his bet on the expedition by filling the holds with secret cargo. To make a profit, all the banker needed was to make sure the goods were sold in Cadiz.[23] The rest, if pulled off, would be a bonus.

Then Henry Avery heard a disturbing piece of news that changed his life forever. The fleet was being readied to sail from La Coruna to Cadiz to sell the hidden merchandise and cut its losses. Before then, all the Protestants in the fleet would be fired. Spain had uncovered O'Bruin's treachery in the lack of Catholic sailors making up the promised crew. Spanish authorities urgently started recruiting locals to replace the English Protestants. Spanish naval officers were readied to board the fleet and "punish all of the criminals aboard." Madrid withdrew the admiral's license to salvage and privateer in the Spanish West Indies.[24] The game was up. Disbelief and shock turned to rage.

Forget the promise of Americas' treasure, no one was going to abandon Avery on a hostile shore without paying him what was rightfully his. Henry Avery had been watching and waiting all his life for a chance like this. For years he had plotted "how I should dismiss myself from that Drudgery, and get to be, first or last, Master of a good Ship, which was the utmost of my Ambition at that Time; resolving, in the mean Time, that when ever any such Thing should happen, I would try my Fortune in the Cruising Trade."[25] The moment had come. Reasoning was pointless. It was time for violence.

The *Charles II* was a stout frigate of fifty guns, and sailed extraordinary ably. On Sunday, May 6, 1694, Henry Avery started a whispering campaign among trusted men in the fleet crew and prepared his coup. He "went from ship to ship and persuaded the men to come on board him." If they would help him man the *Charles II*, "he would carry them where they should get money enough." By now, the seething British and Dutch sailors were "ripe for his Design."[26] At 10:00 P.M. on the night of May 7, Avery swung into action.[27] The mutiny passed smoothly thanks to the captain's weakness for strong booze. "It must be observ'd, the Captain was one of those who are mightily addicted to Punch," Captain Charles Johnson wrote in *A General History of the Pyrates*:

> So that he passed most of his Time on Shore, in some little drinking Ordinary; but this Day he did not go on Shore as usual; however, this did not spoil the Design, for he took his usual Dose on Board, and so got to Bed before the Hour appointed for the Business: The Men also who were not privy to the Design, turn'd into their Hammocks, leaving none upon Deck but the Conspirators, who, indeed, were the greatest Part of the Ship's Crew. At the Time agreed on, the *Dutchess*'s Long-Boat appear'd, which *Avery* hailing in the usual Manner, was answered by the Men in her, Is your drunken Boatswain on Board? Which was the Watch-Word agreed between them, and Avery replying in the Affirmative, the Boat came aboard with sixteen stout Fellows, and joined the Company.[28]

Avery's coconspirators bolted the *Charles II*'s hatches leading belowdecks, cut the cables, loosened the sails, calmly weighed anchor, "and so put to Sea without any Disorder or Confusion." Gunshot from the Spanish fort missed its mark.[29]

Once out to sea, Captain Charles Gibson, now very ill with a fever from excess drinking, and "half asleep, and in a kind of Fright," was awoken from bed. Avery instructed Captain Gibson to get changed, so he could let him in on a secret. "You must know, that I am Captain of this Ship now, and this is my Cabin," Henry merrily informed the deposed commander, "therefore you must walk out; I am bound to Madagascar, with a Design of making my own Fortune, and that of all the brave Fellows joined with me." "I am a Man of Fortune and must seek my Fortune," Avery ended, before asking if the captain cared to join his fanciful scheme.[30] Gibson and sixteen other men declined and were put over the side on the ship's boat, with a bucket to bail out its leaking bottom.[31]

Two years later, when justice caught up with some of the mutineers, they were accused of piracy because they:

> Feloniously and Pyratically did steal, take and carry away from the said Charles Gibson, the said Ship, called, The Charles the Second, her Tackle, Apparel and Furniture, of the Value of One thousand Pounds, Forty Peices of Ordnance of the Value of Five Hundred Pounds; One Hundred Fusees, of the Value of One Hundred Pounds; Fifteen Tun of Bread, of the Value of One Hundred and Fifty Pounds; and two Hundred pair of Woollen Stockings, of the Value of Ten Pounds, in the possession of the said Charles Gibson then being; the Ship, Goods, and Chattels, of the subjects of our said Sovereign Lord the King, and the Late Queen.[32]

The crew of Henry Avery, the pirate king, were never going to get a fair hearing. Sir James Houblon was one of the most powerful men in England. How Houblon and O'Bruin's greed were ready to leave Avery and many of the men of the Spanish expedition without pay and jobs on the dock of a hostile foreign port was brushed under the carpet.

Avery and his fellow abused Protestants had not turned pirate—so far. The eighty mutineers of La Coruna jumped ship not because they were ruthless buccaneers and murderers but for self-preservation, to protect their safety and promised income. Avery seized the *Charles II* in revenge for conduct unbecoming against him. The ship was theirs instead of salaries owed and to punish Sir James, Admiral O'Bruin, and Spain for unjust treatment.

Only when the frigate had passed the Roman Tower of Hercules on the promontory of La Coruna, the oldest lighthouse in the world, and left behind the fields of maize and vineyards, did Avery share his ambitions with his merry men, far out to sea. It did not take long for them to be immortalized in ballads sung from tavern to tavern across England.

Come all you brave boys whose courage is bold
Will you venture with me? I'll glut you with gold.
Make haste unto Corunna; a ship you will find
That's called the Fancy, will pleasure your mind.[33]

The *Charles II* was renamed the *Fancy*. The legend of the pirate king was born.

True-Bred Merchants

D aniel Foe could have had it all. A life of privilege and stability. If only young Daniel had not gotten too big for his boots and shown a reckless gambler's instincts. Like Robinson Crusoe, who ran away to sea, after giving up on his father's wish that he would join the clergy at Morton's academy,[1] Daniel Foe turned to the merchant's life to which he was bred. It was his best option as a dissenter for whom so many doors were closed. His hand was forced. Just like young Henry Avery. Foe would show the world he meant big business.

In these heady days, England was turning from a land of farmers into a nation of shopkeepers and traders. A financial revolution swept the British Isles. Merchants were the heroes of a new dawn, Foe told himself, and trading was the most "Noble way of Life," a road to education and worldly sophistication.[2] "A True-Bred Merchant," he later wrote, "Understands Languages without Books, Geography without Maps, his Journals and Trading-Voyages delineate the World; his Foreign Exchanges, Protests and Procurations, speak all Tongues; He sits in his Counting-House, and Converses with all Nations, and keeps the most exquisite and extensive part of Human Society in Universal Correspondence."[3]

While his father, James, ran the family's mini empire from London, Daniel did the running. Commerce meant endless travel. Foe loved getting to know his country inside out and branching overseas in adventures, which inspired his later writing.

Daniel Foe was well set with cash and contacts to build a booming business. When his father died, leaving his son £1,000 and warehouse stock, Daniel had the perfect springboard for the good life.[4] Not only did his marriage to nineteen-year-old Mary Tuffley on January 1, 1684, come with an enormous dowry of £3,700—over $520,000 today[5]—it opened doors to the Tuffley's commercial orbit.

In later life, Daniel's enemies mocked him as a lowly hosier, which hit a raw nerve and was as unfair as it was untrue. Foe soon branched out into wholesale business, trading in whatever imports and exports turned a profit. He knew all about the fashions of the day, how black crape cloth brought over to England by French refugees started to be used for ladies' dresses, then for servants, and finally menswear. The true-born merchant did owe a debt of gratitude to woolen hosiery for getting him going and firing his imagination. He bought in bulk from his trading partners, Samuel and James Stancliffe of Halifax in the West Riding of Yorkshire, Dissenters like him, and from the Cruso family in Norwich, immigrants from Hondschoote in Flanders whose fond memory he immortalized in his famous novel *Robinson Crusoe*.[6]

Daniel Foe chased wealth wherever money could be made. He sailed to Ireland in 1689 to sell Porto wine, beer, tobacco, hosiery, and Spanish snuff. Spirits were being drunk in ever-greater amounts in Britain, rather than just beer and ale, so importing wine and brandy brought in great rewards. Foe started shipping in "40000 Pipes a Year" of wine from Oporto in Portugal. The future writer was proud of the fine palate he boasted from tasting French claret, entirely for work, of course.[7]

Travels made Foe familiar with "fine Lucca Olives" exported from Marseilles to Narbonne and Bordeaux in France, where four hundred ships in the river were loaded with wine for England. He bought wine from Lisbon and the fruitful mountainsides of Malaga and learned Spanish living near the customs house in Seville and Cadiz, the port of call for Spanish America. Daniel watched how "Spaniards walk, with their Hands on their Swords," and scorned Spaniards' laziness in sea trade, letting the Dutch and English control their foreign trade, "employing our Ships in their own Affairs from Port to Port." This was exactly the heart of the business that got Madrid and Henry Avery entangled in the Spanish Shipping Expedition. The opening up of the American colonies promised transatlantic riches. From 1688, Foe dispatched tobacco to London on the *Batchelor* through Maryland and worked with agents in New York and Boston.[8]

By now, like all good gentlemen, Daniel Foe boasted a house in both town and country. Freeman's Yard, a small court on the north side of Cornhill, was his London home and business. A warehouse took up the ground floor where his precious wines were locked up in a vault under the warehouse; living rooms and his counting house stood on the upper stories. Freeman's Yard was well positioned a short stroll away from the Royal Exchange, and, so he later remembered, among "two or three most famous Perriwig-makers, five or six spacious Coffee-Houses, three or four Illustrious Cake-Shops and Pastry-Men, one or two Brandy-Shops, and the like; and these not in the small Shops, or meaner parts of it, but in the Capital Houses, of great Rents and large Fronts, in the very Prime of the Street."[9]

Steam rose out of the doors of the coffeehouses dotting the back lanes. In what were known as "penny universities"—a cup of coffee was yours for a penny—patrons read the broadsheets, talked politics, soaked up the latest gossip, and struck shipping deals. By 1692, the Foes were living comfortably with their two children, Maria and Hannah, and five servants. When the mood took the family, they retreated to their country pad at Tooting in Surrey in their red and gold horse-drawn coach, a coat of arms painted on the door panels—three griffins and the motto *Jure Divino* (Divine Law).[10]

Just when he had it all, the walls started to cave in around Daniel's overambitious dreams. Later, he would regret his "foolish inclination of wandering abroad"[11] and wish he had been able to give his younger self a piece of wisdom.

> Increasing in business and wealth, my head began to be full of projects and undertakings beyond my reach; such as are indeed the ruin of the best heads in business . . . I must go and leave the happy view I had of being a rich and thriving man . . . only to pursue a rash and immoderate desire of rising faster than the nature of the thing admitted; and thus I cast myself down into the deepest gulph of human misery that ever man fell into, or perhaps could be consistent with life and a state of health in the world.[12]

Daniel Foe regretted his reckless dealmaking, playing with borrowed money above his pay grade. He lost substantial cash insuring ships and cargoes captured by French privateers. Near the town of Deal in Kent, one of his trading ships was blown ashore and should have been saved when the storm quietened down. The locals, "those mountain thieves," however, had other ideas, and "have not rifled the loading only, but torn the very ship herself to pieces before help could be had . . . And in smaller time than one would think possible, a whole ship has been plundered and gutted, and the goods carried up country and irretrievably lost."[13] Foe's profits were lost to English piratical wreckers.

Increasingly, the lure of the sea played the defining role in his business empire. One desperate measure would restore his family fortune. Foe would go treasure hunting. Like Henry Avery, Sir James Houblon, and Admiral Arturo O'Bruin, Daniel Foe fell for the daring-do tales of Sir William Phips, who had returned to England in July 1687 with over £200,000 in gold and silver salvaged from a Spanish vessel off Hispaniola, the Dominican Republic, and handed his investors profits of 10,000 percent. The adventure hooked Foe, who could not believe the riches just waiting to be mopped up below the waves.

Witness Sir William Phips's Voyage to the Wreck; 'twas a mere Project, a Lottery of a Hundred thousand to One odds; a hazard, which if it had failed, every one wou'd have been asham'd to have own'd themselves concern'd in; A Voyage that wou'd have been as much ridicul'd as Don Quixote's Adventure upon the Windmill: Bless us! that Folks should go Three thousand Miles to Angle in the open Sea for Pieces of Eight! why they wou'd have made Ballads of it, and the Merchants wou'd have said of every unlikely Adventure, 'twas like Phips his Wreck-Voyage.[14]

In 1692 Daniel Foe got wind of Cornishman Joseph Williams, who had invented a new type of diving engine. Foe bought ten shares from Williams and was appointed secretary and treasurer of the venture. With an investment of £54 he was instructed to buy a boat as the base of the group's diving operations. Foe started juggling his finances. He used the £54 to pay off part of his debt to Thomas Williams, a Lombard Street goldsmith and sold the diving consortium his own ship, the *Desire*, instead.[15]

The plans went from bad to worse. By mid-August, the speculators were in Falmouth, ready to make a submarine assault off the Lizard on a Genoese wreck laden with silver that sank on Cornwall's Bumble Rock in 1667. A few hundred yards to its west lay the tantalizing prospect of a Spanish trader lost in Polpeor Cove in 1619 with silver ingots worth £100,000.[16] The wrecks and their windfall of £2,500 were the stuff of Foe's wildest dreams.

The dream swiftly turned into a nightmare. Along the shores of the Lizard, Foe and Williams discovered other minds had reached exactly the same idea. They had been beaten to the punch by "some with one sort of diving engine and some with another; some claiming such a wreck and some such and such others."[17] To make matters worse, autumn gales were whipping up the English Channel. "What fury the sea comes sometimes against the shore here," he wrote. "How high the waves come forward, storming on the neck of one another."[18] The get-rich-quick scheme collapsed.

Daniel Foe was in trouble. Joseph Williams, the inventor of the dive engine, sued both Foe and Thomas Williams, the goldsmith given the money for the salvage boat.[19] Ever on the lookout for a chance, Foe filled his ship with Cornish cargo along the River Fal estuary for the trip home from the ill-fated Lizard to London.[20] Foe was on the edge of a cliff. It was time to disappear.

Throughout 1693 and 1694, Foe took himself out of harm's way—chasing creditors—to Orkney and Shetland in Scotland, at first keeping the books for a business catching, curing, and marketing white-fish, mainly cod, and later herring. The ocean, as in Cornwall, still captivated him. "If thou reject the Bounties of the Sea, No more complain of Poverty," he wrote.[21] On the shores of Orkney, Foe found momentary peace. "Nothing can be pleasanter of its Kind in the World, than to stand on the Shore and see the Sea in calm, fine Weather," he reminisced.[22]

Once again, though, Foe ended up trapped in a failed business. The cost of management, setting up warehouses and accommodation for employees, building fishing boats and renting space to moor them had been miscalculated. Catching cod by hook and line failed to harvest enough fish to balance the books. The operation could not compete with the Newfoundland trade, which may have worked much further away, but ships could be loaded there in one fifth of the time and far more cheaply.[23]

Misfortune in business "unhinged me from matters of trade," Foe admitted. Throughout the 1680s, the tradesman had allowed his mind to wander, distracted by thoughts of literature. While he was supposed to be putting food on the table, he wrote his *Meditations, Historical Collections: Or Memoirs of Passages Collected from Several Authors* and a pamphlet attacking the Ottoman Turks. An interested audience started to turn its head when Foe was invited to join a small society of "Noble Design" that included men of power and influence—the Marquess of Halifax, Lord

Maitland, the Earl of Dorset, Lord Cavendish, Colonel Finch, and Sir Charles Scarborough. Foe was humored as a precocious young talent. Out of nowhere, he found himself listening in on intimate anecdotes about King Charles II and his court spouted by bigwigs with access to the monarchy.[24]

Foe appreciated the irony of how he had climbed up the greasy pole, despite being a much-hated Dissenter. "A wit, turn'd Tradesman! what an incongruous Part of Nature is there brought together," he described himself, "consisting of direct Contraries? No Apron Strings will hold him; 'tis in vain to lock him in behind the Compter, he's gone in a Moment; instead of Journal and Ledger, he runs away to his *Virgil* and *Horace*; his Journal Entries are Pindaricks, and his Ledger is all Heroicks; he is truly dramatick from one End to the other, through the whole Scene of his Trade; and as the first Part is all Comedy, so the last Acts are always made up of Tragedy."[25]

It was on the road, during his travels across the south coast, wheeling and dealing in the great ports of Bristol, Falmouth, and Plymouth, that Daniel Foe crossed paths with the equally ambitious Henry Avery. They worked the same tracks and same contacts. Both shared a string of personal coincidences that made them blood brothers united by tragedy, life's knocks, politics, and dreams.

Both were born in 1660. Foe's mother died when he was a boy of ten, Avery's when he was just six.[26] Daniel Foe the outsider had to fight tooth and nail to earn every inch of luck. Avery may have been born into a worthy estate, owned by a father who was a trusted sea captain and made enough to retire young, but he crossed the bar into the next world when his son was eleven years old. Rage burnt in both their souls. Each yearned to make their mark on the world.

As well as talking about world trade, what it meant to be British, and foreign threats, Henry Avery and Daniel Foe shared an obsession with sunken treasure. Avery first went wreck hunting in search of the Spanish galleon the *Nuestra Señora de la Concepción* in 1687. Foe had been romanced by Joseph Williams and his newfangled dive engine to hunt Spanish and Italian silver closer to home off the Lizard in Cornwall. Avery and Foe were men of adventure and risk. They lived on the edge.

Daniel Foe may have chosen trade, "the most Noble way of Life," as his profession, but his merchant ways risked ending in rags, not riches. Trying to overachieve brought disaster, and far worse was to come. The true-bred merchant would have to find another way of making a living to stave off tragedy, this time with the pen rather than the sail.

PART TWO

Red Sea Riches

T he *Fancy* took three months to reach the edge of the richest sea lane in the world. The island of Madagascar off the east coast of Africa was the launch pad for the pirate's round. There, men going on the account careened their ships—scraping foul barnacles off hulls—and patched up leaking planks. When needed, captains took out greater security by nailing an extra layer of outer planks to their pirate ships to spare them from being eaten alive by warm-water shipworms, the silent assassins of the seas. Madagascar was the perfect service station to load water, store food, clean guns, and write wills.[1]

When Henry Avery's forty-six-gun *Fancy* slipped into the well-sheltered anchorage of Sainte-Marie Island, located off the east coast of Madagascar, two pirate sloops idling in the bay beached their boats and ran for the woods in fear. The heavily armed *Fancy* was a British frigate, after all. It was also the fastest ship in the eastern seas. A 1694 ballad described its special design:

> Her Model's like Wax, and she sails like the Wind,
> She is rigged and fitted and curiously trimm'd
> And all things convenient has for his design.[2]

Avery was banking on inflicting dread and mayhem on enemy shipping. The freshly turned pirate smiled as hard-cut men scarpered. Henry Avery was no chancer. His plot was deeply planned. The sight that met him as he neared shore reassured him that Sainte-Marie was the right place to put the final pieces of the puzzle together. The wrecked ships littering the shoreline were all that were left of successful raiding in the Red Sea and Indian Ocean. Madagascar showed all the right signs of roguish success. Not far from the sunken hulks were scattered "Cargo's of China ware, rich Drugs, and all sorts of Spices, lying in great heaps on the Beach."[3] Passing pirates cared little for the mass bulk goods stowed in seized ships. It was gold and silver they wanted to get their hands on. The rest of the valuable plunder was ditched on the shores of Sainte-Marie Island, left to rot in the sun, wind, and rain.

Avery's crew had already gotten a taste of the good life piracy could offer. The *Fancy* first stopped for salt at Bonyvis and at the Isle of May took aboard twenty bullocks.[4] The beef was salted to last as long as possible. Avery helped himself to water, bread, and rice from three ships at the wrong place at the wrong time and persuaded nine of their men to join his ranks: the *Fancy* was still understaffed for the fight ahead. Avery was careful what ships he ransacked. He saw himself as a loyal subject of the British Crown. His moral code did not tolerate attacking English shipping because "I Honour St. George, and his Colours I were [wear]. . . . He that strikes to [the flag of] St. George the better shall fare," he promised.[5] Avery's quartermaster carefully issued bills of payment for the snatched food.

Next, the *Fancy* headed for Guinea on the west coast of Africa. After Avery ordered the English flag to be raised, local merchants were lulled into a false sense of security, mistaking the *Fancy* for any old trader. The ruse worked to perfection, so that "when they came aboard, they [Avery's crew] surprized them, and took their Gold from them, and tied them with Chains, and put them into the Hold."[6] Henry Avery the pirate added slaver to his résumé.

Off the Princes' Islands, the Portuguese trade station of São Tomé, 350 miles off the coast of Gabon, the *Fancy* took two Danish merchantmen in an hour-long fight with its 120 men.[7] One was armed with twenty-six cannon, the other with twenty-four guns. The more powerful three-hundred-ton *Fancy*, with its forty-six cannon, lost just one of its eighty men in the skirmish. The Danish traders were heavily loaded with supplies and money—fifty tons of brandy and about 640 ounces of gold dust—heading for their forts in West Africa. Thirty of its Danish and Swedish crew jumped ship to join the pirates. Avery bought rum, sugar, and fresh provisions. One of the ships was burnt at Vandepo, the other sunk by cannon shot at Cape Lopez off Gabon along the equinoctial line. The *Charles II* turned *Fancy* had been at sea for six months since fleeing La Coruna.

A month later the *Fancy* stopped off at the Portuguese island of Annobon in the Gulf of Guinea for water, oranges, and fifty hogs, paid for with money and small arms. After another twelve weeks, Henry Avery stepped onto the tropical beaches of Madagascar and breathed deeply the smell of eastern promise. He had arrived at the starting gate of an adventure of a lifetime. By now, his company included fifty-two Frenchmen, fourteen Danes, and the rest English, Scotch, and Irish. It was ten months since the *Fancy* sped away from Spain.

Peering out at the bay of Sainte-Marie Island from his deck, Avery spied an eight-sided fort on each side of the harbor mounted with forty guns looted from a Portuguese ship. A loose cluster of huts and dozens of warehouses dotted its defensive shadow.[8] Madagascar was a pirate's paradise, ideal for hiding from enemies in uncountable coves and fine natural harbors, and perfect for finding whatever stores a crew heading out on the account needed. The white sandy beaches flowing into the warm blue Indian Ocean were long, smooth, and gently sloping, perfect for removing the *Fancy*'s guns and careening the hull, scraping away infestations of sea barnacles and weeds, and fixing leaking planks.

Madagascar abounded in natural goodness and "affords all the Neces-saries of Life, and yields to none either in the Wholesomeness of the Air, or Fruitfulness of the Soil: The Seas around it are well stor'd with Fish, the Woods with Fowl, and the Intrails of the Earth are enrich'd with Mines."[9] The fields were filled with God's bounty—pineapples, oranges, lemons, bananas, coconuts, yams, and rice. Pirates could take their pick from honey, chicken, turtle, fish, and beef.[10]

Sainte-Marie was the only spot in striking distance of Arabia and the Indies where pirates could find home comforts. Caribbean buccaneers started using Madagascar as a supply base to chase Spanish Manila gal-leons across the Pacific in the 1680s.[11] Now, in 1695, Henry Avery saw that the island was still reassuringly lawless and ungoverned. No Euro-pean superpower's flag flew over the fort's walls. This free-for-all was the go-to place to prepare an assault on the east coast of Africa, sail into the Indian Ocean as far as Sumatra in Indonesia, ransack the Red Sea, or make your way up the Malabar Coast and into the Gulf of Oman. The endless possibilities were mouthwatering.

Doing business in Sainte-Marie's pirate town meant dealing with the shadowy figure of Adam Baldridge, the son of a planter and master power broker in East Africa. It was the Anglo-American Baldridge who built the island's first wooden fort in January 1691, after fleeing the authori-ties when he murdered a man in Jamaica.[12] Baldridge set up a trading post on Sainte-Marie and gained the friendship of the locals with the promise of Western goods and military power. His fort's design—first wood and then stone—mirrored the European slave-raiding and gold-trading outposts that studded the coast of West Africa. Only the forts of the Netherlands, Portugal, England, and France were financed and managed from above by joint stock companies, shareholders, and royal approval. The small trade hub on Sainte-Marie was built from below by the underbelly of society to cater to pirates and seamen gone rogue.

Adam Baldridge had a good business going. There were no taverns or whore houses in Madagascar. The only Western home comforts were sold and bartered by Baldridge, whose stores were stocked by Frederick Philipse, a Dutch merchant who emigrated to New Amsterdam in the 1650s—the English colony that in 1664 would become New York. There, Philipse married a wealthy widow who owned a fortune in ships and building lots in Manhattan.[13]

Baldridge bought low in Madagascar from pirates fencing their plunder of Indian textiles, Chinese silks, calico cloth, drugs, spices, diamonds, gold, and hard currency. In exchange, he sold the sea raiders everything from clothes, rum, and gunpowder to gardening tools and Bibles.[14] Baldridge could charge whatever he fancied. He ran the only store in town. Wine was bought eagerly on Sainte-Marie at fifteen times higher than the price in New York. Rum bought for two shillings a gallon sold for £3 a gallon.[15] It was money for old rope.

With the kind of cash most sailors could only dream about, the pirates of Madagascar "liv'd most dissolute and wicked Lives, stealing away, and ravishing the Wives and Daughters of the Natives, living by this Means, in a State of continual War."[16] The pirates married "the most beautiful of the Negro women, not one or two, but as many as they liked," Captain Johnson wrote in *A General History of the Pyrates*, "so that every one of them had as great a Seraglio as the Grand Seignor at Constantinople."[17]

To most pirates, Madagascar was a land of the free—Libertalia— where no kings and queens held sway, just the vote of the many.[18] Henry Avery knew better. All the trappings of East–West plunder and trade were cherries on the cake of the island's main business. Philipse's ships did not sail over 8,500 miles just for gold and silver but for a commodity far more wanted in America: African slaves.

The Dutch East India Company started rounding up "strong, robust and rudely built" Africans in Madagascar in the late 1650s to sell to plantations on Mauritius, Batavia, and Cape Town. The French needed slaves too for their new colony on Bourbon (present-day Réunion), over one hundred nautical miles west of Sainte-Marie Island, and the English for St. Helena and Sumatra in far-off Indonesia.[19]

When the Europeans first arrived, the locals were cautious and untrusting. The Malagasy would light a fire on the beach to lure a ship to shore. European merchants spent several weeks bargaining beads, novelties, copper, and brass wire or Spanish pieces of eight for enslaved Africans. As the pirates started to flex their muscles toward the end of the seventeenth century, muskets became the bartered currency of choice. A man cost "one buccaneer gun and one trade gun each, with two measures of powder (pounds) and 30 flints with 30 balls. For a woman, two trade guns, a quart of powder, 30 flints and 30 balls. For a boy, a buccaneer gun, a pint of powder, 30 balls and 30 flints."[20]

The Jamaican deal maker Baldridge liked to see himself as a savior in the locals' warmongering. Once he landed in East Africa, a "great store of Negros resorted to me from the Island Madagascar and settled the Island St. Maries, where I lived quietly with them, helping them to redeem their Wives and Children that were taken before my coming to Sainte Marie's by other Negros to the northward of us about 60 Leagues."[21] Avery had learnt that in line with much of Africa, the Malagasy people were divided into numerous little princes and alliances, which were continuously at war. Prisoners were either killed or sold into slavery. The slaver Robert Drury called the Malagasy's frequent quarrels "the epidemical Evil of this island."[22] Without European and American greed, though, there would never have been a demand for a slave trade in the first place.

Making an alliance with a pirate lord, and his unbeatable firepower, was a guaranteed stamp of victory. In return, men like Baldridge got hold of as many enslaved Africans as they liked. Some were put to work locally planting rice, fishing, and hunting, but most were trafficked off the island. "Tyrant like," the pirates "lived, fearing and feared by all."[23]

Where merchants not sailing under royal license were treated like illegal criminals all along the coast of West Africa, the base of the major European nations and their monopolies, East Africa was a delicious loophole. Enslaved Malagasy were run into British colonies in the West Indies, Massachusetts, and New York from the 1670s, disrupting the Royal African Company's English command of the transatlantic slave trade.[24]

By the time Henry Avery took a very close interest in the comings and goings in northeast Madagascar, the merchants Frederick Philipse and Stephan Delancey were at the height of their powers ferrying goods, people, and mail from New York, and leaving Africa with cargoes of pirate plunder and saleable "ballast": human beings. Life was cheap in Madagascar: an enslaved person cost around ten shillings, compared to £3 or £4 in West Africa.[25] In a letter written by the New York trader Philipse to Baldridge, he confirmed the huge markup the pair made in New York, where "negroes in these times will fetch thirty pounds and upwards in the head . . . It is by negroes that I finde my chiefest Proffitt. All other trade I look upon as by the by."[26] Other merchants claimed that they could buy "a lusty Fellow . . . for an old Coat."[27]

Let the crew think what they may, and "take liberties" with the local women, but Henry Avery knew exactly what the big-ticket prize was in Madagascar. Voices in taverns across the New World spoke of the island as a free revolutionary state—if you were white and heavily armed. To Avery it was a slave-trading center, pure and simple. A plan started to play out in his mind about how to escape with any loot he netted in the seas of Arabia and India or how to cash out if the big gamble backfired. Madagascar would be crucial to his plans.

While his crew blew off steam, the English mutineer gathered intelligence from the loose-lipped Baldridge, planned his cruise, and bought supplies. Down by the shore, some of Avery's crew rolled barrels of fresh water into the *Fancy*, stored provisions in the hold, and salted a hundred head of beef bartered for gunpowder and small arms. Getting the ship, crew, and scheme just right took a month of downtime in Madagascar.

Avery knew exactly what he wanted to catch on the pirate's round. A reality, not a dream. Many of the 1,500 marauders that plied the eastern seas were chancers who headed out without a tip-off for the port of Surat in northwest India, Cape Comorin on the continent's southern tip, or made their way as far as the Malacca Strait in Indonesia, the crossroads of the Indies and China trade.[28]

Avery was not interested in Spanish galleons or Chinese junks piled high with blue-and-white crockery and spices to plump up dinner tables. The scheming mutineer's journal was crammed with intelligence and ideas about the wealthiest man on the planet: Aurangzeb. Aurangzeb, the ruler of 158 million people,[29] who united all the Indian subcontinent under one imperial power, the Mughal Empire, for the first time in history. His courtly palaces dripped in jewels, pearls, and gold. The peacock throne, valued by a French jeweler at £6 million, was studded with precious gems and the largest diamond ever seen.[30] The Badshahi Masjid, which he paid for, its doors able to welcome sixty thousand worshippers, was the largest mosque in the world. Aurangzeb's India was home to the largest cities on earth.[31] While Henry Avery plotted from an East African shanty town, India had eclipsed Qing Dynasty China to become the biggest economy in the world.

The signs of India's wealth swirled around Avery. Many pirates and local princes cavorting in Madagascar sported colorful cotton and silk clothes. Piles of spoiled pepper littered the beaches. Saltpeter used to make gunpowder was a virtual currency on the island. All were made in India and looted from Indies' merchant ships.[32]

Tapping into the profits these goods promised inspired the West to sail East and to "discover" the Indies. Dutch, English, and French joint-stock trading corporations, blessed by royal appointment, bent over backward to romance the Mughal emperor. Aurangzeb, though, did not need Europe. India produced everything he needed. "Europe bleedeth to enrich Asia," the East India Company merchant diplomat Sir Thomas Roe, and England's first official ambassador to India, complained.[33]

Daniel Defoe—that true-bred Englishman—also railed against Indian printed calico cloth worn by fashionable English "Callico Madams." The fabric was "a Foreigner by Birth; made the L . . . d knows where, by a Parcel of Heathens and Pagans, that worship the Devil, and work for Half-penny a Day," he fumed. Calico madams should be condemned as "an Enemy to her Country . . . Tis a Disease in Trade; 'tis a Contagion, that if not stopp'd in the Beginning, will, like the Plague in Capital City, spread itself o'er the whole Nation," Defoe warned.[34]

The truth was that if Europe wanted to do business with India, it had no alternative but to trade on Aurangzeb's terms. Take it or leave it. India's 1.5 million square miles of land fed the continent with everything it desired and more. By the 1690s, the Dutch East India Company and English East India Company were almost a century into a highly profitable, long-distance deal. India's top exports were cotton textiles, raw silk from Bengal, pepper from Kerala, saltpeter, rice, and sugar from Bengal, alongside cheaper hull fillers of indigo, wax, coconut goods, ginger, and turmeric. The English and Dutch companies combined exported 13.5 million pounds of Indian pepper to cheer up Western cooking. The English imported 1,760,315 pieces of cotton cloth in one year in the 1680s.[35]

The Mughal Empire enjoyed a taste for porcelain from China; coffee from Arabia; Ethiopian ivory; Arabian horses; seashells from the Maldives; pearls from Bahrain; American tobacco; and small amounts of top-notch woolen, silk, and velvet clothes; wines and spirits; glassware and fancy goods. In truth, these were shiny baubles. To buy Indian goods, the English and Dutch companies shipped vast fortunes of bullion east. Into Hindustan flooded a large part of the world's gold and silver. Dutch and English company ships' holds sent more than thirty-four tons of silver, and nearly half a ton of gold, to India every year. The silver arrived in boxes of Spanish reales minted in Peru and trans-shipped through Amsterdam or London to the Mughal mints in Surat.[36] The circular logistics were staggering.

With so much wealth toing and froing between the Red Sea and India, Henry Avery was banking on the *Fancy*'s excellent chances of outrunning any ship in the eastern seas. His crew was hungry for success and he expected them to put up the mother of all fights. And Avery needed a hit. The crew, unpaid at La Coruna, had now gone nearly a year without cash. Avery had talked big, promising his men enough riches to retire on. What would they prefer? The meager £12 most Anglo-American sailors made working their way to Africa or the £300—maybe even £3,000—a pirate score promised?[37] Greed settled tempers, just as Lord Bellomont, governor of New York, warned London. "The vast riches of the Red Sea and Madagascar are such a lure for Seamen that there's almost no with-holding them from that vile practice of Turning pyrates," he wrote.[38] To keep the men sweet, Avery needed to deliver. Fail to live up to his words and the pirates would not hesitate to end his reign and cast him away on some desert island.

Avery kept the small details of his big plot private. He knew that once a year the Mughal emperor sent a fleet of treasure ships to the Red Sea loaded with fifteen thousand Muslim pilgrims on the hajj to Mecca.[39] The good and the great of India traveled with jewels to donate in memory of the Prophet Muhammad and Allah. "It is known that the Eastern People travel with the utmost Magnificence," Captain Charles Johnson recorded in *A General History of the Pyrates*, "so that they had with them all their Slaves and Attendants, their rich Habits and Jewels, with Vessels of Gold and Silver, and great Sums of Money to defray the Charges of their Journey by Land."[40] And they returned with masses of gold and silver paid for by the Mughal goods sold in the great port of Mocha and the richest trade goods of Arabia—heaps of aloes, frankincense, gold, ivory, myrrh, and saffron, as well as gift-laden pilgrims. The Mughal fleet had no parallel in Christendom. Henry Avery was primed to head to the southern tip of the Red Sea and intercept the Mocha trade. All he needed was one big hit.

For many years, one quirk of Aurangzeb's sea trade had caught the pirate's curiosity. The Mughals had their eye off the ball when it came to India's ocean. Shipping was small fry. Avery had licked his lips when he read a letter by the Italian traveler Pietro Della Valle, who shared how "The Mogol is a very great and wealthy King, whose Revenues arise from his own Lands and not from the Sea; and one to whom that little which is to be had from the Sea . . . is nothing."[41] The Mughal Empire's import duties raked in less than three million rupees a year, under 1 percent of the state's revenue.[42] Land and agriculture were king.

An Armenian merchant whom Avery fed and oiled handsomely in São Tomé had spat his fine wine out in laugher when he regaled the pirate with his recollection of how a large part of the sea trade was left to the women of the court. A sober Henry Avery stored away that precious shred of information. In a sea battle, he knew that he could bet on his well-drilled crew. The chase was on. Next stop: the Red Sea, the pirates' richest lottery ticket on earth.

Bottomless Plunder

Henry Avery had promised his disgruntled crew riches. Now he had to come good. Navy crews might grumble and gossip about bad conditions and late pay, but a pirate mob would vote you off deck or turn nasty and take your head if the pickings were slender.

After a month's down time in Madagascar, the *Fancy* set sail for the Red Sea. On their way, the pirates left in their wake a trail of rumors. From Madagascar, Avery headed for the island of Johanna, in the Comoros Islands in the Mozambique Channel.[1] Around three hundred leagues to the northwest, and a fourteen days' sail, the *Fancy* topped up with fresh water, bulls for salting its meat, and fruit. The islands were a popular stopping-off point for English East India Company traders as well. Avery took the chance to cruise around the channel in search of prizes.

While replenishing stocks and buying hogs, Avery wrote a warning to his fellow Englishmen. His letter—the only surviving example to bear his signature—declared that in February 1695 he was in a ship of forty-six cannon with 150 men "bound to Seek our fortune." The pirate's letter, nailed to some tavern door, made it absolutely clear to passing ships that he was not in the business of attacking the ships of his home nation. The letter was an extraordinary piece of foresight, a get-out-of-jail-free card to play if he was ever cuffed and accused of attacking British trade. So Avery wrote:

I have Never as Yett Wronged any English or Dutch nor never Intend whilst I am Commander. Wherefore as I Commonly Speake w'th all Ships I Desire who ever Comes to yr perusal of this to take this Signall that if you or any whome you may informe are desirous to know w't wee are att a Distance then make your Antient [flag] Vp in a Ball or Bundle and hoyst him att y'e Mizon peek y'e Mizon Being furled I shall answere w'th yr same & Never Molest you: for my men are hungry Stout and Resolute: & should they Exceed my Desire I cannott help my selfe.[2]

Tacked to the end of the letter, Avery warned that 160 armed Frenchmen at Mohill, Mayotte in the Comoros Islands, were preparing to attack passing ships. "Take Care of your Selves," Avery ended touchingly.

More immediately, Avery had the problem of dodging heavily armed East India Company ships, whose skippers were under instructions to take would-be pirates. The *Fancy* was chased out of the Comoros by three company ships. One of its captains sent his own letter to warn the English in Surat that "he was too nimble for them by much, having taken down a great deale of his upper works and made her exceeding snugg, which advantage being added to her well sailing before, causes her to sail so hard now, that she fears not who follows her. This ship will undoubtedly [go] into the Red Sea, which will procure infinite clamours at Surat."[3] Avery had customized his ride. Like future blockade runners during the American Civil War, all unessential decoration and cabins were removed to make the lightened fanciless *Fancy* sail smooth and fast.

Off Johanna, Avery captured a junk, unspectacularly loaded with rice.[4] It was a far cry from what he was after. The pirates emptied the cargo and sank the ship. Next, they passed over the equinoctial line running through southern Somalia. In the town of Mahet, in the Gulf of Aden approaching the Red Sea, the locals refused to trade. The frustrated *Fancy* crew was forced to turn back to Johanna for fresh water and supplies. Despite taking a small French vessel, emptying and sinking it brought little satisfaction. The mood aboard the *Fancy* was turning sour. The crew returned to Mahet and took its revenge by torching the town.[5]

Back in the Gulf of Aden, two English privateer ships of eighty and ninety tons and about sixty men each, an old bark from Dunfanaghy and Captain Richard Want on a Spanish ship, asked to join Avery's team.[6] Avery agreed. The three sails ploughed through bad weather that tore down one of the ships' top masts. The next stop was what the English liked to call Bob's Key in the Red Sea, three weeks away.[7] Bab el-Mandeb Strait was not known as the Gate of Tears for nothing. It was a dangerous chokepoint between East and West. The merchant Captain Alexander Hamilton was well aware that "the Navigation of the Ethiopian Sea is very dangerous, and their Maps very deficient." Much of the ocean was off the chart. A Dutch skipper sailing between Batavia and Mocha in the Red Sea "affirmed to me, that he saw several large Islands, and many Rocks and Sands in those Seas that were not placed on his Maps." The southward-flowing currents swirling between banks and rocks were another hazard to worry about.[8]

Bob's Key felt like home, though. It was one of the wealthiest sea lanes in the world and a place where "the Pirates finding great Booties . . . had a Project to be Masters of the Key to that Door." After anchoring there for a day and a night, when the *Fancy* was forced to replace its top mast, three more American ships—a bark, brigantine, and sloop—arrived, hoping to strike it rich on the pirate's round. They too "signed articles to share & share alike."[9] Henry Avery, now an admiral of a flotilla of 440 men and six ships—including Thomas Tew's *Amity*, Joseph Farrell's *Portsmouth Adventure*, Richard Want's *Dolphin*, William May's *Pearl*, and Thomas Wake's *Susanna*[10]—waited at the southern turn of the Red Sea for about five weeks, every day expecting the Mocha fleet to sweep south, striking for the coast of India, and be trapped in the pirates' web.

Every year a fleet of twenty-five Mughal ships headed south from India for Mecca.[11] Their main reason was religious pilgrimage. Making it to Mecca was one of the five pillars of duty for all Muslims, male and female, and the crowning glory of Islam. Mecca and the port of Jeddah, where pilgrims landed, was also the setting of one of the world's great commercial fairs. Merchants from the Ottoman empire joined the faithful in August and September with extraordinary payloads of bullion to buy mountains of coffee and textiles. The outbound Surat ships ferrying the faithful also carried cargoes of four million rupees of Indian textiles, which brought in 50 percent profits.

The pirate who had little to show for his mutiny had high hopes of netting a tremendous prize. The crew was itching for a massive payload. Avery had sent his scout boat to Mocha to spy out what ships were in port.[12] Mocha, on the coast of Yemen, was the most famous emporium for buying coffee on the planet. Not because of nature's bounty, but thanks to its location. The town may have been rife with malaria and made do with a terrible anchorage, forcing ships to anchor and bob a mile offshore,[13] but being sandwiched between Jeddah, the port for Mecca, and the foot of the Red Sea made it a commercial gem. The Dutch and English set up offices and warehouses there.[14] Profit attracted trade and wealth, and the port town made ever-greater money exporting aloe, myrrh, frankincense, and gold. Dutch and English ships added spices, textiles, and chinaware to its markets. You name it, Mocha sold it, from nutmeg, cinnamon, cardamom, and pepper to turbans, silk, iron, opium, coconuts, tortoiseshell, coral, horses, and slaves.[15]

The intelligence from Mocha was good news and made Avery lick his lips. Around forty sails were readying to head home for Egypt and India, and "six Sail of them were Jeda Ships & very rich."[16] All he had to do was sit tight at the foot of the Red Sea and await the Surat fleet to gather there as the monsoon set in, then pass by crammed full of gold, silver, aloes, frankincense, ivory, myrrh, saffron, and wealthy pilgrims dripping in gems. Then the trade would slip straight into his arms.

Fate played a different card—at first. Fourteen days later, their prey swept through, silent and unseen, the twenty-mile-wide Bab el-Mandeb

Strait untouched one moonless Saturday night in September 1695. The Mughal fleet gave the pirate mastermind the slip through the Gate of Tears. The pirates missed the convoy by a few hours.[17] Avery's reputation and command were on the line.

Only when the pirates took a small junk on Sunday did the upsetting news come to light. Avery called a meeting to decide whether the flotilla should continue menacing Red Sea shipping or go over the horizon hunting the Mocha fleet. The decision was overwhelming. The chase was on. The *Dolphin* bottom was sunk and its men boarded the *Fancy*, which took an American brigantine in tow. Captain Farrell and the *Portsmouth Adventure* joined the flagship. The two other pirate ships were left to catch up as best they could.[18]

As fine a captain and navigator as Henry Avery was, he would need a huge dose of luck to track down the Mughal fleet. It could be anywhere in the two thousand miles of Arabian Sea between Bob's Key and Surat on India's western shore. Or maybe it was sitting pretty in the dozens of harbors dotting the sea lanes between the Red Sea and India? Avery kept his cool, knowing full well that "this was a Booty worth watching for, tho' it had been some Months longer . . . and [we] began to despair of Success; but the Knowledge of the Booty we expected spurr'd us on, and we waited with great Patience, for we knew the Prize would be immensely rich."[19]

Just when the grumbling was growing belowdecks, fourteen long days later—as hope was fading—sails appeared on the horizon. The ship circled round to a ship's bows, ten leagues from the coast of India, and fired a broadside and shot.[20] The smaller ship of 250 tons, armed with just six guns, surrendered almost at once. Avery's men found "a pretty quantity of silver & gold on board . . . to the Value of 30 or 40000 *l*. with other Merchandise."[21] The haul was worth an impressive £50,000–£60,000 (about $8.6 million today).[22]

The pirates' first big prize was the *Fateh Muhammed*, owned by Abdul Ghafur, the wealthiest and most influential merchant in all of India who controlled a quarter of shipping in Surat. The shipping magnate owned thirty-four ships and boasted his own private wharf. Visiting merchants waxed lyrical about the magnificence of his grand house with its famous pleasure gardens.[23] Alexander Hamilton, the English trader who spoke several Asian languages and spent thirty-five years in the East Indies, knew Ghafur as a man who "drove a Trade equal to the English East-India Company, for I have known him fit out in a year, above twenty Sail of Ships between 300 and 800 Tuns, and none of them had less of his own Stock than 10000 Pounds, and some of them had 25000."[24]

Taking the *Fateh Muhammed* was a big hit and a strike that would make a loud noise across the Indian Ocean. The pirates had messed with one of the country's most powerful merchants. There was only one more powerful man on the continent: Emperor Aurangzeb. The intelligence Avery shook out of the captain of the *Fateh Muhammed* was perfect news that "the Jeda ships, were all gone another way, only the Admirall of Mecca a very rich Ship was still behind."[25]

The *Fancy* towed Abdul Ghafur's ship toward shore and a day later was bobbing at anchor off St. Johns, forty leagues or eight to nine days' sail from Surat, counting its booty, when the crow's nest spied a sail, this time enormous and traveling at full speed.[26] It was September 28, 1695. The 1,600-ton ship was the *Ganj-i Sawai* (or *Gunsway*), the largest in all Surat and royal property. The hold was full of cash, the proceeds of the goods of Hindustan sold in the seasonal markets of Mocha and Jeddah. So a popular ballad remembers to this day:

> The Grand Mughal of Islam was from holy Mecca bound
> And all on board, a treasure hoard, worth two hundred mil-
> lion pounds
> So Avery and comrades the Portsmouth and the Pearl
> With stripped down masts, their ships were fast
> And they chased them 'round the world
> A bounder, rake, a cad, a knave was he
> Sail with Long Ben Avery.[27]

The *Gunsway* hoisted the Mughal's colors and prepared to defend its honor, turning its starboard guns toward the far smaller *Fancy*. Sixteen months after dropping out of the Royal Navy to turn pirate, the mayhem was brutal but brief. At first, Avery fired his guns from a safe distance away. Some of his crew, desperate to get into the thick of the action, worried their commander would not risk tackling the well-armed machine, had gone soft, and "was not the Hero they took him for."[28] They were wrong. Avery's mind was already made up: he had "resolv'd to attack her if she had been full of Devils as she was full of Men."[29]

What should not have been a fair fight—David versus Goliath[30]—ended being a "hopeless battle," so the captain of the *Gunsway* reported back to the emperor.[31] The Mughal ship was armed with four hundred soldiers, eighty guns, and four hundred muskets[32]—so powerful a floating fortress that it needed no convoy for protection. This was the date with destiny Henry Avery had dreamed of since he was a teenager, a moment in time to become rich and famous. The *Fancy* bore down on the ill-prepared Mughal crew. Not only were the Indian mariners poorly trained, their guns were not primed for action. The first eighteen-pounder cannon grazed the *Fancy*'s mizzen mast but did the pirate flagship no damage. The *Gunsway*'s next broadside overshot the pirates completely. The Mughal crew "fir'd them so confusedly that we could easily see they did not understand their Business," the pirate crew realized.[33]

Then disaster struck. Gun fire burst one of the Mughal's cannon. Splintered metal flew across the deck, its own friendly fire killing three or four men and wounding countless others. The *Gunsway*'s deck was a scene of blood, screams, and chaos. In turn, Avery had the luck of the gods. The *Fancy*'s eleven broadsides made matchsticks of the *Gunsway*'s mainmast.[34] The emperor's pride and glory was a sitting duck.

The pirates wasted no time swarming all over the *Gunsway*. In boarding they met the greatest resistance, when the emperor's men "fired very warmly upon us all the while & threw fireworks into us to set our Sails etc on fire."[35] Only one of the *Fancy*'s hard men was wounded.

Their adrenaline rush was pumped up for nothing, however. Captain Muhammad Ibrahim took one look at the frenzied English, Dutch, Danish, and French pirates and fled belowdecks. The rest of the crew dropped their cutlasses and followed his cowardly retreat, "running down under their Hatches, crying out like Creatures bewitch'd."[36]

Desperate to delay the inevitable and save his skin, Ibrahim dressed in turbans the Turkish concubines he had bought for his pleasure in Mocha, thrust swords in their hands, and ordered them to fight.[37] The *Gunsway* was Avery's for the taking in two hours with the loss of just one life. Twenty-one of the Mughal emperor's subjects were killed, including Nur Muhammad and his bodyguard, Seyyid Yusuf and his concubines, and Muhammad Yusuf Turabi. Twenty more were wounded, not least the spiritual teacher Muhammad the Blessed.[38] Today was the day of all days.

The Mughal emperor's treasure ship was vast. It took a week of searching and reveling "in a bottomless Sea of Riches" before the newly anointed pirate king was satisfied that every plank had been lifted and rummaged through. Only then was the *Gunsway* set free to limp back to port in Surat, its merchants and travelers "absolutely ruined."[39]

Cowardice aside, the Indian fleet had done itself no favors by sailing erratically, breaking away from the convoy's safety in numbers as it pleased. The "fleet of Hindustan" had little understanding of sailing in formation. Commanders behaved like little gods, competing to get to market first and be first home to sell their goods to eager buyers. Abdul Ghafur's ships cruised under different rules. Because the shipping magnate enjoyed special exemptions from customs' taxes at the port of Mocha, his merchants could afford to hang back at market and hoover up late arriving freight at rock-bottom prices. Since his vessels were the fastest on the Surat–Red Sea run, they usually outran the early starters home to India anyway.[40] It was win-win economics. In September 1695, though, the ploy backfired terribly.

Royal freighters like the *Gunsway* also played by their own rules. More like the royal court at sea than grubby traders, they transported relatives of the emperor and aristocrats, whose main aim was to be entertained by musicians while they drank coffee and sucked Persian fruit. The eight hundred pilgrims aboard also slowed down the floating palace's progress. In a later run to the Red Sea in April 1701, the *Ganj-i Sawai* lagged four miles behind the fleet. Its Dutch escort had no way of protecting the emperor's treasure ship, not least because other Hindustan traders it was also supposed to defend had swooped in front of it. The Dutch complained about this "accursed manner of sailing" and "very bad habit."[41] Tracking all the fleet ships safely during the month it took to cross the Arabian Sea was an impossible headache. And in 1695 the *Gunsway* had pulled back to Mocha at first and let the convoy speed off, when it heard news that English pirates were at large.[42]

Henry Avery knew full well just how badly drilled Mughal crews were. From insider information, he had also learned that much of the sea trade was left in the hands of women courtiers. The more powerful ladies of the court owned junks of 1,200 tons. Yet according to Dr. D. Pant (of India's University of Lucknow), at their very heart Indians suffered from hydrophobia.[43] Whereas the Chinese emperors forbade citizens from sea trade throughout most of the nation's history to protect their borders, Hindus traditionally did not take to the sea because interacting with uncivilized barbarians in foreign lands was unworthy.[44]

Now to Henry Avery, the spoils of this loophole. Pirates had pulled off some big hits before, especially Thomas Tew of Rhode Island in Bab el-Mandeb Strait. No single pirate, however, had taken such a massive prize before.[45] The "Sail brought in worth an Empire's Ransom—Women and Gold Boys, Plenty of both . . . a Blaze of Jewels, Beauty, Gold."[46] The *Gunsway* was carrying home "fifty-two lakhs of rupees in silver and gold,"[47] in some accounts said to be equivalent to one hundred thousand pieces of eight and one hundred thousand chequins.[48] The loot was "above the Value of a Million of Money in Silver and Rich Stuffs."[49] Aurangzeb's royal court put the loss at £600,000 ($149 million today).[50] The East India Company reckoned the crime at £325,000,[51] no doubt desperate to estimate low, well aware that the emperor was likely to hold the company responsible for fully repaying the loss. Either way, it was the greatest prize in pirate history.

The newly minted wide-eyed pirates, desperate for cash ever since Sir James Houblon fooled them, did not hang around. Avery left Tew behind in his slow-sailing sloop to fend for himself. Four ships sailed to Rajipur. In sight of the English East India Company factory there, the pirates watered and split their shares. Some of the 160-strong crew pocketed £1,000, others £800, £500, or £300.[52]

Tew was never seen again. He had been the first commander to pounce on the homeward-bound Mughal fleet. His attack was fatal after "a Shot carry'd away the Rim of Tew's Belly, who held his Bowels with his Hands some small Space; when he dropp'd, it struck such a Terror in his Men, that they suffered themselves to be taken, without making Resistance."[53] Like almost all the great pirates, Thomas Tew would never enjoy his ill-gotten gains.

Avery's mind switched from striking it rich to survival. Word of his raid would reverberate like gunfire from port to port across the Indian Ocean to the Red Sea and into the Atlantic. Few places would be welcoming havens. The *Fancy* and brigantine sloped off toward the safest hideaway east of the Cape of Good Hope, the pirates' lair in Madagascar. Thomas Wake would meet them there: he had his eye on a twenty-two-gun-armed ship he wanted to buy on Sainte-Marie Island and head out to sea again.[54] The intoxicated captain was high on the sweet taste of success.

On the way, Avery's men voted to swap their cut of the looted silver for the brigantine crew's gold. Traveling on shore with less gold, rather than large lumps of silver, would help them escape faster. When the exchange was over, however, Avery discovered that the brigantine's men had cheated his crew. They had clipped the edges of their gold coins and pocketed the shavings. The pirate king was no man's fool. They would pay for their greed. Not only did Avery demand the clippings back at the end of a pistol, but he seized his original silver. The sorry swindlers

were left with £2,000 to share among themselves and were cast away on
the ship's boat to teach them a painful lesson.[55]

In later, less likely, versions of the story, no doubt spread by the embarrassed crew, Henry Avery persuaded all the ship's captains to lock their
cut of the bounty in the hull of the *Fancy*, the safest floating strongbox
in the flotilla. The treasure was sealed in crates aboard the *Fancy* and
without feeling "any Qualms of Honour rising in his Stomach, to hinder
them from consenting to this Piece of Treachery," they took "Advantage
of the Darkness that Night, steer'd another Course, and, by Morning,
lost Sight of them."[56] The *Fancy* ran off with the lot.

Henry Avery and his men never made landfall in Madagascar. They
watered at Degorees, and fifty leagues north of Madagascar the governor
of the French island of Dascaran was so inviting that the crew decided to
unwind on its shores. The quartermaster restocked the *Fancy* with eighty
bullocks, while Avery locked himself away, planning his escape in his
chessboard of a mind. His French crewmen were keen for the men to
break up in Martinique. Henry did not like the idea. So the twenty-five
French splitters bade their farewell and stayed put on Dascaran. Fourteen
Danes and some Englishmen joined them, fearful that if an English ship
caught them west of the Cape of Good Hope, they would end up hanging
on the end of a rope.[57]

By way of Ascension Island—1,000 miles off West Africa, and 1,400
miles from South America—where they stocked up with fifty turtles,[58]
the pirates voted to head for America, where their names and faces were
unknown. There they would change their identities, buy land, and live
a life of ease.

The *Fancy*'s pirates now owned "wealth enough, not only to make us
rich, but almost to have made a Nation rich." The *Fateh Muhammed* and
Gunsway also carried costly goods, "which we did not know the Value
of, and besides Gold, and Silver, and Jewels, I say, we never knew how
rich we were; besides which, we had a great Quantity of Bales of Goods,
as well Calicoes as wrought Silks."[59]

Henry Avery had delivered on his promise to glut his loyal crew with gold. None of them would ever have to work again. Or their children or grandchildren. As Avery made his getaway, his great strike started to ring across the West. Songs and ballads sang out of taverns and inns from Edinburgh to Boston. *Villany Rewarded* would later wax lyrical how:

> We Robb'd a Ship upon the Seas,
> the *Gunsway* call'd by name,
> Which we met near the East-Indias,
> and Rifled the same;
> In it was Gold and Silver store,
> of which all had a share,
> Each man 600 pounds and more
> *let Pirates then take care.*
>
> Thus for some time we liv'd, and Reign'd
> as masters of the Sea,
> Every Merchant we detain'd
> and us'd most cruelly
> The Treasures took, we sunk the Ship,
> with those that in it were,
> That would not unto us submit,
> *let Pirates then take care.*[60]

Raping the Gunsway

In the eyes of the world's rulers, there was nothing romantic about Henry Avery's theft of government property, the *Charles II* frigate in La Coruna, or heist on the Indian Ocean. Pure and simple, it was robbery and mass murder. All the while, the legend was spreading like wildfire in the popular imagination. To some, he was a pirate king. To others, the Robin Hood of the oceans. The public loved the drama, adventure, and success of a working-class hero.

In the eyes of the Mughal emperor, the theft of a fortune on a "sacred ship" doing Allah's work on the hajj was borderline heresy.[1] What enraged Aurangzeb beyond his gold and silver were reports of a "monstrous unheard of Story,"[2] that in between counting their booty the crew of the *Fancy* ran riot in an orgy of gang rape. In Surat and Bombay the pirate king was tarred as a spineless rapist who needed dragging to justice.

What started out as torture had escalated fast on the emperor's floating treasure chest. Once the *Gunsway* had been rummaged from stem to stern and its gold and silver, sales from goods in Mecca and Mocha, secured aboard the *Fancy*, the crew turned to the merchants' and passengers' personal wealth. The mood turned ugly when the victims refused to talk. In an earlier shakedown in the Red Sea, a group of irritated pirates had turned malicious when a Captain John Sawbridge, on a voyage to Surat with a cargo of Arabian horses, complained about his rotten treatment. The quickest way to stop his whining and force him to hold his tongue, the looters figured, was to sew his lips together with a sail needle and twine. The captain died soon after.[3] The *Gunsway*'s passengers and crew knew what treatment was coming. The pirates would get what they wanted by any foul means.

Henry Avery had no alternative but to let pirate nature unfold. The men were high on success, wealth, and an orgy of violence. Getting the crew to see reason and not run riot was a fool's hope. Locked away in his cabin on the stern of the *Fancy*, the thought of taking revenge on the families that had done him wrong in his youth for company, the pirate king's head dropped at the depraved sounds screaming across the waves. Wickedly raping innocent maidens was not part of the Avery code. Still, he knew that he could lose his position or worse if he tried to stop men being men, pirates being pirates.

All that changed when one of Avery's lieutenants banged on his cabin door and forced the captain to jump onto the *Gunsway*. In its great cabin the looters had found a lady and her entourage. The lieutenant "fear'd the Men were so heated they would murder them all, or do worse." Avery needed to intervene fast. The lady was the granddaughter of Emperor Aurangzeb, cowering alongside "her Houshold, her Eunuchs, all the Necessaries of her Wardrobe."[4] As the story of the Indian princess later grew from sea to sea, legend had it she was sailing with a vast dowry heading to marry the king of Persia.

Inside the great cabin, Avery was met by "such a Sight of Glory and Misery was never seen by Buccaneer before." The emperor's granddaughter sat on a couch, dressed in gold and silver thread, and crying from fright.[5] The arrival of the pirate king made her tremble for her very life. Avery was accused by some of failing to control his lust.

The earliest account of the princess, shared by a Pennsylvania merchant two years after the event in September 1697, agreed she was preparing to be married off and that the crew of the *Fancy* "killed most of the men and threw her overboard. They brag of it publicly over their

cups."[6] In another tale, Avery fell head over heels in love. "I never saw
so fair a Creature, There's a bewitching Softness in her Eyes," he supposedly melted. "She sinks into my Soul . . . High Heav'n has sent you
here, Imperial Maid, to found a Race of Kings, To be the Mother of a
mighty Nation."[7]

The most down-to-earth odds are that a hyperrealistic Avery was
smart enough to realize savaging a high-ranking member of the Mughal
royal court would bring unfathomable heat to his escape plan. Rape
was not his style. And at this stage in his career, the pirate king lusted
after just one thing: hard cash. Avery had immediately noticed one
quality in the princess: the great cabin was "cover'd with Diamonds,
and I, like a true Pirate, soon let her see that I had more Mind to the
Jewels than to the Lady."[8]

Upon seeing the "Lady in Tears," young and beautiful, Avery felt deep
compassion, and "pay'd the Respect that was due to her high Birth."[9]
Henry ordered his lieutenant to place a guard in front of the cabin door.
He was more than ready for some civilized company. A comedy of errors
quickly started playing out. The princess assumed the pirate king had
bolted the door to have his wicked way and then kill her. To delay the
deed, she pulled off "her Jewels as fast as she could, and give them to
me; and I, without any great Compliment, took them as fast as she gave
them me, and put them into my Pocket."[10]

Two more women from her retinue, all crying, knelt in front of Avery
with their hands raised, begging for their mistress's life. The pirate king
proceeded to ravish not the princess but her wealth. By calm, reassuring
gestures, the pirate king made it clear that assault was not in the cards, as
long as she handed over all her jewels and money. The mood lifted. Henry
Avery the pirate was welcomed as the hero who saved the life of the
emperor's granddaughter, for which he would be thanked handsomely:

> She got up, smiling, and went to a fine Indian Cabinet, and
> open'd a private Drawer, from whence she took another little

> Thing full of little square Drawers and Holes; this she brings
> to me in her Hand, and offer'd to kneel down to give it me . . .
> and she gave me the little Box or Casket, I know not what to
> call it, but it was full of invaluable Jewels.[11]

Delighted with the bonus bulging in his pockets, the discovery of
which Avery reasoned there was no reason to share with the crew, he
started inspecting the decks and state of the ship. Broken crates and
crow-barred deck planks littered the gangways. A little later the princess's slave beckoned for Avery to hasten back to the great cabin. His
return was welcomed with unusual respect as her unlikely protector. A
meal had been prepared, and for the first time in months Avery tucked
into food fit for a king and sipped out of delicate blue-and-white Chinese porcelain.

The unexpected respect bestowed on the pillager of the *Gunsway*
included another going-home gift. After the meal was finished, the
princess approached a finely decorated wooden cabinet and pulled out
a hidden drawer. The pirate king found himself staring at around three
thousand coins of Pegu, a port city in Myanmar. Next, she opened several
other drawers, full of wealth "and then gave me the Key of the Whole."[12]
For the first time in years, Avery was dumbfounded. His cast-iron jaw
hit the floor.

By now the crew of the *Fancy* had spent a day and a half rum-
maging the *Gunsway*. For sure, Avery could have happily spent a while
longer enjoying the princess's hospitality, but it was time to move. The
lieutenant had pulled the captain aside and privately warned him that
"the Men would be ruin'd, by lying with the Women in the other Ship,
where all Sorts of Liberty was both given and taken" if they did not lift
anchor.[13] The princess and all the prisoners were let go to return to Surat
empty-handed.

As much as Avery protested to friends and authorities in years
to come, no one ever believed his restraint when he met Emperor

Aurangzeb's granddaughter. Pirates did as they pleased, everyone winked. Avery's honesty did not help his case, especially when he admitted that

> As for the Ship where the Women of inferior Rank were, and who were in Number almost two hundred, I cannot answer for what might happen in the first Heat; but even there, after the first Heat of our Men was over, what was done, was done quietly, for I have heard some of the Men say, that there was not a Woman among them but what was lain with four or five Times over, that is to say, by so many several Men; for as the Women made no Opposition, so the Men even took those that were next them, without Ceremony, when and where Opportunity offer'd.[14]

Soon after the *Gunsway* limped back to port in Surat, the Indo-Persian historian Khafi Khan heard all about the horrors of the pillage. He later confirmed in his *Selected Records of the Wise and Pure* how the crew of the *Fancy* stripped the men and violated the women, both old and young. Several honorable women from the family of Idrisi Sayyids chose to hurl themselves "into the sea, to preserve their chastity, and some others killed themselves with knives and daggers."[15]

While there was no escaping the real frenzy of rape, Avery swore black and blue that he never touched the princess. He did admit finding a lady who was "more agreeable . . . and who I was afterwards something free with, but not even with her either by Force, or by Way of Ravishing."[16] The pirate king felt deeply wronged.

Henry Avery did not violate the Mughal princess. The very thought would have broken his personal code, reminding him of the painful years he endured when love betrayed him in his youth. The pirate king, in full control of his emotions and actions, was backed up by the firsthand witness account of crew member William Philips, a former trooper in Lord Devonshire's regiment, who turned state's evidence.[17] At the trial for piracy of some of the *Fancy*'s crew in London in October 1696, Philips swore under oath that "there were no women of any quality on board nor any ravished as is reported."[18] Why would the jury be surprised that the pirate undoubtedly committed perjury on the stand?

Still, Henry Avery would go to his grave accused of having "plunder'd . . . something more pleasing than the Jewels"[19] in the emperor's granddaughter, whom he found to be "the Brightest Jewel of his East."[20]

In truth, the pirate king had far weightier matters on his mind than women. There would be plenty of time for fun and games. Right now was the time for absolute focus—sink or swim.

Strong Men of Nassau

Henry Avery had his hands on the golden goose. Keeping his head on his neck would be a tougher trick. Most pirates were brought to justice and met a sticky ending. For now, all the world's seas flowed before Avery. Too many options can be a dangerous thing.

The pirate stealthily steered past Hog Island. In the English waters of the Bahamas, his crew were under strict orders to call him Henry Bridgeman. The *Fancy*'s gold, silver, and diamonds were spirited away under false floorboards in the captain's cabin.

Palm trees bowed toward the battered ship and newly crowned pirate king. Sea oats shimmered in the early morning breeze. Blue skies and light winds. It was going to be a beautiful day. The final leg into Nassau's calm harbor was tricky. It took a skillful old hand to squeeze through the narrow channel. On either side, shifting sandbars waited to chew up and spit out wayward traders, nationality be damned. One false move off West Point and all the months of jeopardy would have been for nothing.

It was April 1, 1696. A day to make fools of the smartest of men. Luckily, Henry Bridgeman knew all about New Providence. He understood what made the darkest of souls tick and was skilled in turning any man to his way of thinking.

New Providence was the perfect place to make landfall. It strad-
dled the ancient sea lanes between Carolina and Jamaica, Britain's
colonies on the East Coast of America and the tropical Caribbean
to the south. Havana, Cuba, was just a three days' hop away. From
Nassau you could watch the panorama of New World trade gliding by.
Catch me if you can, Bridgeman whispered into the moody trade winds.

The Bahamas was paradise. It had everything. So the king's collector
of customs, John Graves, championed the region's bounty:

> They are the most healthy Islands of all our Settlements; and
> tho' the Ground be very rocky, it will produce whatever is
> put into it, the best of Cotton in all the Indies. Dying Wood,
> Canes, Indigo and great Quantities of Salt made by the Sun
> out of the Sea. Tortoise-Shell, Oyl of Whale, Seal and Nurse,
> &c Spermacaeti-Whale sometimes. Amber-Greece often
> washed up on the Bays.[1]

New Providence, the heart of the islands of the Bahamas, at twenty-
eight miles long and eleven miles wide, was big enough to lay low.
Ships of less than five hundred tons could tiptoe through the shallow
sandbanks into Nassau's harbor if they knew where the underwater
canyon lay, sculpted by nature to a depth of twenty-four feet. It was
said that Britain's entire Royal Navy squadron could fit into the port
at any one time.[2]

The town's ponds and rock reservoirs, kept cool by thick overhanging
trees, brimmed with fresh water. Fish were plentiful. On land you could
trap your pick of coneys, cows, sheep, hogs, or goats. The Bahamas'
oranges, pine nuts, grapes, pomegranates, bananas, and plantains were
ripe for the picking.[3]

Best of all, New Providence had a sweet reputation for aiding and
abetting villains. The pirate mantra—"Ask me no questions and I'll tell
you no lies"—could have been invented for this dodgy outback. Henry

Avery, now in the guise of Henry Bridgeman, knew the bad folk of New Providence were as rotten as a shipwrecked barrel of apples. In fact, he was banking on it. The Bahamas' motley mob were experts in fishing wrecks sunk along the Florida coast, rushing to salvage Spanish, British, Dutch, and French valuables lost to hurricanes and storms. It was easy and generous work that beat breaking your back tilling the hateful earth.

Bad navigation and the Old Bahama Channel's dangerous currents had chewed up many a trader. Pride of place went to the crown jewel of the islands, the Spanish galleon the *Nuestra Señora de las Maravillas* sunk in January 1656.[4] Seville's skippers and merchants squirreled away so much illegal contraband on fleet ships that no one had a clue how much loot sank on the *Maravillas*. Word had it that millions of pieces of eight still carpeted the Little Bahama Bank. A man could retire on the back of that kind of filthy lucre. Just because the Bahamas did not have an official government did not stop its governors rubber-stamping salvage permits it had no right to authorize. All for a fee and a cut of the loot. Corrupt thinking led Avery to this rogue's lair.

The New Providence of 1696 was a long way from becoming the world's wickedest republic of pirates, its chaotic lanes home to Benjamin Hornigold, Blackbeard, Calico Jack Rackham, Charles Vane, Mary Read, and Anne Bonny. By the fall of 1717, eight hundred pirates would rendezvous in New Providence to divide spoils, fence looted cargos, and party away their ill-gotten gains. At times the lair swelled to a thousand cutthroats, commanded by a changing who's who of crazed leaders.[5] Brawn and brains were respected, but strength always won control. All pirate captains understood that on these shores, the "strongest man carrys the day."[6]

"Bridgeman" had a knack for reading places and people like others read books. As an ex–Royal Navy salt turned skipper of the meanest pirate ship on the high seas, he needed to decide in a blink of an eye who he could trust and what gossip peddled in some mosquito-infested East African tavern was hogwash. His gut rarely let him down.

Peering through his eyepiece, Long Ben—so his crew called Avery on deck—made out a few dozen makeshift huts inland of the trees screening the coast. Disgruntled logwood cutters had recently fled to New Providence in the hope of a life free from stiff Spanish and British iron-fisted authorities on Hispaniola. Loggers made first-rate builders. In Nassau they split cedar and pine logs, dug thatch palmettos into postholes, and set up rectangular huts. The cozy log walls were padded with wattles of woven mangrove stakes daubed with limestone clay. Roofs were covered with overlapping stripped palmetto leaves so rainwater could run straight off when storms ripped through the town. Nothing fancier was needed.

Bridgeman spied what was little more than a shantytown on the make. Locals were gathering salt to stop shipboard meat from rotting too quickly and to hawk to passing Newfoundland and New England cod-fishing traders. The New Providence of 1700, with a hundred houses and a church, was still a few years away. Up the slope, piles of masonry were being cut and plastered into foundation trenches to build the town's desperately needed stone Fort Nassau with twenty-eight cannon, paid for by port customs' profits. Its gates would only open in February 1697.[7]

The man who put the world's economy on a knife-edge drew deeply on his pipe filled with Virginia's finest tobacco. The gray smoke billowed into the charred rafters and out the chimney stack. To freedom. Henry Avery was thinking about liberty as well. Not dreaming. The hard knocks of family life as a child, and betrayal by the Royal Navy, had shattered any dreams Avery once cherished. These days he was a cold-blooded hyperrealist.

Avery had just become the first pirate commander to chase down a Mughal emperor's treasure ship. Overnight, he and his crew were millionaires, celebrities, notorious. The pirate would enjoy the moment before deciding his fate. Wise heads among his crew favored staying in the

Americas, lording it in the nouveau riche New World, ready to again take to the waves when they had betted or wasted away their windfall. The French had jumped ship at Dascaran in East Africa and vanished into the wild, where money lasted forever and the women were plentiful and not picky about pirates' poor hygiene and foul mouths. The British crew had sailed with Avery to Nassau, hankering after more civilized ways.

There was much to be said for staying in the Americas—the laid-back lifestyle, the tropical mood, the sun on your back standing next to the tiller. No doubt about it. But the people were vermin. And the culture. What culture? Avery had rolled out his deadly plans with all the guile and strategic know-how that his navy training taught him. His scheming was not over yet. Ever since stripping the stricken *Gunsway* off Surat, Avery had been thinking about payback. To the family of his old governor who cheated him out of his fortune. To his country for betraying his men in La Coruna.

How much power can a man buy with a fortune like mine? Avery pondered. And power meant returning home to England. England, the land of his fathers, and Bideford in Devon, thick with bittersweet memories. Yet again, Henry Avery would prove the world wrong.

The nectar of the pirate's sweet tobacco was a welcome respite from the anarchy of New Providence. The town had no proper governing body and little order. Human waste and garbage choked the alleys. A whiff of rot hung over the town. Avery had no plans of settling down in the midst of a stinking dump.

New Providence was not yet the bustling market where anything was possible, an early American dream where pirates fenced stolen porcelain from China, spices from the Indies, cotton and calico from India, and laundered their ill-gotten gains. But it was getting there. Just looking around the small tavern, off-the-clock crews with cash to spend could find all kinds of entertainment to relieve their weary souls. Gambling, drinking, whoring—Nassau obliged with them all.

Nassau's women were greatly outnumbered by men. Those who did not fancy mending clothes, doing laundry, working in the stores, or cooking could earn big. The town's prostitutes charged whatever they wanted. A desperate pirate might pay five hundred pieces of eight (around $3,000 today), just to see a woman naked.[8] Rumor had it that before turning pirate, Anne Bonny made her money on her back in downtown Nassau.

Besides pleasure, salty sea folk came to Nassau to refit and resupply their tired ships. Outside the tavern window, Avery saw the bones of repairs, abandoned hulls, and burned-out prizes littering the shores. The island's wide, open beaches were perfect for careening hulls, beaching ships, listing them to one side and scraping off the foul barnacles and shipworms that infest the tropical Caribbean. In a few short years, New Providence would become the Americas' capital for colonial drifters and buying plunder at rock-bottom prices. Everyone would live by the one rule, "The strongest man carrys the day."[9]

Henry Avery sipped his glass of wine—no Catholic sobriety for the pirate king. He may have been tarred as an enemy of all mankind, but he was still a defender of the Crown—the British Protestant Crown—till the death. Loyal royalists believed in making merry, and nothing was merrier than drinking the good health of the monarchy from an aristocratic claret. Claret also happened to be the most expensive top-shelf booze going. Henry Avery would not be drinking to his good fortune in drain-water beer or hellfire Jamaican rum. He planned to polish off a couple of bottles of Château Haut-Brion and get rip-roaring sozzled. If it had been good enough for King Charles II's wine cellar, it was good enough for the pirate king.

Avery had complicated reasons for wanting to head home to England. He had always played by a high-minded code. Even though the world was condemning him as the darkest soul on the waves, a heartless cutthroat who would do anything to anyone for a few pieces of eight, Avery had battled to keep his crew on the right side of his law.

When Henry decided to seek a fortune by preying on enemy ships, he swore he would never hunt British prey. He remembered the letter he wrote and nailed to a tavern door on the island of Johanna, midway between Tanzania and Madagascar, promising fellow allies that "I have never yet wronged any English or Dutch, nor ever intend to whilst I am commander."[10]

The pirate king loved England unconditionally. Sure, many rotten eggs tried their damnedest to ruin the homeland, but what nation did not? The pirate king's true reason for heading home, deep down—not that he would ever admit it to his mean crew—was to see Mrs. Avery again. If he said a word, his ship's company would think he had gone soft in the head. Since leaving La Coruna and going on the pirate account, Henry had not written a line home. A communication blackout had been the only safe way to cover his tracks and protect his loved ones.

Night after night, the thought of his wife stuck back home in Ratcliffe Highway in east London, sweating to make wigs by candlelight for the land's good and great nobs, left to wonder whatever happened to her husband, gnawed away at Henry's guilt. They would meet again. And then Mrs. Avery could stop shredding her fingers with lowly domestic work. With the Mughals' gold, she would hang up her thimble, wear silk, and move out of the rat-infested hovels of the sailor town to smart St. James's. Dare Henry dream a little? Everything was going too well.

Henry Avery's plan had gone just how he hoped. On paper, Nicholas Trott, governor of New Providence, was an upstanding pillar of the community. Avery knew better. He had gained intelligence about the top dog's true nature. Trott liked to frog-march around the harbor with his crisp leather ledger tucked under his arm, all-important. But make no bones about it, Avery knew that the governor was a snake in the grass without a shred of experience serving king and country. He was promoted by guile and family connections, earning the governorship of Bahamas to buy him off when his cargo of tobacco spoiled after a heavy-handed

English customs officer impounded it in Bermuda and the Trotts threatened to sue. He took the governorship and generously promised to let the king's lords off the hook.

Trott had been in office since August 1694, dreaming of his own empire. For an empire you needed people and muscle. Trott smartly pledged twenty-five acres of free land to any settler who arrived before March 1695, topped up with extra real estate for a wife and children.[11] Charles Town was remodeled and renamed Nassau after one of King William III's grand titles. The rising fort would be Trott's legacy and insurance policy to lock himself in if anyone came for his head. In this small pond, Trott was a fat fish. The strongest man in town carried the day. For now. The king of the pirates would play nice, try diplomacy. If that failed, he would have no qualms strangling Trott's neck till his eyes popped out.

The rumors swirling around the Caribbean left no doubt that Nicholas Trott was the greatest villain in the Bahamas. The snake would do anything to fill his boots. Hardly had he stepped onto New Providence's shore as governor than the Dutch trader the *Juffrow Geertruÿd* (Miss Gertrude), was cast ashore, loaded with seventy-four thousand Spanish pieces of eight and a rich cargo. Sixty-five of the ship's crew rowed for seventeen grueling days straight without a drop of water. New Providence should have been their sanctuary.[12]

And how did the dear governor welcome the heroic survivors? Seizing an opportunity for a quick buck, Trott confiscated their arms and sent out a sloop to salvage their silver. When the Dutch complained about being treated like pirates, Trott shrugged and warned them that he was the king of Providence. He could do whatever he pleased. Sure, the governor would release the Dutchmen. As soon as they coughed up forty pieces of eight a man, thank you very much.

Henry Avery was also aware that Trott had grabbed land when merchants and landowners refused to pay his fabricated fees. The devious governor would soon get his hands on Hog Island for the throwaway price of £50.[13] The arrow-shaped, three-mile-long island sheltered the entrance to Nassau harbor from wind and wave. Whoever owned Hog Island controlled entry in and out of New Providence—and so all the trade.

The stench of Trott's lawless rule was already worrying Anglo-American authorities. Richard Coote, the powerful 1st Earl of Bellomont and governor of Massachusetts Bay, knew plenty about leveraging the buck in these backwaters. The same rotten politician would soon bend over backward to financially back Captain William Kidd to hunt down pirates and prey on enemy shipping in the Red Sea, but later throw him to the wolves, plotting his capture and hanging for piracy to save his own sweaty, triple-chinned neck. The foul-tempered Coote's angry letter warned London what a mess the colonies were and that "Trott is the greatest pirate-broker that was ever in America."[14]

To Henry Avery, dropping into Nassau and dealing with Nicholas Trott was no big risk of being slung into a dungeon for piracy. Trott was no gamble. Here was a man who could be bought, greedy to top up his demeaning £30 a year governor's salary. Money meant power. Power meant status. The question was, what was his price?

To be sure his reckoning was sound, that morning Avery had moored the *Fancy* six leagues away and sent Thomas Hollingsworth, Robert Clinton, and Henry Adams to New Providence on the ship's boat with a personal note for the governor.[15] Avery, in the guise of Bridgeman, pretended his ship was a slaver bending the rules, as so many did, trafficking enslaved Africans and 126 elephant tusks of around two tons without the seal of approval from the Royal African Company that owned the Crown monopoly over the trade.[16]

The *Fancy*'s tall tale claimed the crew needed permission to take on provisions before going straight. Avery sent a purse stuffed with pieces of eight to make sure the governor got the point. In return for the courtesy of letting him land, the governor could expect a tip of twenty silver pieces of eight and two pieces of gold from each crew member. Bridgeman would pay double as captain.

Trott's fawning reply played the innocent to perfection. With a nudge and a wink, he embraced Avery's crew as "Soldiers of Fortune" who "had done no Christian Nation any damage & were the king's agents." Trott sent Hollingsworth, Clinton, and Adams back to the *Fancy* weighed down with a cask of wine, a hogshead of beer, and a cask of sugar, as well as permission for Captain Bridgeman to land at his leisure.[17]

The pirate king chuckled at the memory of Governor Trott waiting on the dock when the *Fancy*, firing all its guns, glided into Nassau in a show of strength. The message was clear: respect my terms or I can blow you out of town. In all his finery—puffed up gray wig, white cotton cravat, matching blue waistcoat and jacket with brass buttons—Trott marched these shores like an aristocratic milord.

Avery knew that Trott knew what game was afoot. Before puffing out his chest and playing at power, the governor had been a humble merchant and henchman on Bermuda. Trott only needed to glance at the *Fancy*'s English and Irish crew, clad in a riotous rainbow of silks from India and headscarves from Africa warding off the high-rising sun, for the penny to drop that the ship was no slaver but had been fishing for treasure in the Indies. Which could mean only one thing: piracy. Even if Trott turned a blind eye, the shrapnel riddling the *Fancy*'s side planks from fighting the powerful *Gunsway* was a clear giveaway of mischief.

The two strongest men in town retreated to a back room in the Wheel of Fortune inn. No verbal arm wrestling was needed. Trott did not give a damn. Especially after Avery sweetened the deal by offering Trott the *Fancy*. The ship had served the pirates ably, but was a pitiful ruin on its last legs. Avery needed to be rid of it.

The smiling beacon of hospitality opened the town to Avery and his men, who tried to keep a low profile. Captain's orders. When you pay for wine and women with exotic gold and silver coins from Yemen and India, though, heads turn, tongues wag. Avery watched his men make very merry after two years at sea. They were piling on the charm, but he knew their moods could switch in an instant. They were pirates, cut from the toughest teak. One wrong look or word and the cutlasses would swing. Best to get the crew out of town as fast as possible before the legend of Henry Avery the pirate king, raging across the seven seas like a Caribbean hurricane, reached the Bahamas.

New Providence brought great fortune to all that fateful day of April 1, 1696. Avery had heard it said that colonial governors needed to make £400 a year to stay on the right side of the law.[18] Trott was a pauper by comparison. The governor's face was one of comic shock when Avery opened his battered wooden chest and dumped 1,860 pieces of eight on the tavern table, which almost cracked under its weight—twenty coins for each of the ninety-three crew.

Avery gambled rightly that Trott would have a field day with the ivory cargo camouflaging as a part of a slaver voyage in the *Fancy*'s hold. Elephant tusks were the most valuable West African good after gold. The governor could flog the white gold for a small fortune to a passing merchant. It would end up in an artist's studio in Amsterdam, Paris, or London, its soft, satiny surface sculpted into swanky artworks, medallions of aristocrats and nobility, dentures, or the odd dildo.

Avery knew full well that the clincher for Governor Trott would be the *Fancy*'s big banging guns, forty-six cannon, and a hundred barrels of gunpowder. French forces had recently seized the island of Exuma, 140 miles away. Rumor had it they were heading for Nassau with three warships and 320 men.[19] Fear filled the air. Nassau had no men-of-war and Trott's stone fort was a building site. But with dozens of guns lining the shore, the French would think twice about rape and pillage.

Trott was as pleased as punch as he strolled out of the Wheel of Fortune inn that night, his back straining under the weight of silver. By the time the governor grounded the *Fancy* on Hog Island and started stripping its bones bare, he had raked in a small fortune. The strong man was rich and had hardly needed to lift a finger.

As the weeks unfolded, there would be only be one winner. Henry Avery's crew scattered. The pirates were spotted openly walking the streets of Philadelphia, thick as thieves with judges and sheriffs, the *Gunsway*'s riches buying influence and power. Others preferred spending their loot in New York, Connecticut, and New Jersey. A few of the crew stayed local. Daniel Smith and Benjamin Griffin settled in Bermuda. Seven of Avery's crew married in New Providence and bribed Nicholas Trott to sign royal pardons. The pirates went straight.

All the while, the rumor mill churned alarmingly. The wrecking ball of Avery's recent past was catching up with him. East India Company agents were seeking the pirate king in Bombay and Calcutta. The Royal Navy was thinking about dispatching battleships to hunt for the *Fancy* in the waters between West Africa, Madagascar, and Arabia. Bounty hunters crisscrossed the world from the Indian Ocean to the English Channel. Henry Avery was the most wanted man in the world. The world's first global manhunt was underway.

As the number of guns for hire searching for the pirate grew, and the proclamations flew from port to port, the legend of Henry Avery the pirate king echoed through the world's taverns, smoky coffee shops, and fashionable ladies' salons. Avery had shown the world how to unpick the richest treasure box on earth and the wealth waiting to be stolen from heathen pockets.

Every pirate wanted to match Avery's strike. The golden age of piracy had begun. Men of fortune flooded the Red Sea and Indian Ocean. Captain William Kidd, the man sent on a mission in September 1696 to hunt down and destroy pirates marauding between the East Coast of America and the Red Sea, joined the free for all by seizing the *Quedagh Merchant*.[20] Four years later, the pirate hunter ended up on the end of a rope at London's Execution Dock, the scapegoat for the evil chaos that Avery's pirate gang unleashed.[21]

Henry Avery wanted to keep his precious head on his neck. So far his plan had worked like a dream. Nicholas Trott was eating out of the palm of his hand. Avery was now the strongest man in Nassau.

The burning question, needing resolving urgently, was how to slip through the closing net. Should the pirate king hide out in the Caribbean or head to England and payback? A life of luxury in the West Indies—the Wild West—or risk it all and be damned back for retribution on far more dangerous British soil?

World's End

World's End in a godforsaken bog appealed to the man who lived in the shadows.

No respectful Londoner visited Essex's dripping marshes. The air was dank and unhealthy, the byways a no-man's-land between life and death. Too much open space. Water everywhere. In the river, in the moist air, in the soil. This charmless place was not fit for gentlemen.

Only a year ago in 1695, the man with the dark brown hair, hooked nose, sharp chin, and gray eyes that missed nothing was on the rise. The insomniac darted from market to coffeehouse, ears eager for news of the day and tidbits of gossip. Indiscretions uttered by loose lips were knowledge. Knowledge was power. Daniel Foe had traded a fortune and lost, and now he was back, looking for commercial know-how, whether it was bought or eavesdropped.

Foe's old life was over. Gone was the elegant cravat, flowing gown, and full-bottomed wig. Gone the country house, the coach and horses. Despite the setbacks, his mind was no pit of despair. At the grand age of thirty-six, Foe dared to dream once more.

Appearances had to be kept up to impress the baying mob that he was not washed up. Foe bolted and locked the tile factory's sliding oak-paneled door and dusted down his long brown gown with shiny brass buttons. The brownish-red striped waistcoat with sharp lapels and rounded hem, pulled crisply down above dark green knee breeches, were survivors, like him, from his years flogging hosiery in the family business.

Another day was over. And each passing day his wounded soul healed a little more in his climb out of hell. Foe would show his enemies, a phoenix flying out of the smoldering ashes of his battered business empire. Perching his dark gray tricorn hat on his head, the tradesman stuffed a pinch of Virginia tobacco into a white clay pipe and sucked the infernal fumes, allowing himself a little satisfaction.

Thinking always brought up ghosts. Foe would never forgive his transgressions. He had blown sweet Mary's £3,700 dowry ($520,000 today) on shoddy investments. Disdain had replaced the kindness of her father, John Tuffley, who pushed Foe's interests in the wholesale trade and introduced him to London's livery company.[1] Joan, his mother-in-law, had taken him to court for outstanding debts.[2] For a while he had it all. And it slipped through his fingers like the waters of the Thames flowing in front of him from Tilbury down to the English Channel.

Daniel Foe's grand vision was genius. But when it came to the daily grunt of handling money, he was rashly irresponsible. Some of his big schemes were spiked by nothing more than ill luck. Deals buying and selling with the Lombard Street goldsmith and that Love Lane merchant manufacturing saltpeter for gunpowder should have brought in easy cash. Why had those wolves in sheep's clothing not given him more time to pay off their investments? No need to have sued at the King's Bench.

Other schemes, the more Foe thought about it, were pure stupidity, the rush of blood that comes with youth. He yearned for adventure and he would never have forgiven himself if he had failed to buy into Joseph Williams's plan to dive with his engine on a Genoese silver cargo sunk off the Bumble Rock in 1667 and a Spanish ship castaway in Polpeor Cove in 1619 with £100,000 of silver ingots.[3]

Daniel Foe was a whiz at international sea trade, contracts, and contacts who just got unlucky. So he told himself. The Lizard dive scheme had a greedy logic. But his wildcats? Each day, castaway in the boggy marshes of Tilbury, Foe whipped his soul for investing in those seventy hissing Abyssinian civet cats. Wasn't it a surefire hit? London's elegant crowd were mad for the perfume made from the buttery oil extracted from their anal glands. It sounded foul to Foe, but this was a get-rich scheme if ever he saw one. Greedily he made a deal with Jacob Dela-fontayn Jan Zoon, who was offloading the beasts. To the stinky scent's qualities, experts told him it cured diseases of the head and brain, fits and vapors, bad hearing, barrenness, and depression of spirits.[4] Quack medicine or not, these promises would do his sales no harm. Foe was hooked.

Hardly had the cattery in Stoke Newington been in business for a few months when Foe was dogged by skullduggery. Instead of sinking the cash he raised into the perfume venture, he started juggling his purse again, diverting his capital for a little while to pay off heavy-handed credi-tors. Foe was already thousands of pounds in debt when he was thinking about acquiring the cattery.

To pay for the land in Tilbury, his river island empire, Foe flogged the cat scheme to his mother-in-law, Joan Tuffley.[5] The penny soon dropped that her beloved daughter's rogue of a husband technically did not own the wildcats. What choice did she have but to sue for fraud? Daniel's family still believed in his abilities, not his bad choices. The word in the coffeehouses was to watch out for Daniel Foe. Bit of a knave and a gambler that fellow.

Little did London see the fire burning ever higher inside the tradesman. How many of the gay crowd laughing in the capital, across this land, this world, knew what it was like to live forever looking over your shoulder? Wondering where the next crack of the whip would come from? The next door to shut in your face.

Coming from Dissenter stock molded Foe's every thought, action, and word. Foe had good reason to be scared of his own shadow. Popish plots and the threat of James, the Duke of York, seizing the throne were sometimes invented and, at others, a real fear. In 1678, when Foe was just eighteen years old, Titus Oates had blown the whistle on a plan to shoot King Charles II. The king laughed off the assassination threat until the corpse of one of his Protestant magistrates, Sir Edmund Berry Godfrey, turned up in Primrose Hill. He had been strangled. A sword with a Catholic cross-shaped hilt had been plunged through his heart. Twenty-two Catholics were rounded up and executed.[6]

Foe was a man of words but also action when pushed to the cliff's edge. In a desperate plot to throw the Catholic King James II off the throne, Foe had joined the illegitimate son of the deceased Charles II, the Duke of Monmouth. In his mind, the duke was the true heir to the crown. Rashly leaving behind his new wife in London, Foe had taken up arms after Lord Monmouth landed at Lyme Regis, ready to march on London and seize the throne from James.

Monmouth's uprising and poorly trained army was a shambles. His forces had been cut to shreds in a disastrous skirmish at Sedgemoor near Bristol on July 6, 1685. Monmouth was executed a few weeks later.[7] Before Foe fled to the Netherlands to save his skin, he was shocked to his boots to see his old school pals from Morton's academy—the rebels Battersby, Jenkins, and Hewlin—hanging from trees along the Bridgwater to Glastonbury Road. Daniel Foe, twenty-five years old, went into exile.[8]

A decade later, his high principles still never wavered. His hatred for the Catholic King James festered like an open wound. "For my part, I thank God, that when he was King" from 1685–1688, Defoe later wrote, "I never owned him, never swore to him, never prayed for him, never paid any act of homage to him, never so much as drank his health, but looked on him as a person who, being Popish [Catholic], had no right to rule."[9]

A life of hard knocks had cast Daniel Foe away as an outsider. He was forced to chase a living as a lowly merchant, all the while buying and selling were not in his heart. Foe felt like Julius Caesar, always watching for the next dagger in his back, so he wrote. Fear made a man desperate, a man vigilant, reliant on shreds of information to stay safe.

☠

Forget the past, Foe told himself, striding toward his house on the riverside of Tilbury Fort. Time to start afresh. And what possibilities the future promised. Foe had been pardoned for fighting with the Duke of Monmouth. Most of his creditors were at bay. Even if they tried to find him in the Essex marshes, he had hidden the large mole next to his mouth under white powder, and these days he was going by the more aristocratic-sounding Defoe.

The cash was starting to roll in once more as well. Thanks to a word in the ear of one of King William II's courtiers, Charles Montagu, 1st Earl of Halifax and chancellor of the exchequer, Defoe had landed the plum job of accountant for the new tax on glass. The merchant Dissenter had thought up a number of ways to help the Crown meet the soaring costs of the war with France. Not only did the tax job rake in £100 a year for Defoe, it got his foot on the political ladder.[10] Who knew how far the tradesman might climb?

Defoe's mind never stopped whirling. He hatched a thousand plans, and the hundreds of ideas he committed to ink were starting to reach influential ears. He had it on good authority that the king was keeping a close eye on his rising star. Was he too much trouble to handle, though? Defoe had put his name on the line by publishing *A Discourse about Raising Men* in 1696, supporting King William's plea that England's parishes be forced to send more men to fight France. Once the tradesman started writing, the floodgates opened. Ideas haunted Defoe's dreams. Not that he had much interest in sleep.

The flat Essex marshes, cut by deep ditches, were the perfect place for Defoe to hide away and keep a low profile. A perspective glass, an early telescope, hung from his waist wherever he went. It was more valuable to him than a sword. The Dissenter had spent a lifetime lurking in the shadows. Science helped him spot trouble from afar, jackals coming to claim debts.

Defoe spent much of the day in his tileworks, two miles inland from the River Thames near the villages of West Tilbury and Chadwell St Mary. The factory he owned from juggling ill-gotten investments was in rude health. One hundred poor workers made him £600 a year.[11] With his all-or-nothing nose for the next big fashion, Defoe's twenty acres manufactured thin red bricks and elegant S-shaped roof tiles. Until the dissenting entrepreneur came along, expensive pantiles like these could only be imported from the Netherlands. Now they were all the rage in well-to-do homes.

Defoe's goods were in hot demand, his tiles supplying the Royal Hospital for Seamen in Greenwich. London was still rebuilding after the Great Fire gutted the city three decades earlier in 1666. The industrialist's bricks went into new streets. Defoe's rich vein of contacts in merchant shipping circles, especially his friendship with the trader Dalby Thomas, future governor in West Africa of the Royal African Company, saw his materials end up in chapels and slave prisons in England's forts strung along the Gold Coast.[12]

Secretly, Defoe was convinced his boggy soil was prime real estate. An outbreak of war with France would surely loosen the nation's purse strings. The wheeler-dealer was gambling on netting a handsome profit when the army would be forced to buy up the land around Tilbury Fort. This was the gateway to London, to England, where Queen Elizabeth I rode to take on the mighty Spanish Armada in 1588. Any invasion would need to march passed these very riverbanks. The battle for England would be won or lost right here. His Majesty's forces just had to invest in a massive artillery arsenal at Tilbury. It was the perfect setting. Then the outrageous price he would ask for his land would end his worries forever.

Only the army decided to develop Woolwich, not Tilbury, for its Royal Artillery base and Royal Brass Foundry for its guns. Defoe was shafted once again. In the meantime, he could not rest for a moment. The likes of Marescoe, Stamper, and Ghisleyn, who advanced Defoe funds to buy his Tilbury factory, were on the prowl for their pound of flesh.[13] The Dissenter was a long way from settling his financial worries.

☠

The sun was setting when Defoe's tavern came into view. On the ground floor, he raked in cash from thirsty soldiers billeted in Tilbury Fort and from his own factory workmen who seemed hell-bent on blowing their salaries on beer. The hard core headed out drinking on Saturday nights and "lie there until Monday, spend every penny and run into debt to boot, and not give a farthing of it to their families, though all of them had wives and children."[14] The tavern was a masterstroke, even if Defoe said so himself. He could hide in plain sight among the throng of faceless out-of-towners and watch the world go by, always from the shadows.

The World's End tavern stood a stone's throw from the gateway to London's Custom House.[15] Defoe looked like any other tradesman. Half the day he worked down at the wharf, loading his bricks onto ships and waving them off to the corners of the earth. All the while, he kept a beady eye on the flood of people coming in and out on every tide by the Gravesend ferry.

Defoe's rooms above the tavern enjoyed a majestic view of the shipping flowing along the great artery of the Thames. Large hoys of sixty tons carried Kent cherries to the capital. Barking fishing smacks flew up to market, loaded with mackerel from Folkestone. One of the river's finest sights were the powerfully built collier fleets, up to seven hundred sail at a time, coming upriver weighed down with Newcastle coal for London. Coasters trafficked wheat and Cheshire cheese from the Solent and Wash. Big merchant ships chugged in Oporto wine and Virginia tobacco, huge East Indiamen tea, and that flashy Indian calico that was ruining England's homespun cloth market and made Defoe's blood and pen ink boil.[16]

All the masters and sailors stopped in the World's End tavern to refresh their parched throats. Day after night, Defoe listened to tales of shanghaiing sailors, slavery, and cannibalism in Madagascar. Most of all, the inn was abuzz with the daring deeds of English pirates.

The epoch-making 1695 was the year of years when the golden age of piracy began. Henry Avery's capture of the *Gunsway* off Surat had left the Mughal Empire spitting feathers at England's failure to reign in its degenerate thieves. From the swift deck of the *Fancy*, Captain Avery had run down Emperor Aurangzeb's juggernaut of a trader heading home loaded with exotic goods from the Red Sea port of Mocha and with grand courtiers returning from the hajj pilgrimage to Mecca.

Would you know it, a single cannonball cut down the *Gunsway*'s main mast, leaving the pride of India a sitting duck, Defoe had heard many tongues wag. London's gossip mill was grinding out rumor after rumor. Did you know Avery got away with £600,000 in gold, silver, and jewels? Shocking. Is it true the crew raped the courtiers and the captain had his wicked way with the emperor's granddaughter? Then they ran off to the island of Madagascar, living like lords. No, they escaped to New Providence and Boston. My brother's uncle heard the pirates returned to Bristol, where the gang split up, some going to ground in Ireland, others in Cornwall, and more running north of the border to Scotland.

One thing everyone agreed on: Captain Henry Avery had pulled off the big one. He had seized a king's ransom and vanished with an unfathomable fortune. Then in the early summer of 1696, Henry Avery the pirate king became a ghost.

Daniel Defoe was transfixed. Writing pamphlets might make him a political player, earning prestige at the highest tables in the land. But it did nothing to satisfy the romantic adventurer inside him. Defoe had another vested interest in what he knew was more than a tall tale. Henry Avery and he were actually acquainted. Defoe liked to think they were even friends, albeit from a very different, more innocent, time.

Defoe had often run into Avery on his travels to deepest Cornwall when he was just another budding tradesman dreaming big. The Dissenter saw a kindred spirit desperate to break away from the sorry trappings life had dealt him and show the world.

Deep into the night, the pair used to chat about everything—family, trade, empire, the sea, travel, adventure, and the future. They shared a string of personal coincidences. Both men were born in 1660. Defoe's mother died when he was a boy of ten, Avery's when he was just six. Both were orphans. Defoe was an outsider who had to fight tooth and nail for every inch of luck as he made his way up life's greasy pole. Avery may have been born into a worthy estate, owned by a father who was a trusted sea captain and made enough to retire young, but he crossed the bar into the next world when his son was just eleven years old.

Avery's fate was thrust on him by a dishonest neighbor, Defoe's by birth. And so, Avery and Defoe became blood brothers in their most impressionable years, and whenever they met drank away their troubles. Who could have imagined how infamously high they would both rise?

Even hidden away in the marshes of Tilbury, word of Henry Avery's piratic daring reached Daniel Defoe's ears in 1696. Over and over, he had read the lines of the ballad *Villany Rewarded* about his old friend's adventures:

> We with our Comrades, not yet ta'en,
> together did agree,
> And stole a Ship out from the Groyne,
> to Roam upon the Sea:
> With which we Robb'd, and Plunder'd too
> no Ship that we did spare,
> Thus many a one we did undo,
> let Pyrates then take care.

Our Ship being well stored then
   for this our Enterprise,
One Hundred and Eighty Men
   there was in her likewise:
We Pillag'd all we could come nigh,
   no Nation did we spare,
For which a shameful death we dye,
   let Pirates then take care.

To Daniel Defoe, Henry Avery's pirate mob had it all: adventure, wealth, an escape from unjust rules. To the great merchants Defoe dealt with in London, Avery may have been tarred as an enemy of all mankind, but his life inspired the Dissenter. The seed of an idea had taken hold in Defoe's mind. That year he started filling his diaries with tales spouted by every sea dog with a loose tongue he met in the World's End tavern. Some were pure nonsense fueled by too much booze. Others, just maybe, had legs. A pirate book? Now *that* would sell like hot cakes.

In his tavern, Defoe learnt about the pirates' republic rising from the shores of Sainte-Marie Island off the east coast of Madagascar, a secret lair for captains like Avery sailing to and from the richest sea lanes in the world, crisscrossing the waters between Mocha in the Red Sea and Surat in India. Defoe knew all their names. He had even met some of them. In October 1696 he could not help but disguise himself and sneak into the back of the trial of Henry Avery's crew at the Old Bailey, taking realms of notes.

The stories of Joseph Dawson, Edward Forseith, William May, William Bishop, James Lewis, and John Sparkes seemed like the stuff of make-believe. All stood accused of seizing the *Gunsway* and its sparkling cargo, the likes of which had never been stolen on the high seas.[17] When the men were hanged on Execution Dock, Defoe was among the rubbernecking mob watching everyone and everything as the tide at Wapping washed over their bodies staked to the high-water mark. Also on the sidelines, Defoe had given the faintest of nods to a tall, well-set man of about forty, gray-eyed and swarthy, paying his last respects to the men at the end of the rope. Much of his face and flattish nose were hidden under a light-colored wig.

☠

Daniel Defoe never forgot a face. Three nights before, when he had surveyed the crowd in World's End before heading to his desk, there in the corner was the same man. The face he had befriended decades ago in Falmouth. Henry Avery was back from the dead.

For the most wanted man in the world, with a £1,000 bounty on his head, the arch-pirate looked in rude health, relaxed, calm. Was there a man on Earth who would dare cross him? The pirate king was back in Britain, hiding in plain sight in the shadow of the hangman's noose.

Defoe thought it wise to invite Avery into his private quarters, behind closed doors. They broke open the good stuff and stayed up all night reminiscing. An awestruck Defoe wanted to know everything. Why had Avery gone on the account, turning his back on the Royal Navy? What was it like commanding a pirate mob? He did not go so far as to ask about Avery's future plans for keeping his head on his neck. Theft on the high seas was one thing. Raping the emperor of India's entourage was unforgivable. Surely there was no way of worming his way out of that orgy of violence?

For the first time that night, Henry Avery's shoulders had drooped when the story came up and his skin paled. The pirate hung his head. There was no escaping the brutal truth. And Avery never lied. Daniel Defoe listened and memorized every detail. How when the pirates' hooks went over the side of the *Gunsway*, Henry had feared the worst. That moment should have been his crowning glory. Instead, depression racked his body and he took to his cabin, locking the latch. Let humanity unfold as it will, he had decided. There was no other choice. The *Fancy's* pirate crew were no longer under his command. They were rich. To the victor belong the spoils.

The Mughal ship was full of high-born maidens traveling back from paying their respects to Allah and Mohammed in Mecca. Avery did not want to see the orgy of rape. It was bad enough hearing the screams ringing out across the water. The crew had fallen into the pit of human depravity. It was true, Avery shrugged. The only women who escaped being assaulted were the ones who jumped overboard or stabbed themselves to death, drifting slowly down into the Indian Ocean's abyss. East and West would never forget or forgive the rapists' bloodbath.

Even though Henry Avery kept well away from the carnage that broke his personal code, sparing the princess herself, he knew that he would be made to pay. Forever held guilty. The horror stories spread far and wide. They said he even led the charge, "taking the Great Mogul's Daughter, ravishing and murdering her, and all the Ladies of her Retinue."[18]

Avery may not have touched, let alone raped, any of the *Gunsway*'s aristocrats, but he was the brains behind the assault. The dual disgust of piracy and rape was something East and West could not overlook. Because of the enormity of the haul seized from the *Gunsway* and Mughal India's rightful fury at the crew's anarchy, Avery would spend the rest of his life on the run, always scanning the crowd. His crew's rush of blood to the head in the heat of battle, after so many months of dull failure, was pirate human nature, Avery told himself. What went down on the *Gunsway* pained him to the core. But he would not let the crimes of his own men destroy his plans. Henry focused on his big picture. He had clawed back his wealth. Now, finally, it was payback time for his enemies in England. Captain Avery had zigzagged away from the scene of the crime to stay alive and always knew unfinished business would pull him to his old homeland.

Defoe listened hard. He did not judge. In fact, he felt sympathy for his old trading friend. The Royal Navy was a den of dossers commanded by despicable stiff upper lips with wobbly chins. The institution needed reforming badly. Truth be told, Defoe admired the pirate for his guts in going on the account, for his glory. He was even jealous. Apart from supporting the Duke of Monmouth at the Battle of Sedgemoor, what the hell had Daniel Defoe done with his life?

Defoe, eager to impress the pirate king, could not help overplay his cards. It was true that he had started sending dispatches to the government through the Earl of Halifax at the glass tax office whenever he saw anything suspicious in the marshes. But it was hardly earthshaking action. Henry Avery was a household name. Daniel Defoe was still a nobody.

Now a little drunk, Defoe remembered the words he had scribbled into his journal earlier that week. Pompously, he preached the importance of people like himself to king and country. "Intelligence is another point of mighty consequence," he slurred, leaning close to Avery, "and can scarce be purchas'd too dear." He stopped, pretending to search for the right words, even though he had total recall of every line. "For it is the soul of Government," he went on, "and directs all its actions properly, and without it you consult in the dark, and execute blindfold. You know not what to act, what to fear, where to attack, or where to defend."[19]

Avery was curious and quizzed his friend about his ideas, his plans. No doubt about it, Defoe was obsessive, often unstoppable. Sink or swim. The pirate king also happened to make it his business to know that Defoe typically sank nine times out of ten.

When Daniel Defoe vainly promised that the king and country could use a man like Avery, the pirate king smiled and thought nothing of it. This was a quagmire out of which he alone would have to dig his way out. After surprising Mrs. Avery in Ratcliffe, he planned to ride south to visit some old acquaintances in Bristol and persuade them to launder some Indian diamonds.

Defoe was still rambling on. Something about arranging for Avery to exchange some of his loot for a royal pardon. Which he, Daniel Defoe, would personally arrange and deliver on a plate. No charge.

Avery was barely listening. The evening had been just fine, a relief to talk to a trustworthy kindred soul after months of worry. Avery did not have the privilege of hope. Defoe was a dreamer, Avery a man of action. All the pirate king needed was to stay a few footsteps in front of the bloodhounds chasing the warrant out for his head.

Wanted: dead or alive.

India in Chains

D espite the worries shared with Daniel Defoe at the World's End tavern, Henry Avery had no idea just how great a noise his name was making across the world. Taverns toasted him as the Robin Hood of the seas, an underdog who bloodied and broke the establishment's nose. Entertainers on street corners sang his name in ballads for a few pennies dropped into their hats. In the coffeehouses, learned men devoured the latest news about the political storm waves the *Fancy* churned up. Elegant ladies whispered in tea salons about whether pirates were dashing heroes, dastardly, or just plain rapists. It was all too thrilling.

The more the streets raved, the more the corridors of power raged. Furious letters fired off between London, Surat, and the colonies wriggled hard to protect England's reputation. India was beyond incensed. The homeland where Avery and his pirates were born was not to be trusted. The only antidote was the head of the pirate king. London needed to be seen to take Avery's assault on the *Gunsway* deadly seriously. The enemy of all mankind had to be brought to justice. The future of the Indies trade and building a British empire hung in the balance.

☠

Samuel Annesley, president of the East India Company's Council in
Surat,[1] saw the writing on the wall. Henry Avery's scandalous sacking of
the *Gunsway* was not going to blow over. Surat and Bombay demanded
justice. Or better, blood. The demand for vengeance was not just about
stolen cash, it was about sacrilege, an attack on a faith, Muslims fulfilling
the holy pilgrimage to Mecca, and dishonoring women.

Annesley had ridden out past pirate attacks and finger wagging
bruised but in one piece, until now. Officials in London thought the
Avery raid was a one-off, but Emperor Aurangzeb's India had been
humiliated time and time again by 1696, the year of the *Fancy*'s fateful
voyage. The Mughal Empire's ships had been raided in 1684 and 1689.
And it was all the fault of the English. As much as the East India Company's pens scribbled that the accusations were slanderous, the reality
on the ground made it too dangerous for Annesley to even step outside
without a guard.[2] Annesley was worried enough to warn the Company's
office in London early on that:

> Was it not on account of the piracys, we should live here in
> as great, or greater honour, credit and respect than ever, to
> the promoting thereof we do find all our endeavours checkt
> exceedingly by these our enemies endeavouring all they can,
> both at Court and here with the Government, to make us and
> these villains equall under the generall name of the English
> nation . . . if it please God to strengthen us that any of these
> rogues do fall into our clutches, we shall certainly make them
> publick examples to the whole world for the justification of
> our nation's honour and your Honours.[3]

No sooner had the *Fateh Muhammed* and *Gunsway* limped home to
Surat in September 1695, stripped bare, than Annesley—after learning
many painful lessons—shut up shop. The mob was stirring, a popular
uprising was in the air. Annesley screamed for the factory gates to be

locked. Just as the fanatic crowd of ruffians poured out of the city's bazaars, usually happily selling English goods for rich profits, Ushoor Beg, Surat's military commander, and his troops clattered on horseback up to the fort. The *harcoora* (third officer in town), mufti expert on Islamic law, and prominent Mughals had plucked lines from the Koran to justify the English being put to death in revenge for the murder and torture of so many, including the execution of Annesley.

The governor of Surat, Itimad Khan, caught between fulfilling his emperor's orders and following his own interests, decided to put Annesley and sixty-two other East India Company men in chains and lock them up in their factory grounds for the next eleven months. Their windows were boarded over. Darkness enveloped the British in India. Annesley later remembered those bleak days with horror. "It is needless to write of the indignities, slavish usages and tyrannical insultings wee hourly bear day and night," he complained.[4] A guard of two hundred soldiers surrounded the factory. England, already an island guest in India, was now cut off from the outside world. In the cold light of day, the governor had saved Annesley and his men from being torn to shreds at the hands of the mob.

Ashore, all Europeans were banned from carrying arms and traveling in litters. An Englishmen caught by the rabble on the street died of his wounds. Ships were forbidden from hoisting national flags. Trade was at a standstill, the safety of homeward-bound fleets in the lap of the gods. The very existence of the East India Company in India and the English trade was in jeopardy. "How often have we been falsely charged," Sir John Gayer, governor of the East India Company, huffed and puffed. "Nay, how often hath it been proved so, and yett upon every fresh alarm of a pyrate on the coast all is still laid upon the English, and the Company's Chief and Council, and gentlemen of quality, must like the meanest and basest criminals be clapt up in irons, chained together like a company of doggs to secure their lives being made a sacrifice to the rabble."[5]

As soon as he had the chance, Annesley bitterly protested to the governor of Surat at the absurdity of accusing the East India Company of piracy:

> For nine years past, have been the same false aspersions on us, and all along wee have at last appeared merchants and not pyrates. If wee were the latter, would wee live amongst them and bring so many 100,000 rupees' worth of goods to the City? He might consider how unreasonable and ridiculous it would be to expect anything of the nature from persons meriting such a character. Were wee pyrates, would wee rob under our own colours and tell everybody who wee were ? No, rather if wee had plundered the ship wee should have sunk her, that 100 years after none should have known what had become of her . . . Is their King [Aurangzeb] answerable for any of his runagate subjects that may do mischief abroad? No more is our prince or we for those of his that have shook subjection to the laws and pyrate it up and down.[6]

The reasoning worked. Annesley was allowed to write to Bombay asking for his master's help in London. While he waited for an answer, the seasons came and went. The lifetime servant to the East India Company had plenty of time to fume about how events had spiraled so perilously.

After so many years of trouble with the arrogant English, Emperor Aurangzeb was more enraged than at any time in his thirty-eight years on the throne. The lid of the powder keg blew off when returning crewmen of the *Gunsway* swore that some of Avery's crew were former East India Company men employed in Bombay. The Mughal court had long been convinced that the East India Company's servants tipped off British pirates about the Mocha fleet's movements,[7] so "the balance of the money required for the maintenance of the English settlement is obtained by plundering the ships voyaging to the House of God [in Mecca]."[8]

Henry Avery's antics seemingly showed they were right all along. Even the company was forced to admit that "tis certain the pyrates which these people affirm were all English, did do very barbarously by the people of the Gunsway . . . All this will raise a black cloud att Court, which we wish may not produce a severe storme."[9] Not that Annesley would admit it openly, but he knew full well that some of the lowly officials in the English factories took far too close an interest in the pirates' enterprises. They trafficked in plundered cargoes, and one factor working on the Malabar Coast even bought a ship taken by pirates at sea.

The emperor would rather give up the revenues paid by the Europeans for the right to trade in his land than endanger the safety of pilgrims going to Mecca on the holy hajj. The emperor demanded a solution. Or the English could forever rot behind bars.

To the Mughal, all piracy on the high seas, their plots and actions, pointed in one direction: England. The bulldog British had shrugged off the complaints of the "natives" for decades, Annesley knew all too well from the company diaries. In 1630 King Charles I had encouraged Captain Richard Quail to raid on his *Seahorse* the ships and goods of Spanish foes in the Red Sea, knowing perfectly that the Spanish kept to the Atlantic and did not venture into the Red Sea or Indian Ocean. It was a good cover for royal piracy. When Quail snagged a Malabar prize, the East India Company's servants in Surat were forced to pay full compensation.[10] Back home a new enterprise was born.

Five years later, Endymion Porter, Gentleman of the king of England's bedchamber, sponsored a pirate venture rubber-stamped by the king. The not-so-good *Samaritan* and *Roebuck* were secretly fitted out and headed for the Red Sea in April 1635. The *Roebuck* took two Mughal traders at the mouth of the Red Sea and stripped them of a large sum of money and goods. Yet again, the East India Company was held responsible as His Majesty's representative in India. Its employees were imprisoned in Surat until they paid full compensation. The company complained stiffly. Back home in England, one of Porter's merchants was thrown in jail and swiftly bailed by order of the king. Charles I promised to try the case personally, at his leisure. It never happened.[11]

Endymion Porter saw dollar signs swimming in front of his eyes and signed a new partnership with Sir William Courten to set up private "trade" with the East Indies. Even though it was a breach of faith against the East India Company's charter, it received a royal blessing. King Charles even subscribed a slice of the £10,000 seed money. Courten went on to plunder two ships from Surat and Diu and tortured their crews. The company's servants in Surat were unsurprised when they took the heat for the loss. Yet again, they were thrown behind bars for two months. Freedom cost them 170,000 rupees and a solemn oath to respect Mughal shipping from now on or else.[12]

Nothing changed. The pirates' strike rate accelerated. In 1684 Abdul Ghafur lost his first of many ships to pirates. Two more traders flying English colors, mounting forty-four and twenty guns, helped them-selves to cargoes in the Red Sea valued at 600,000 rupees. Dutch and French traders competing with London's East India Company in Surat seized the opportunity to "spitt their venom" to push for the English to be kicked out of India for good.[13] It was a hazardous moment for the company's ambitions. England's strong-arm tactics at that very moment were demanding special trade privileges and taking measures to turn the emperor to their way of thinking. When Aurangzeb refused, the company blockaded India's western ports and access to the Red Sea. Twelve ships of war sped from England to India armed with two hundred cannon and six hundred troops.[14] The emperor condemned the company as pirates and, in turn, blockaded their port in Bombay, forcing the English to prostrate themselves and pay an imperial fine of 150,000 rupees in 1690.[15]

All the while, the real pirate menaces swarmed across the Indies like wasps. The year 1689 had seen the East Indies' trade "pestered with pirates" fitted out in the West Indies. Sea rovers chanced their hands off the Malabar Coast, in the Persian Gulf, at the mouth of the Red Sea, in the Mozambique Channel, and as far as Acheen on Sumatra in Indonesia.[16] The losses were staggering. A successful hit team of two English and one Dutch pirate ships that inched into St. Helena in 1689 were weighed down with so much booty that they could barely sail. A passing slaver reported how:

> They were prodigal in the expences of their unjust gain, and quenched their thirst with Europe liquor at any rate this Commander (the slaver) would put upon it; and were so frank both in distributing their goods, and guzzling down the noble wine, as if they were both wearied with the possession of their rapine, and willing to stifle all the melancholy reflections concerning it.[17]

The 1690s started just as badly. A ship owned by the wealthy merchant Abdul Ghafur was seized in August 1691 at the mouth of the Tapti River with nine lakhs in cash. Once more, the East India Company's fort was put under arrest and an embargo issued against English trade, no matter that the pirate rogue responsible was really Danish.[18] England was tarred as the great friend of pirates. Plead its innocence as the company might, and write home in strong terms to stop their country's sea rogues, piracy was spiraling out of control.

A royal order signed in 1692 to give East India Company commanders new powers to seize pirates at the king's pleasure had no effect. The pirates were well-drilled seamen who could outsail, outsmart, and outfight most ships. The prizes on offer were so great and the risks so small that even company men joined the sea rovers.[19] That same year of 1692, two more of Ghafur's ships, the *Karimi* and *Ahmadi*, were plundered of 500,000 rupees' worth of Spanish reales.[20]

By the time Henry Avery reached the Red Sea in 1695, and Captain Thomas Tew joined forces with the *Fancy* at Bob's Key, Tew had already hit the jackpot.[21] In a sloop of sixty tons and seventy men, he had twice left New York to ravage the Red Sea and netted a personal windfall of £12,000.[22] Now he was back for more. Thomas Wake had joined Avery's Red Sea flotilla despite having taken the king's pardon for piracy in the late 1680s and supposedly gone straight.[23]

Now that Annesley's wrists were unfettered and he at least had a stack of pens and paper, the diplomat merchant started firing off letters to London, urging the Company's governor to take serious action. At court, the Englishmen's ally, Prime Minister Asad Khan, and an enthusiastic taker of handsome backhanders, worked hard to cool the emperor's rage. "King of Kings, the English are great merchants and drive a vast trade in your country," he advised his ruler. "There are a great many hat men [European] thieves in these seas, but such busyness is not from the English cast, nor ever will be."[24] The wise and expensively bought words lifted the death sentence against Annesley and his men. The question now was how to deal with the deviant English.

At the end of October, Annesley warned London that there was "nothing so afflictive as the publick dishonour of our King and country by barbarous infidels who have violated the public faith given us by the Governor's hospitality and protection due to strangers." Gifts of 30,000 rupees here and there and a few Persian horses on New Year's Day were not going to cut the mustard after Henry Avery's latest mischief. Annesley proposed a fresh approach: making East India Company ships available to guard the Mocha and Jeddah ships to and from the Red Sea. For the pleasure of the convoy, the Mughal emperor would pay 400,000 rupees a year. Annesley flattered his boss, Sir John Gayer, General of the East India Company, that the plan would make him the first military commander "to secure the navigation of the Emperor's subjects from piracy." Annesley held his breath. Nothing happened. The factory in Surat remained surrounded and the Indies trade paralyzed.[25]

India House in London took no action for over five months until its lords realized that the trade was dead. The government was petitioned to take hard action and send warships to smash the pirates' lair at Sainte-Marie Island and hopefully Henry Avery trapped there. With England's treasury empty from the heavy costs of the war with France, and the government struggling to cover its own costs, the idea fell on deaf ears.

While the lords dithered about how to handle the pirate menace, the East India Company's reputation as trustworthy trading partners went from bad to worse. At the end of 1695 the Imperial Court ruled to allow the trade to begin again. In return, England, France, and the Netherlands would need to commit to sending ships to search and seize the pirates or pay for the *Gunsway's* losses.

A way out of the mess arrived by good luck and timing. In 1695 a sea captain from New York called Captain William Kidd was fishing in London for a privateering commission. Kidd had cultivated influential ears, including Richard Coote, 1st Earl of Bellomont, who had just been appointed the governor of Massachusetts Bay to replace the wreck hunter Sir William Phips and clean up New York, a rampant friend of pirates. The city was a smuggler's den for traders competing with Pennsylvania's sea trade. If that meant making money aiding and abetting pirates, so be it. Colonel Benjamin Fletcher, the city's governor from 1692 to 1697, ran a protection racket that allowed any sea rogue to buy a safe pass to land anything in the port for $100 or twelve pieces of Arabian gold.[26] Women and men fleeing the witch trials in Salem found a welcome sanctuary in New York too.[27]

Lord Bellomont was a Rottweiler who quickly sniffed out New York's eagerness buying pirates' plunder in Madagascar and fencing it for sale. Some chancers, such as Captain Thomas Moston of the *Fortune*, covered their tracks by sailing as a privateer with a commission signed by

Governor Fletcher. New York merchants coordinated their movements with pirates who fitted out their ships in the town. The notorious pirates John Hoar and Richard Glover both worked in and out of Madagascar with Fletcher's commission as well. No collectors checked cargo holds arriving from East Africa and the governor kept ships' names off the official register of ships for the right price.[28]

As he continued to dig more and more shocking dirt, Lord Bellomont discovered that pirate ships were also manned in New York. Captain Thomas Tew, who sailed with Henry Avery's flotilla, was protected by a privateering commission from Governor Fletcher. On his return to New York from the East Indies in his successful two cruises before joining the pirate king, "he was received and caressed by Governor Fletcher, dined and supped often with him, and appeared with him publicly in his coach," the Earl of Bellomont was appalled to learn. "They also exchanged presents, such as gold watches, with each other."[29]

Following the New Providence playbook, another pirate, Captain William Mason of the *Jacob*, gave Colonel Fletcher his ship after taking three prizes in the Red Sea and the crew pocketed $1,800 a man.[30] The good governor sold his windfall of a pirate ship for a delicious £800. Mason's crew bought protection at a rate of $100 dollars a man. When Josiah Rayner, one of Avery's crew, landed with £1,500 of treasure, he was seized by the sheriff but freed by Fletcher after greasing his palm with a considerable reward. The pirate bought land in this province and put down roots.[31]

The Earl of Bellomont was infuriated and fired off a letter to London complaining how:

> those villains do . . . carry their unjust gains to New York,
> where they are permitted Egress and Regress without con-
> trol, spending such coin there in the usual lavish manner of
> such persons as might sufficiently convince the government
> that they came not well by it, and they stick not to report also

that by Piscashes [gifts] to the Governor they pass without being molested.[32]

Lord Bellomont knew all about Henry Avery and the plummeting fortunes of the East India Company in Surat. Captain Kidd would be the solution and a money-spinner at the same time. The Earl of Bellomont approached Sir Edmund Harrison; Secretary of State Charles Talbot; Attorney General Sir John Somers; Naval Treasurer Edward Russell; and Henry Sidney, the Earl of Romney, to join the scheme. The lords paid four fifths of the costs of the venture, while Bellomont, Robert Livingston, the New York politician and entrepreneur, and Kidd, covered the final fifth.[33] The scheme could not fail: together these mighty lords virtually ran the government. Shrewsbury was secretary of state and served as regent when King William was overseas. Somers was the Lords Justice and Orford the First Lord of the Admiralty. Sidney was one of the Immortal Seven who had invited King William to become monarch and served as master-general of the Ordnance, responsible for the arming of England.[34]

When he was presented with this heavyweight support for a noble plan, King William III signed a proclamation on January, 26, 1695, empowering Captain Kidd to set out on the custom-built pirate-hunting ship the *Adventure Galley* in search of:

> wicked and ill-disposed persons, and do against the law of nations commit many and great piracies, robberies, and depredations on the seas upon the parts of America, and in other parts, to the great hindrance and discouragement of trade and navigation . . . and do hereby give and grant to the said Robert Kidd . . . full power and authority to apprehend, seize, and take into your custody . . . as all such pirates, free-booters, and sea-rovers . . . with all their ships and vessels, and all such merchandise, money, goods, and wares.[35]

Kidd headed to the Americas in March 1696 at exactly the time when Henry Avery was approaching the Bahamas. What should have been the perfect solution to Surat's problems brought even worse misery. Kidd and his crew confused the 350-ton *Quedagh Merchant* for a French enemy ship, helped themselves to its cargo of silk, muslin, calico, sugar, opium, iron, and saltpeter valued at £100,000, plus the bonus of personal gold, silver, and jewels. Unfortunately, the owner of the *Quedagh Merchant*, Khoja Minass, was a rich Armenian merchant from Surat who had close commercial dealings with the English East India Company, which often hired out this very ship for trade voyages.[36] Captain Kidd had embarrassed powerful men and in 1701 would end up hanged in London on the same gallows as five of Henry Avery's crew.

☠

Back in Surat, Samuel Annesley waited for news, any news. On June 27, 1696, the Mughal's guards left the factory in Surat. The port was back open for business. Ten long months after Henry Avery had smashed and grabbed the *Gunsway*, London finally dipped its quill in ink. A royal proclamation for the capture of the pirate king and his crew was issued on July 17, 1696, whereby:

> we do hereby charge & command all his Majesties Admirals, Captains & other officers at sea, and all his Majesties Governors & Commanders of any forts, castles or other places in his Majesties plantations or otherwise to seize & take the said Henry Every & such as are with him in the said ship & cause them to be punished as pirates upon the high seas & in case of resistance to sink & destroy the said ship.[37]

Crewmen who informed on Avery's hiding place or the location of the *Fancy* "shall have his Majesties gracious pardon for their effertes."

Then came the sweetener: a £500 reward for their trouble from the Lords Commissioners of His Majesty's Treasury. The East India Company, under intense scrutiny, needed to send the Mughal emperor a convincing sign of their serious intent. So, on July 22, it issued its own declaration "for the vindicating of the honour of the English nation & manifesting our abhorrency & detestation of such piratical & villanous practices." On top of the royal £500, the company padded the reward with another 4,000 rupees "to such person or persons as shall so size the said Henry Every, & bring & the said ship into any of the English factories."[38] All in, the bounty on the pirate king's head came to a mouthwatering £1,000 (around $150,000 today).

As reports of the crimes of Henry Avery and his crew, and their movements, poured into England, the Lords Justices updated their proclamation on August 10, 1696. The same carrot of a royal pardon and reward were on offer, but the powers added that Avery had changed his name to Henry Bridgman and listed some of men in the *Fancy* as James Cray, Thomas Summerton, Edward Kitwood, William Down, John Roddy, John Stranger, Nathaniel Pike, Peter Soanes, Henry Adams, Francis Frennier, Thomas Johnson, Joseph Dawson, Samuel Dawson, James Lewis, John Sparks, Joseph Goss, Charles Falconer, James Murray, Robert Rich, John Miller, John King, Edward Savill, William Philips, Thomas Hope, and Thomas Belisha. The Crown believed each man ran off with around £1,000. As well as the big payoff, informers would now enjoy a top-up off £50 for each of these pirates collared.[39]

Despite its pleading for help, when the slow post finally arrived with the warrant for the pirates' arrest, the humiliated East India Company did not even publicize the royal proclamation against Avery or tell the governor or court in Surat because

> if wee acknowledge that these country ships were lately robbed
> by Englishmen and the plunder conveyed to England they
> may require satisfaction of us, and ye proclamation specifying

ye number of men to be 130 and each of their shares of the plunder 1000£ will direct them what to demand.[40]

Sir John Gayer did finally agree that sending an East India Company convoy to escort the emperor's Mocha fleet to the Red Sea from now on was a jolly good idea. Still, business ruled. The emperor would have to pay the English and Dutch convoy twenty thousand rupees for a round-trip on a large ship and five thousand or less for small ships. Half the cash would come from the imperial treasury, the rest from the merchants trading in each voyage.[41]

By August 1696, tongues were wagging. Pirates who had joined Henry Avery at La Coruna, when the *Charles II* was stolen, and been caught and started talking rather than be tried and hanged. When news of arrests reached the East India Company, it asked the Lords Justices of England for any gold, silver, and jewels recovered "not be disposed of but put into the possession of the said Governor & Company in order to be preserved for the use of the proprietors in India."[42]

Rather than scaring off British sea rogues, the proclamation and bounty against the pirate king, the *Fancy*, and its men emboldened and inspired a host of fresh plunder. Samuel Annesley shivered with a cold sweat when he heard news that pirates had roamed into the waters of Calicut in Kerala on the southeast coast of India on November 23, 1696, attacked the *Outermost*, and hoisted Danish colors, "firing broad-sides and volleys of small shott, and then laid her on board, and take her, from her." The sea dogs added another three ships to their prizes, one again under contract to the Mughal emperor. The pirates held the ships for ransom, telling worried English and Indian authorities that they acknowledged no countrymen and had sold out from their country. Their wishes were clear:

Having taken those 4 ships they demand 10000 ransom for them or threatened to burn them, and not having the money

immediately, they hoist bloody colours and fire one of them,
and soon after sett 2 ashore also on fire.[43]

The next month, December 1696, news reached Bombay that when
the *Mocha* frigate, an East India Company ship, was heading from
Bombay to China with a rich cargo, the crew killed Commander Leonard
Edgecomb, wounded the carpenter, and locked up the supercargo (chief
trader) and the rest of the officers.[44] The *Mocha* would end up under
the control of the notorious English pirate Robert Culliford. Around the
same time, the crew of another company ship, the *Josiah* ketch, sailing
out of Bombay, had "runaway with her by a strange providence" when
the officers were sick ashore.[45]

The East India Company was shocked to its boots. A letter dispatched
in haste to Their Excellencies the Lords Justices of England warned
starkly that

> if thee do not care taken to suppress pyrates in India, and to
> empower the Companyes servants to punish them according
> to their deserts without fear of being traduced for what they
> have done when they return to England, they fear it is prob-
> ably all their throats will be cut by malefactors and all natives
> of the country in a little time in revenge for their frequent
> losses, as well as the trade in India wholly lost.[46]

The noises coming out of the East Indies finally troubled the Company so much that in February 1697 it wrote desperately to the Lord
High Admiral of England, warning that "unless some stop be put to these
villainous practices, your petitioners have too great reason to apprehend
the continuance of such practices will so far exasperate the Indian nation
that they will utterly destroy the factorys and efforts of your petitioners
& totally forbid all comers between them & the English nation." The
company wanted the powers "to seize and take all pyrates infesting those

seas within the limits of the Company Charter. And likewise to empower them to erect a Court of Admiralty in those parts to try and condemn further pyrates . . . for suppressing & preventing the like villanyes as in time to come."[47]

In the end, Samuel Annesley bore the brunt of the mess in Surat. He was accused of fraud and was let go by the company, despite his "solemnly protest . . . that I have never had a rupee in your cash under any borrowed name."[48] Annesley, who had grown gray in the service of the East India Company, felt bitter but relieved. The future of the company was bleak and nowhere were its prospects darker than in Surat.

Annesley went on to make a small fortune as a private merchant. In 1724 he asked his brother-in-law, Samuel Wesley (the nephew of John Wesley, the founder of Methodism), to buy him an estate of £200 or £300 a year between London and Oxford. After forty years in India, Annesley embarked to the place of his birth on an East India Company ship, wearing a loose white suit. Only he never arrived home. When the ship's officers broke into his cabin, they found his boxes neatly packed, his watch hanging on a wooden ceiling beam, and a handful of gold and silver tossed onto the bunk, as if he had just emptied his pockets.[49] The man who was as much a victim of Henry Avery's great heist of the *Gunsway* as the people of Surat was never seen again. Like the pirate king, he vanished into thin air.

Manhunt

J ust one miracle could save the plummeting reputation of the East India Company—the head of Henry Avery the pirate king, the most wanted man in the world. The world's first global manhunt was underway. Trackers were searching high and low for the captain of the *Fancy*, his ship, and crew.

By now, the pirates were gone, scattered in all directions. Prince the boatswain, Robert Clinton, and one parcel of rogues headed to Carolina.[1] William May escaped to Pennsylvania. Two more men tried settling in Jamaica but returned to New Providence where Joseph Moriss went mad, "having lost all his jewells upon a wager." Edward Short was eaten by a shark.[2] Thomas Jones returned to his old ship, while Captain Richard Want of Rhode Island tried his luck again in the Gulf of Persia before apparently making his way to Rhode Island or Carolina, where he blew his money.[3] Back in New Providence, Read Elding, deputy governor from 1699 to 1700, even made one of Avery's crew a marshal,[4] in exchange for a nice little backhander.

Meanwhile, Nicholas Trott, governor of New Providence, was in serious hot water, fighting for his own life. Reports in London reckoned Trott raked in around £7,000 for allowing the *Fancy*'s crew to land in Nassau. Avery and his men had even been entertained over fine wine in the governor's house. When one of the uncouth "slave traders" broke a drinking glass, Trott made him pay for it. The attorney general of Barbados complained that, all told, the governor ripped £50,000 off assorted pirates. His money was squirrelled away in an offshore account in Barbados as well as in New York and Boston. Now, the East India Company was after the friend of pirates. They demanded that "all the estate & effects of this Trott, be seiz'd on, & his person secur'd . . . in order to punish so fowl a crime, & to give opportunity for the said owners, to recover their right, or damages, from the said Governor Trott."[5]

Trott pretended he had nothing to hide and had been hoodwinked by a clever rogue who arrived in New Providence disguised as a trader from the Guinea coast in West Africa. How could the elephant tusks, enslaved Africans, and beads aboard the *Fancy* lead to any other conclusion than a voyage along the Gold Coast of Ghana? The governor pretended he had been in a moral bind. There was no proof of piracy at all. As for the cash he took from Captain Bridgeman and his traders, well, that was nothing more than a legal bond locked away to make sure the Englishmen behaved on his genteel island:

> so without accusation, information & proof, which here was not any, I could not doe more than I have done on suspition; have taken all their bonds with the best security they could procure on ther place, jointly & severally, for every one of their appearance in a twelve months & a day if any things be alleged against them here.[6]

The cash would be held to make sure the men of the *Fancy* kept their whiskers clean and did not break the law. Nothing else. The "honorable" governor backed up his version of events with two documents. Trott told the East India Company of London that as soon as he received Avery's written request to land in Nassau, he called a meeting of his advisory council on March 30, 1696, with Bartholomew Mercier, Thomas Williams, Lieutenant Colonel Thomas Cumber, Thomas Peck, and Captain

Edward Holmes. The council read in Captain Bridgeman's note how his ship was armed with forty-six guns, was carrying two hundred men, and "desires admittance alleging they have done nothing criminall."[7]

The skipper promised to answer for any allegations that might come to light and "to give security or otherwise as the court shall award."[8] The council claimed to have been terribly concerned that had the *Fancy* been forced to land elsewhere, and if such a powerful ship be taken by French enemies, it would be very bad news for New Providence and the Bahamas. Time and time again, Trott emphasized that the crew were English subjects and had to be treated as brethren.

In the end, the council agreed to let the crew land in Nassau but covered the decision with a bizarrely naïve proclamation to make the newcomers behave nicely. The strong men of New Providence therefore

> require & strictly command all persons what soever either strangers or inhabitants to be carefall to keep and observe the peace and to be civill and use Christian like behaviour one toward another and that no person presume to challenge one another, at either gun, pistol, sword or any other offensive weapon . . . . These are to give notice that whosoever shall comitt murder, disable, assault, abuse, robb, ravish, condemn, or affront authority etc whether they be inhabitants of this island or sejourners amongst us shall be lyable to be prosecuted according to the lawes.[9]

To a bunch of mean pirates like the crew of the *Fancy*, Governor Trott's words were a great joke. Not worth the paper they were written on.

The case against Nicholas Trott saw the governor swear that Henry Avery, in the guise of Captain Bridgeman, asked to be admitted into Providence "being quite out of Provisions & repairs," and that they were "Kings Subjects."[10] An affidavit written by a Mr. Barker in favor of Trott's version of events believed that if as great a ship as the *Fancy* had not been given permission to land, "they had certainly attacked yr Island of Providence & had taken it, and therefore certainly it was better to invite a known pirate in to save a place, than by denying them suffer yr Enemy to be Master of such an Island fortify so."[11] Trott had saved the island from being lost to England, so his supporters continued. He was a hero.

Seven months after Captain Bridgeman arrived in New Providence, Trott heard a tale from the governor of Jamaica about a ship stolen from La Coruna by one Henry Avery, who turned pirate in the East Indies. The penny dropped. Or at least Trott could no long turn a blind eye. The governor finally issued a warrant to his sheriff for the crew of the *Fancy* to be examined before the island's justice of the peace. Even after various testimony was taken, the official "proclaimed they could not informe anything." Finally, Trott's cronies swore black and blue that stories of £1,000 gifted to the governor were "a most malitious memorial."[12] The only money he took was for provisions and liquor for his fellow Englishmen. Who would you best believe? Trott and his witnesses asked. A governor or a band of pirates who would spout any lie to save their necks?

In the end, the scandal did not blow over. From Surat to London, the affair was far too destructive. Nicholas Trott was removed from office and replaced as governor by the Right Honorable Nicholas Webb, charged with clearing up the whole mess and putting New Providence back on an even keel. As soon as he reached town, Webb let it be known he would never accept "any ill-gotten bribe" and put a twenty-one-day embargo on the movements of all shipping. The port was sealed.

But it was far too late in the day to recover any Indian treasure or find any drunken sea rogues rolling in the taverns. Play time was over. The plunder and pirates were long gone. All Webb could round up were "a few old sailes blocks, a large chain and some other things of small value,"[13] 126 elephant tusks weighing two and a quarter tons, and several barrels of gunpowder. The only semblance of fact, what really went down, were the statements of the council and citizens of Nassau who, unsurprisingly, all swore in favor of their former governor, equally desperate to hide their own guilt and not be forced to hand back the bribes they had pocketed.

All the while, the *Fancy*, rotting on the shoreline, was a daily reminder of New Providence's role in a national disgrace for England. Now, Sir James Houblon and the backers of the Spanish Shipping Expedition of 1693 wanted their property back. They would never see a plank of it. Sir Alex Rigby and Wynne Houblon had asked the Lords of the Admiralty to order an English warship to head to New Providence "& there to take possession of, & bring away to Jamaica, on behalf of the said owners, the ship of Charles, with all that can be recover'd . . . and to recover from the said Governor what shall be found to have been embezzld."[14]

The true fate of the *Fancy* and what it brought into Nassau was hidden under layer upon layer of untruths. Crew member Joseph Goss told the Lords Justices that after reaching the Isle of Providence, "within 24 houres after she had been at anchor she foundered."[15] This was Trott's initial story as well. Try as he might, the governor wrote under oath, he had been powerless to save Sir James's frigate:

> Their ship being very much worme eaten, much adoe to keep above water with pumping. Their sayles & rigging quite worne out, they quitted her, and left her with me. They had lost their best cable and anchor among our islands before they came in with a hard gale of wind, she swept her anchor, and drove on a reafe in our harbour, a small distance from the place she ridd not a cables length. I have offered one hundred pounds to the people to get her off but no ways could. The wind blew so hard some days after that she is bilged thereby she being made so weak for sayleing, she would not endure her own weight with the guns. My intention was to preserve her for who ever proved to be the owners of her . . . And if no other owners appear, I intend the guns which are very good & large for the fort and cittadell which will sufficiently furnish them.[16]

Fifteen months after the pirate ship landed in Nassau, the *Fancy* could still be seen above the waves. On August 2, 1697, Governor Webb made a detailed survey of the foundering ship in the company of William Humble, commander of the Lord's Galley; Mr. Gilmore, provost marshal of the Bahamas; the merchant William Loyett; and Robert Leeson, carpenter of the Lord's Galley. Upon an oath taken on the Holy Evangelist's Bible, Webb confirmed that the *Fancy* really was in bad shape:

> One of the planks of her bottom was absolutely beaten out, and tho the Deponts did find her 3 lower masts standing yet were much damaged & almost useless her boltsprit [bowsprit] broke, & no rigging standing, and neither sailes cables hawsors anchors or Rudder in the said ship, & her bottom soe covered with barnacles, that tis difficult to see any of her lower Planks, but in the hold of the said Ship lay 7 great Guns & two more Great Guns lying between Decks, upon their carriages much damaged . . . upon the strictest search & inquiry wee could make, we could neither find plate goods jewels nor any other valuable thing, Moreover to the best of our Judgements, she is wholly irapairable of ever being refitted soe as to undertake any voyage without greater charge than ever in all prospect.[17]

In the end, the *Fancy* was left to rot in the rotten island state of New Providence. Trott removed some of the ship's cannon for the forty-eight guns mounted on a platform in Nassau needed to guard the island from attack by French ships. Whose truth was the whole truth will never be known. Nicholas Trott was a serial scoundrel. Even before his encounter with the pirate king, he was ensnared in ugly legal proceedings for cheating Dutch sailors wrecked twenty leagues off his island. And even earlier a vicious attack on the former governor of Bermuda forced him to return to London to answer charges. Trott may even have been thrown in Fleet Prison for debtors, the same dark hole Daniel Defoe frequented for fraud.

Trott was a chancer who grew far too big for his boots and was cut down to size. If he was "the greatest pirate-broker that ever was in America," in the seething view of the Earl of Bellomont and governor of New York,[18] Nicholas Webb, his successor, was no better. Nassau's new top dog almost certainly checked his story with Trott before writing his oath and massaging its contents. Webb stayed in New Providence just long enough to thoroughly grease his palms. In 1699 the new governor stepped down and sailed over the horizon to retirement.

Only when he docked in New Castle, Pennsylvania, to freshen up, his crew "ran away with his ship and all his estate, £7,000 in gold and £1,000 in goods. If he was to give an account how he made £8,000 in two years, I believe he would [say] he but trod in the steps of his predecessor Trott," Lord Bellomont raged.[19]

A bunch of bloodthirsty pirates should have been the last people to be believed about Henry Avery's months in New Providence and the behavior of Governor Trott. Since the pirates' accounts largely sang to the same tune, and were delivered in court under fear of the hangman's noose, they are probably closer to the truth about how Trott befriended the pirates, shook their hands, and drank with them.

While Nicholas Trott was swearing his innocence before the Crown, the *Fancy*'s pirates who stayed in the Americas found other governors equally as welcoming as in the Bahamas and New York. The line between rumor and truth was hard to prove and easy for poorly paid authorities in the Americas to shrug off as hearsay. The ways of the colonies were a very different kettle of fish to the rule of England in the British Isles. The rash of proclamations issued in England against the pirate king took an age to reach the New World. The council of Massachusetts only read its copy on May 6, 1697, Maryland on June 7, while the governor of Virginia published his copy on July 1.[20]

Captain Robert Sneed, commissioner of peace in Pennsylvania, was one of the first colonial authorities to get his hands on a copy of the warrant at the end of April 1697—more than nine months after it was signed and sealed. Sneed know full well that some of Avery's crew were living in Philadelphia, including Robert Clinton, Edmond Laselle, Peter Clay, and James Brown.[21]

When the commissioner confronted Governor William Markham about seizing the pirates, Markham shrugged and told the enforcer that the supposed proclamation, which he had not personally seen, had not been "directed to him, so that he was not bound to take notice of it." If the owners of the *Charles II* cared so much about happenings in America, they should have written to him personally. In any case, the governor shrugged, the accused "men had been civil with him, they had brought in money, which was an advantage to the country."[22] The governor's wife and daughter, who one of the pirates had even married, charged the commissioner with being no better than an informer. A disgusted Sneed threatened to resign as a magistrate if Markham refused to enforce the proclamation.

The town sheriff, John Claypool, was equally blinkered, and refused point blank to put out a warrant for the pirates' arrest, which would have no useful result apart from "up & down whistling to scare people."[23] The constables were ordered not to serve any warrants. Instead, Captain Sneed was threatened with jail and his sword and pistols taken away. Soon after, the Lords Justice Proclamation for apprehending Avery's men and serving immediate punishment eventually reached Governor Markham in the Maryland post. Within two hours, the sheriff was spotted heading from the governor's house to the prison and walking with the freed pirates. That night, Avery's men mysteriously vanished from Philadelphia. The pirates still locked up in jail were set free without bail and were spotted roaming about town. In short, the king's proclamation was ignored.

As the months passed, the trail started to go cold, but the pirate atrocities were unrelenting. In April 1697 news reached the East India Company that the *Mocha* frigate with 125 British, Dutch, and French men sank the *Shabandar* off Congo and the five-hundred-ton *Satisfaction* off Zorlone, laden from Bengal. Next the ship seized another ship owned by the long-suffering Abdul Ghafur of Surat. Once again, the loot was taken to the safe haven of New York.[24]

The council at Fort Saint George in Madras would soon learn that off the Gold Coast in Ghana the crew of the four-hundred-ton, thirty-gun *Hanniball*, in the service of the Royal African Company, and trading under license from the Crown, mutinied. They ran away with the ship "and it is supposed that she goes on a pyraticall voyage to the East Indies as was done by Every and his accomplices in the Charles 2d als Fancy." Doing an Avery lured in hardened desperadoes with the promise of thrills and life-changing riches.[25]

Proclamations, slinging out corrupt governors, replacing them with tough operators, and pasting MOST WANTED posters for the head of Henry Avery and his crew across the Americas did little to restore England and the East India Company's reputation. The company estimated the latest damage done to India's traders at five million rupees ($10.5 million). The future of East-West trade and the very British Empire was sinking fast. The Surat council of traders again wearily warned in February 1697 that

> Your Honourable Estates trade and servants liberty, and lives here, are in continual danger, and may be shortly so all over India, we are at this instant prisoners at large, and how soon, no maybe straiter confined, by the Government, or massacred by the rabble, God alone knows.[26]

The pirates were lawless and going nowhere, now "committing robberyes & intreagues upon all nations without distinction."[27] As a crew cruising off Cape Comorin put it, we are "friends to no man but to God

Almighty!"[28] No longer was Henry Avery's plunder about what happened in some heathen backwater. The *Fancy*'s destructive path was on the verge of bringing the entire Indo-British trade crashing down.

The problem was deteriorating by the year. Henry Avery was the toast of the underdog, his adventures celebrated in taverns across Britain and the Americas. To families whose men sweated on the waves, were cruelly pressed into the Royal Navy, or whipped on warships' decks for doing next to nothing, Avery was a hero. All the while, the ringleader himself had disappeared off the face of the earth.

Defending the Crown

While Henry Avery was robbing the emperor of India with cutlass and cannon, back in London Daniel Defoe was starting to wield a pen that would become even mightier than the sword. Just as Avery's life had turned upside down, so Defoe was reinventing himself from merchant to secret agent, dampening down trouble from the shadows.

Defoe had dreamt all his life about being a saintly hero for big causes he was willing to die for. Day in, day out, he feared a French invasion, backed by Spain, and with it the death of the English cloth market, the backbone of the nation's economy and power. Stopping France and the Catholic menace meant fighting tooth and nail to block the Stuart dynasty and their Jacobean supporters from seizing the throne. Defending the Crown, not writing novels, was what made the outsider feel alive.

When Prince William of Orange had docked on the south coast of England in 1689, Dissenters like Foe finally breathed freely in their own land. Defoe was ecstatic. He never forgot the marvelous sight of the Protestant Dutch Armada landing at Beachy Head, especially "when Night came upon them, [and] all the Ships set out their Lights, which made a most glorious Shew upon the Sea. . . . All which at a distance appeared like so many Stars, moving upon the Water."[1] The cosmos had aligned. King James II fled to France in a bloodless revolution and Daniel Foe rode to Henley to see firsthand the coming of salvation. William and Mary were invited to sit on the vacant throne. "Our Deliverance was like a Dream to us," Defoe wrote.[2]

The City of London officially welcomed William of Orange to its ranks on October 29, 1689, and Foe made sure he was among the "royal regiment of volunteer horse, made up of the chief citizens, who being gallantly mounted and richly accoutred, were led by the Earl of Monmouth, now Earl of Peterborough, and attended their majesties from Whitehall."[3] Foe could not believe his good luck when the wit with the golden tongue and familiarity with the Netherlands from many trading voyages was invited to visit the gardens of Kensington Palace and wait on Queen Mary II. Daniel Foe the outsider was on the cusp of entering royal circles. And he would not stop talking and writing until the highest power in the land lent him his ears.

After the Glorious Revolution, a feeling of freedom and hope swept throughout England. All the country needed was to defend its liberty from inside and outside threats. As the seventeenth century reached its end, the king's shine was rubbing off. The country was in uproar, riddled with riots over food shortages and political corruption. The government's decision to withdraw all the nation's silver, whose coin edges had for decades been clipped and clipped again by defrauders, pushing down the value of a coin by 50 percent in the 1680s, and to strike new currency in 1696, was disastrously handled.[4]

The new cash was slow to come out of the Royal Mint, which had siphoned off piles of the silver to pay off its debts. England's economy was in a slump, unemployment rising, and a feeling of mutiny in the air.[5] "Your Majesty is much abused," Sir Richard Newman wrote in *The Complaint of English Subjects*, "the County most grievously injured, and opprest, their Trade is meerly lost, and in their Estates and Minds they are much decayed."[6]

Foe, the champion of the everyday man and woman, placed the blame squarely on the shoulders of the gentry and Parliament, not the king.

William served the will of the people. Parliament only cared for itself.[7] All this was a badly timed distraction to what Foe was certain was England's greatest problem, making sure the country's army was large enough to fight off King Louis XIV of France, his lifelong nemesis.

Foe did much more than ride in parades to honor the king. He had secured the trust of King William and quietly started taking on tasks that he cryptically described as "writing within doors": palace doors. Foe had demonstrated his loyalty and skilled penmanship in defending the Crown in a pamphlet published in 1691, *An Account of the Late Horrid Conspiracy to Depose their Present Majesties, K. William and Q. Mary, to Bring in the French and the Late King James, and Ruine the City of London.* He wrote the text anonymously behind the cloak of "a Gentleman, who was present at their Trials." The poor-quality pamphlet was no official-backed document but Foe's personal crusade to turn the public tide. The true-bred merchant had started wearing the first of his many masks.

An Account reached King William's ears and favor. Swiftly it was updated a year later with *Reflections Upon the Late Horrid Conspiracy Contrived by Some of the French Court to Murther His Majesty in Flanders.* *Reflections* was a very different beast: the paper and printing were first-class, the text free of the blemishes that filled *An Account*, and the author had now got hold of unpublished secret documents slipped under his door by government agents. Foe was charged with whipping up public anger against King Louis for his scheming to murder William and restore the exiled James to the triple crown of England, Scotland, and Ireland. Louis was painted as a would-be merciless devil of the civilized world. Only King William, "one of the most Illustrious Lives upon earth,"[8] could stop the coming darkness.

Foe's words started to be listened to more seriously in the corridors of power from the fall of 1695. The previous spring, Daniel had been all for giving up and starting afresh overseas. Writing in his *Appeal to Honour and Justice*, he admitted planning to move to Cadiz when suddenly

Providence, which had other Work for me to do, played a
secret Aversion in my Mind to quitting *England* upon any
account, and made me refuse the best Offers of that kind, to be
concern'd with some eminent Persons at home, in Proposing
Ways and *Means* to the Government for raising Money to
supply the Occasions of the War then newly begun.[9]

Foe, who had dreamed of profiting from diving engines and civet
cat perfume, put his mind to thinking up ingenious schemes for funds
to help pay for the Nine Years' War. His scheming answered to Thomas
Neale and Dalby Thomas. Neale, the royal groom-porter, was in charge
of gambling in the royal palace and sat on government committees.[10]
Dalby Thomas was a close personal friend of Foe's and doing very well
trading in Africa and the West Indies. Foe had made powerful allies.

These were the times of the "projectors," men of inventiveness and
ingenuity turned entrepreneurs. The tax on glassware and bottles that
came into force in September 1695 was a solid start. Foe eagerly pocketed the £100 a year salary to keep the scheme's books. He was moving
in heady circles and decided he needed a more captivating name. From
October 1695, he took the more fitting, fancier, and memorable surname
of De Foe and finally Defoe.[11]

To anyone watching closely, Defoe's movements started to look suspicious. Although he had traveled the length and breadth of the land
making deals most of his life, his observations now took on a deeper
motive. In Sussex he visited gentlemen's estates to investigate their
reserves of oak timber needed for the Admiralty or timber merchants
supplying the Royal Navy to build warships to fight France. Down south,
near Hastings, he mulled over the worrying reminder of "the bones of
one of the Dutch men of war, which was burned and stranded by the
French"[12] in the Battle of Beachy Head in 1690. Near Southampton,
Defoe checked the river on the west side of the town, which ran "by the
edge of the great forest, call'd New-Forest; here we saw a prodigious

quantity of timber, of an uncommon size, vastly large, lying on the shoar of the river, for above two miles in length, which they told us was brought thither from the forest, and left to be fetch'd by the builders at Portsmouth-Dock."[13] Wood stocks for warships were in good health.

These were dangerous times for King William and his supporters. While the hunt was in full swing to find the pirate king in 1696, King Louis was loaning ships and soldiers to James, the fallen ruler of England, to fight for his "rightful" throne. James was spearheading a French invasion secretly planned by Jacobites. Taking Britain would be all the simpler and less bloody if William was out of the picture. Several plots had already failed; 1696 would see the big one.

Treason was in the air. The Duke of Berwick, the Earl of Aylesbury, Captain George Porter, Sir Thomas Roe of Islington, Sir William Parkyns, Sir John Friend, Captain Robert Charnock, Lieutenant Edward King, Sir George Barclay, and others were planning to topple William once and for all. The cabal never met in the same place but made sure to "run into each other" in the Nags Head in Covent Garden, the Sun in the Strand, and the Globe Tavern in Hatton Garden. The plotters spoke in code. King William was called the "Spark" and the assassination plan was known as "striking at the Head."[14]

The Catholic enemies planned to hijack William when he was returning from hunting in February 1696. The careless king was a man of habit who liked to cross the River Thames back to the palace by ferry at leafy Kew. The Scottish army officer Major General Sir George Barclay would ambush the hunting party in the narrow reaches between Brentford and Turnham Green on the outskirts of London. The conspirators would then attack London Bridge, the Exchanges business center, Savoy, Whitehall, and the Tower of London. The king's Horse Guards would be taken out.

At least forty men would lead the attacks armed with blunderbusses, muskets, and pistols. From several inns scattered across Brentford and Turnham Green, the Jacobites would attack by horseback and foot:

Immediately, upon the Coach's coming within the Lane, they were to shut the Gate, and the Conspirators were to divide into three Parties: Some before in the Habit of County-men were to throw down the Pales . . . in the narrowest Passage, to prevent all possibility of Escape: Then Mr. Charnock with his Party were to attack the Guards in the Rear, and Rookwood and Porter with another Party in two Wings were to attack both sides of the Guards. The other Party to Aim only at His Majesty's Coach, which Party consisted of 8 Persons, and was to be under the Particular direction of Sir George Barclay.[15]

Seven or eight bullets would be shot from blunderbusses into the king's coach. Then it would be over and the sea and roads open for James to march on London and reclaim his birthright. This time the glory would be theirs. The invasion of England from France hinged on the mission's success. If William survived capture, a ship was waiting to rush him across the Channel into a dark dungeon and eternal oblivion.

At the last minute, though, the scheme was betrayed to the king. No sooner had William set off to hunt than "the guards were all come back in great haste, their Horses being all in a Foam." The spy Matthew Smith had infiltrated the Jacobite schemers at great peril and, as he boasted in his book, *Memoirs of Secret Service*, in 1699, "I am confident nothing will be concealed from me, and dare pawn my Life upon it." Through his intelligence services, a quantity of arms were later discovered under a garden wall at Sir William Parkyns's house. Nine of the assassins were executed.[16] This time England's spies got lucky. One thing was certain: the enemy would strike again. Great minds and strong men were needed to foil France.

London had its back to the wall. Britain was rife with clandestine criminals planning terrorism and riots. Daniel Defoe knew full well that the French king "spends more Money in Intelligence than all the European Princes besides."[17] Just as he had told his friend Henry Avery one very drunken night, he had warned the Crown for years that "Intelligence is another Point of mighty Consequence, and can scarce be purchas'd too dear: For it is the Soul of Government, and directs all its Actions properly, and without it You consult in the dark, and execute blind-fold."[18]

King William and his tight circle of advisors needed eyes but also minds and hands. The most pressing issue of the day was still how to force Parliament to give him a budget to keep a large army to fight off Louis. That meant a permanent army of forty thousand men. In November 1697 a hammer strike of a pamphlet, written anonymously, titled *An Argument Shewing That a Standing Army Is Inconsistent with a Free Government*, shouted out how a tired public was turning against William. The supporters of the exiled James II were desperate to see William's forces cut to the bare minimum, while the Tory squires whose taxes paid for the costs of war voted with their wallets. England should avoid all overseas battles.

William's reputation as England's savior was taking a drubbing. Good old xenophobia raised its ugly head. The new king was not just a distrusted foreigner; whispers swirled that he was in a relationship with two close male confidants.[19] William stood aloof from his English and Scottish subjects. Much of the time he was not even in England but on the Continent playing wargames or making merry. There was a deep communications gap between the king and the public. The quiet Prince of Orange who had been welcomed as a national hero began to be resented as a foreigner who needed Dutch troops to guard his life and back him in an unpopular war with France.

Defoe was one of very few diehards who devoted himself to the service of William's cause. In his new role as a government propaganda writer and confidential agent, Defoe was called on to write swift answers to political enemies, or what he called the "Grumbletonians."[20] In 1697 Defoe unleashed the power of his pen in a loyal broadside fired off in ink, not gunpowder, with *Some Reflections on a Pamphlet Lately Published*. The arguments against the king for a British Isles free of troops were an illusion, Defoe wrote. In the end the army was kept but diluted down to less than ten thousand men, far below the minimum fifteen-thousand-strong force William wanted. Ten thousand soldiers were next to useless. Defoe had proven his loyalty to the cause, however.

By April 1698, when Defoe was sent north of the border to seek information for Charles Montagu, 1st Earl of Halifax, chancellor of the exchequer and regent in the king's absence, Defoe was not just talking and writing, he was going undercover. Word had reached London that the Company of Scotland Trading to Africa and the Indies was trying to bust the East India Company's monopoly, now severely weakened, perhaps mortally, by Henry Avery's pirate attacks. In late 1697 the *St. Andrew*, *Caledonia*, *Unicorn*, *Enterprise*, and *Dolphin* were preparing to leave the Firth of Forth with 1,200 settlers, cargoes, and provisions to set up a Scottish colony at Darien on the Isthmus of Panama, a strategic bridgehead between Colombia, Mexico, and Florida. Announcements were plastered on coffeehouse walls in Edinburgh and Glasgow in early June 1698 telling the settlers to say their goodbyes and prepare to sail.[21] Some of the dreamers included crewmen from Avery's adventures aboard the *Fancy*.[22]

The timing could not have been worse for English interests. Montagu was pushing through a £2 million plan to create a new and more powerful East India Company. Defoe invented a trading excuse to visit Scotland and scoured Edinburgh's coffeehouses and the waterfront at Leith for gossip and intelligence to report back to the chancellor of the exchequer. Paradise for the Scots, meanwhile, turned out to be hell on earth. Swampy Darien was a land of torrential rain, yellow fever, and death. Ten people died every day. English and Spanish merchants refused to trade with the New Caledonians. When the Spanish planned to attack the failing colony, the newcomers fled. Fewer than three hundred survivors made it home to Scotland.[23] The scheme was a disaster. Defoe made his mark. He had arrived as a government spy. The king had a new champion.

The ill winds of change that blew across the political landscape while Defoe was in Scotland brought the spy a fresh dose of terrible luck. Montagu was suddenly out of political favor. Soon after, the glass duty was scrapped and Defoe's £100 salary gone. Thomas Neale and Dalby Thomas were caught embezzling funds for the Million Lottery. Neale was expelled from the House of Commons in early 1699 for bribery in the previous election and died that December. Dalby Thomas was taken into the custody of the sergeant at arms in February 1699.[24]

Defoe's great allies and power players fell like a house of cards. The ex-merchant was out of his depth without his political supporters within doors, but his hand was forced. From now on he would be increasingly drawn into the murky world of intelligence and propaganda writing. For king and country.

Vanishing Act

"Oh yes, Oh yes, Oh yes. All manner of persons that have anything more to do at this session, draw near and give your attendance," the court crier shouted. Sir Charles Hedges banged his gavel. The case against Henry Avery's crewmen—Joseph Dawson, Edward Forseith, William May, William Bishop, James Lewis, and John Sparkes—pushed "double Fetter'd" in iron chains into the Old Bailey in London,[1] was getting out of hand. The crowd pressing on the windows and doors had no respect for the law. None at all. The low muttering coming from the politicians and broadsheet press hounds in the public gallery was not how the judge of the High Court of Admiralty liked to hear cases. All respect had gone out the window. It was October 31, 1696.[2]

This was no normal hearing. The Privy Council expected the axe to fall after the disaster of a first trial had the audacity to find the accused not guilty. Hearings for piracy were not normally held at the Old Bailey, the country's palace of justice.[3] This was different. A show trial was expected to send a clear message to the Mughal emperor and the world: Britain was not responsible for a bunch of deviant pirates gone rogue in the Indies. Still, the world was watching. Sir Charles, sitting under festooned flags and the king's royal crest, DIEU ET MON DROIT (My Divine Right), chose his introductory words very carefully. Since foreigners would look upon the outcome as a mirror of the conduct of an entire nation:

> Our enemies will be glad to find an occasion to say, that
> such miscreants as are out of the protection of all laws, and
> civil government, are abetted by those who contend for the
> sovereignty of the seas. The barbarous nations will reproach
> us as being a harbour, receptacle, and nest of pirates; and our
> friends will wonder to hear that the enemies of merchants
> and of mankind, should find a sanctuary in this ancient place
> of trade.[4]

Now Sir Charles could hardly hear himself think. He banged his gavel manically and called for an early lunch. In his chambers the judge pushed his door slider to OUT and collapsed in his armchair, not before ordering up a spot of roast beef and half a bottle of claret. Essential reinforcements would improve his mood, or at least give him peace and quiet to reread the holy mess of his notes.

Defoe's *General History of the Pyrates* described how Henry Avery "made as great a Noise in the World . . . and was looked upon to be a Person of as great Consequence; he was represented in Europe, as one that had raised himself to the Dignity of a King, and was likely to be the Founder of a new Monarchy."[5] The noisemaker had now fallen silent. Where the devil was he? In his absence, Sir Charles was expected to find six of his arrested crew guilty in his kangaroo court.

This much the judge had worked out: soon into his brief stay on New Providence, Henry Avery realized the noose was tightening. The news was traveling fast on the trade winds from colony to colony. The bloodhounds would surely soon follow. The question was how fast until the sands of time ran out and nowhere in the Indies, Africa, Americas, or Europe would be safe?

Governor Nicholas Trott could only be trusted as long as the bribes held out. India was a powder keg ready to blow. England would have to respond with fire. Avery needed to pack his bags and create a smoke screen. Where to hide low? New Providence, as good as any English colony and its coming law enforcers, was out of the question. Dropping out into the dark forests of Madagascar was seriously attractive. New York, Rhode Island, Boston, and Jamaica were all British enclaves. A recipe for being hanged. The pirate king did what no one expected, Sir Charles Hedges read in his notes. He headed straight for the lion's den: England.

The judge's notes were stacked in chronological order. Under oath, John Dann of Rochester, a Royal Navy deserter who joined the Spanish treasure hunt in La Coruna in 1693,[6] and became an eager crew member of the *Fancy*, had sworn a detailed account of Avery's heist on the high seas in exchange for his life and the £1,000 offered by the state and East India Company. "We'll see about that," Sir Charles muttered to himself. As he read, he could not but help be grudgingly impressed by the old rogue Avery's boldness.

In May 1696 Henry Avery overpaid £600 for the small but sturdy fifty-ton sloop the *Seaflower*, commanded by Joseph Farrell, formerly captain of the *Portsmouth Adventure*, which raided the *Gunsway* alongside the *Fancy*. The *Seaflower* was manned by a crew of fifteen men and armed with four guns, just enough to protect its passengers and gleaming cargo without raising suspicions. Popular Americas' consignments of tobacco and furs covered over the valuable loot.[7] With fair winds, the pirate sailed through New England and Virginia[8] and landed in the fishing harbor of Dunfanaghy, the remotest backwater of northern Ireland he could find, after less than a month's sail. In County Donegal a bored customs official was delighted to be gifted £10 for each of the sixteen passengers, while three gentlemen and a woman paid £20 a head. All the official had to do was look the other way and tell anyone who asked that it had been another sleepy month.[9] As well as Avery, the *Seaflower* shipped home Philip Middleton, John Dann, John Stroger, Nathaniel Pike, Peter Soanes, Henry Adams, Francis Frennier, Thomas Johnson, Joseph Dawson, Samuel Dawson, James Lewis, the boy James Hamond, John Sparks, Joseph Goss, Charles Hawkins, Thomas Somerton, and James Murray.[10]

Sir Charles carefully reread the sworn testimony of the pirates turned king's witness. John Dann claimed he lost track of his captain after Avery announced, six miles outside Dunfanaghy, that he was off, going his own way. After all the months living and fighting together in the sweatbox of the *Fancy*, the pirate king was unemotional and matter-of-fact. Not even a handshake. Gone with the wind. Avery gifted Farrer the *Seaflower*; the captain would sail for Londonderry, then head back to America. Dann made his way with the dodgy port official Maurice Cuttle to Dublin with seven more of the pirate crew. Their ultimate destination, before being collared, was Letterkenny. [11]

In the end, Dann kept moving. He landed at Holyhead in northern Wales, traveled up to London with Thomas Johnson, and at the start of August 1696 made it all the way home to Rochester. After an epic adventure and journey, he got sloppy. Before sleeping off his exhaustion late into the morning in a local hotel, he had thrown his clothes onto a chair. When a maid tried folding Dann's jacket while he was still snoring, the next morning she found it padded with 1,045 gold sequins and ten gold guineas. The mayor of Rochester threw the pirate in jail and then sent him to London. [12]

Sir Charles was well into his roast beef, and two glasses of fine claret down, when he started coughing uncontrollably. You had to hand it to Henry Avery—quite a mover and shaker that chap. The judge read how Dann, cheekily asking for his £500 reward after being given the king's pardon for spilling his guts, had claimed to be called Long Ben when he was arrested in possession of his loot. It looked like the real Long Ben, Henry Avery, had greased some of his crew's palms with gold to pretend to be him and throw up his own smoke screen.

When the judge regained his composure and wiped a few drops of gravy off his gown and paperwork, he read how a second sloop from New Providence, the *Isaac*, [13] slipped into Westport on the western tip of Ireland on June 7, 1696. The thirty-ton ship was commanded by Thomas Hollingsworth, the same pirate rogue who served Henry Bridgeman's letter to Governor Nicholas Trott in Nassau that April. *Clearly a man of some substance*, Sir Charles mused. Aboard were sixteen of the old crew of the *Charles II* and then the *Fancy*, including Robert Richy, John Miller, George King, Edward Savill, William Phillips, and Thomas Joye, mostly Scotsmen.[14]

A week later, Thomas Bell, sheriff of County Mayo, got wind of a strange landing and sped to Westport. He got lucky. Hollingsworth and two of his crew were still there. Bell's eyes went out on stalks when he saw that "they had no other loading but gold & silver which they conveyd away." Henry Avery's captain had already sold his sloop to the Galway merchants Thomas Yeeden and Lawrence Deane. The sheriff took off to have a word with Yeeden and Deane, who he caught in the possession of "two bags of about forty pound worth of mony not passable in this kingdom . . . & took their bond of a hundred pound to have the same forthcoming to answer the governments pleasure."[15]

Bell's enquiries paid off when he tracked down two more of the sloop's crew, James Trumble and Edward Foreside, "in whose hands he found about 200 l. and seizd on their persons and goods." The loot was made up of 2,700 silver Spanish cob coins. Bell's intelligence understood that £20,000 in gold and bullion had been landed at Westport.[16]

By now, the sloop had scarpered, but warnings of strange goings-on along the west coast of Ireland was spreading fast. Farmer Glover, general supervisor of the revenue in Galway, had joined the hunt in Westport. In a comedy of errors, the sloop landed in Galway while he was traveling to Westport. Glover did his best to get to the bottom of what had been imported, which he was informed included "three tunn & a half of Brazelett wood [brazilwood that grows in the Bahamas] & a great quantity of coyne & bullion."[17]

The custom's officer at Westport had been suspicious when "he dischargd at one time 32 baggs & one cask of mony each as much as a man could well lift from the ground." What was the spooked man supposed to do? No one had any experience dealing with an oddity like this. No one knew who the newcomers were, "some saying she was a privateer, others a Buckaneer or that she had landed some of the Assassinators" aboard, plotting to murder King William.[18] Plenty of good folk in western Ireland were Catholic sympathizers who would happily see the Protestant pretender's throat slit.

As soon as the passengers landed, they had offered any rate for horses, £10 for some not worth forty shillings, and thirty shillings in silver for a horse with a "lightness of carriage." The officer had decided something queer was afoot and seized the sloop until the captain comfortably paid a bond for its release.

Mr. Lee, the collector of customs in Galway, also demanded a bond of security to make sure the sloop would not depart without a license. The crew, having already taken their share of gold and silver, scattered. Lee had not asked for custom's dues because "that mony paying no duty & being frightened in thither by a privateer; there being no place there to make a report he could not hinder the men to carry off their fortunes, but on oath denys the knowledge of any other goods whatsoever."[19]

Sir Charles was impressed by the Irish diligence in trying to fathom the mysterious background of Henry Avery's two sloops. Another officer, Mr. Vanderlure, the collector in Ballinrobe, on the River Robe in County Mayo, who had joined the hunt, learned that before landing in Westport, a dozen passengers had gone ashore at Achill Head with a considerable quantity of gold and silver coins and gold bullion. The crew lost no time laundering their ill-gotten gains. Vanderlure tracked down a small bag of "5 weight of broken silver" in the hands of officials Humphrey Currin and Samuel Bull and another nine weight of melted silver with John Swaile inland in Foxford. The haul weighed fourteen and three fourths pounds.[20]

Sir Charles was now on his third glass of claret and the confusing testimony was starting to swim before his eyes. The crew may have run from the scene of the crime, but they left behind a trail of curious breadcrumbs. Stuffed into a passenger's bag, Vanderlure heard about "5 yards & half of striped Muslin, 2 yards and half of cottoned cloth, 2 yards of

quilted linen with 10 small cravats & 4 silk handkerchiefs." Humphrey
Currin had seized them in Westport as liable to the payment of duty
and locked them up in the Customs House in Galway. Currin and his
friend, Bull, also bought from the crew "5 pound of broken silver and
9 pound melted coarse silver."[21] No doubt about it, this was a curiously
exotic cargo.

Meanwhile, the sloops and crew of the *Fancy* were moving fast. In
Bristol, England, John Dutton, collector of His Majesty's Customs,
jumped to attention when he heard that a ship had newly docked from
the West Indies. He had just read by the last post around July 22, 1696,
a proclamation against Avery for rape and theft on the high seas in India.
Was the timing pure coincidence? Down by the waterfront, Dutton
confronted Captain Farrer, who swore the ship called the *Seaflower* was
carrying cargo nothing more exciting than four tons of brasiletto wood.
Dutton was suspicious and:

> Upon rummaging the vessel we found casks in her for water
> such as usually belong to men-of-war, & turning one of them
> in the water out came a piece-of-eight, & 5 or 6 more were
> found in the ballast. The captain upon further examination
> said that those people he landed had pieces-of-eight, & they
> took but one trunk ashore with them . . . Immediately upon
> landing they dispersed, pretending to be fearful of a press
> [gang from the Royal Navy]. I, being not satisfied with his
> confession, understanding there was a boy on board who came
> from New Providence sent privately & examined him.[22]

Dutton learned from interrogating the *Seaflower*'s boy that at the
time when it left New Providence, a great ship lay at anchor with maybe
thirty-six guns. The boy thought the ship belonged to Governor Trott.
Dutton was unconvinced and wrote to Sir William Trumbull, a privy
councillor, who advised the king that "I take it to be the ship Every

commands . . . the man-of war in New Providence island is the *Fancy*.
I suspect that Every has dispersed his men & parted with his ship."[23]
The water casks from a man-of-war were part of the frigate *Charles II*'s
original provisions.

☠

Sir Charles had little doubt that the six men in his dungeon were the
guilty crewmen of the *Fancy* that attacked and looted the *Gunsway*. They
would swing for their crimes. Back in court, Sir Robert Newton, head
of the King's Learned Counsel against Dawson, Forseith, May, Bishop,
Lewis, and Sparkes was performing as he always did, with theatrical
gravity. Public influence had let the accused off the hook after they were
found not guilty of piracy in India by a jury:

> for feloniously and piratically taking and carrying away from
> persons unknown, a certain ship called the Gunsway, with
> her tackle, apparel, and furniture to the value of 1,000*l*. and
> goods to the value of 110*l*. together with 100,000 pieces of
> eight and 100,000 chequins, upon the high seas, ten leagues
> from the cape St. Johns, near Surat, East Indies.[24]

In the same court, twelve days later, the Crown defense changed tack,
instead accusing the pirates in a second back-to-back trial of stealing the
Charles II from Sir James Houblon.[25] Joseph Dawson knew which way
the wind was blowing and confessed his guilt. To hell with this sorry
world. He would go out swinging. The rest pleaded not guilty. Newton
laid out for Sir Charles, Lord Chief Justice Holt, Lord Chief Justice
Treby, Lord Chief Baron Ward, Mr. Justice Rokeby, Mr. Justice Turton,
and Mr. Justice Eyre how the accused first carried out crimes on their
own countrymen before attacking foreigners and strangers. The *Fancy*
then "committed many and great piracies for several years . . . in most

of the parts of the known world, without distinction, on all nations, and persons of all religions," Newton claimed.[26]

The final piracy was the "most pernicious in its consequences, especially as to trade, considering the power of the Great Mogul, and the natural inclination of the Indians to revenge." Dr. Newton stopped speaking and theatrically peered around the court for twenty seconds, before punching his point. "For suffer pirates, and the commerce of the world must cease," he emphasized, "which this nation has so deservedly so great a share in, and reaps such mighty advantage by."[27]

The adjournment of the hearing to November 10 felt like an age for the accused. They knew they could not expect a second close shave. This time the jury found the crew guilty. Given liberty to reply, Edward Forseith asked to be sent to India to suffer his fate. William May also asked to be sent to work for the East India Company, having "served my King and Countrey this thirty Years." Maybe they would be able to hop ship on the way or slide out a back door in the factory in Surat? It was a long shot but a glimmer of hope. William Bishop explained that he was only eighteen years old when Henry Avery orchestrated a mutiny on the *Charles II*. What did he know of the evil ways of the world? James Lewis and John Sparks merely pleaded their ignorance and threw themselves at the king's mercy.

The hard decisions had been made for Sir Charles. There would be no pity for these criminals. The noble lord stood to deliver the men's fate:

> The Law for the heinousness of your Crime hath appointed
> a severe Punishment, by an ignominious Death; and Iudg-
> ment which the Law awards, is this, That you and every one
> of you be taken from hence to the Place from whence you
> came, and from thence to the Place of Execution, and that
> there you, and every one of you be Hanged by the Necks,
> until you, and every one of you be Dead: And the Lord have
> Mercy upon you.[28]

And so, on Wednesday, November 25, 1696, the pirates were led to Execution Dock in Wapping. The procession weaved its way through London, slowly so the chattering mob could gawp at what fate befell pirates brought to book. At the head of the sanctioned lynch mob rode a marshal carrying a silver oar, the sign of the Admiralty's authority over estuaries, rivers, and British subjects on the high seas.

The streets were lined with rubbernecking spectators, the River Thames choked with boats eager to be part of history—the execution of the most famous pirate crew hanged in London. The chaplain walked next to the pirates, ever ready to hear their confession of sin. The condemned were steered into the Turks Head Inn for a last quart of ale. It helped some convicts take the edge off. Others finally repented at the eleventh hour.

Executions on the scaffold and gallows, a hideous apparatus of death along the east London foreshore, were timed to fit with the low tide, where the Admiralty's jurisdiction began. Wapping-in-the-Wose (the ooze), so the sixteenth-century antiquarian John Stow wrote in his *Survey of London*, was "a filthy strait passage, with alleys of small tenements or cottages, built, inhabited by sailors' victuallers" and "the usual place of execution for hanging of Pirats & Sea Rovers."[29]

Thousands watched the few crewmen of the *Fancy* led to their deaths. The hangman made sure the rope was short enough so the ordeal would be as painful as possible. A short drop did not break the neck but left the victim to die from a long suffocation. The spasmed body shook in what was known as the marshal's dance.

And so the *Fancy*'s men swung for the evils committed by Henry Avery against Emperor Aurangzeb and the *Gunsway*. Their bodies were then tied to wooden stakes between the high and low water mark.[30] Not until three tides had clogged their lungs with water and mud would the Admiralty's surgeons declare them dead. Their corpses may then have been packed off for anatomical dissection and medical training. As the gallows shook, Daniel Defoe and Henry Avery, hiding in plain sight in the crowd, nodded faintly to one another.

☠

Sir Charles doubted whether the hanging of five of the pirate king's crew would change much. The Mughal emperor would still distrust all England, the fatherland of pirates. Piracy would not be scared off either, not least until a new war broke out and the same deviants could come in from the dark and receive letters of marque to go privateering and legally chase enemy ships and seize their rich booty.

The whole case had been window dressing. Most of the crew did not end up at the gallows that fateful day. John Dann would end up being pardoned by the king in January 1697 for testifying against Henry Avery and his crew's piracy, and Joseph Dawson a month later.[31] Edward Savill was sprung out of prison on the island of Anglesey in Wales to give evidence in the trial of six of the *Fancy*'s pirates before the King's Bench in Dublin. All of them were acquitted.[32] Robert Seely was let out of Newgate Prison under the general pardon for poor convicts in May 1699.[33] For Emperor Aurangzeb, without Avery himself in the noose, the sentence was a hollow political gesture.

In December 1696 the East India Company wrote to advise its general presidents council at Fort St. George to be sure to spread word that English law had done its duty:

> The advice of this exemplary justice, that the Moors may see, we abominate these rapacious villanyes to such a degree as to spare no cost to detain the authors, it having cost us many hundred pounds in their apprehension & conviction by promising 50 l. head for seizing the criminalls to encourage their taking.[34]

The Old Bailey had sentenced Henry Avery in his absence. Neither hide nor hair was seen of the ringleader, however. The global manhunt ramped up its efforts. Thomas Hollingsworth was said to be hiding away in Galway, and Henry Adams and James Murray were in Ireland too. Thomas Johnson, the ex-cook of the *Charles II*, was thought to be in Ireland as well, but expected to go and find his wife in East Smithfield in London. Robert Rich, Robert Ogilby, Patrick Lawson, Thomas Johnson, and James Stevenson all fled north to Scotland. Edward Foresight was seized and let go on his way to Newcastle upon Tyne. Thomas Castleton went home to York, William Bishop to Plymouth or Bideford. Dennis Merrick had left for Bristol and John King to find his merry wife in Windsor by way of Oxford. Joseph Dawson was in Yarmouth in Suffolk.

Jacob Game, Richard Chope, Edward Saville, John Miller, Greshame, James Craggett, James Lewis, and John Donne were scattered across London from the port of Deptford to the pirate's lair in Ratcliffe, east of the city. Nathaniel Pyke was expected to leave London for Chatham Dockyard, as was Thomas Sommerton, and Robert Silly to slip out of the capital for St. James's market, where his father worked as a chimney sweep.[35]

August 1696 saw pirates in chains in London and Ireland and "messengers employed to go abroad in search of such others as can be found" and "desirous by all due ways . . . for the bringing such vile criminalls to exemplary punishment for the satisfaction of the government of Surratt."[36] The thirteen men who signed the call for more human bloodhounds to be set loose on the world included Isaac Houblon, one of the backers of the Spanish Expedition three long years earlier. That month, the proclamation for the capture of Henry Avery and his merry men was posted throughout the British Isles, as far as Scotland and Ireland. By April 1697, twenty more of the *Fancy*'s crew had been rounded up in Ireland, ready to be tried.[37]

The net was filling up. On November 14, 1696, a ship sailing from Virginia, forced into Brest in France, included more of Avery's crew caught with Indian and Arabian gold and silver, £33,333, and chests of rarities hidden in wooden casks with butter stuffed into each end to hide the loot.[38] In Dublin, the Lords Justice of Ireland had rounded up more of the *Fancy*'s crew in the same month to be put on trial before a special commission.[39] Thomas Lane, going by the name of Coviaro, was taken into custody in July 1698 on suspicion of being one of Henry Avery's crew. That October James Craget pretended to know nothing of Avery, although a letter in his possession, written by his wife, looked like he had bought a pardon.[40] The pirate king himself, so a Royal African Company report informed the Commissioners of Trade, was supposedly spotted off the coast of Africa with his crew in March 1699.[41]

On July 2, 1700, Rear Admiral John Benbow, commander-in-chief of the king's ships in the West Indies, and a bounty hunter who once cut off and salted the heads of thirteen African Moors to claim a reward in Cadiz, arrived home from the West Indies with three men-of-war and nine of Avery's crew chained belowdecks.[42] Two more were picked up in Malacca in southwestern Malaysia in 1701.[43] As late as May 1704, an informer called the authorities to look into a Henry Avery, outwardly a salesman at the Golden Ball and Dagger in London's Drury Lane, "a substantial man and householder" who seemed to have more cash than a man of his position ought.[44] A Captain John Breholt even paraded a woman in London in 1707, which he claimed was Henry Avery's wife, picked up abandoned in Madagascar.[45]

A legal opinion researched by Sir Charles Hedges had shown in November 1697 that admiralty courts in the colonies had no power to try and punish pirates.[46] Anyone collared had to be shipped home to await trial. The sole exception was Jamaica, where men behaving in "an Hostile manner, under any Foreign Prince, State, or Potentate," could be "duly Convicted in His Majesties Supream Court of Judicature within this Island, to which Court Authority is hereby given to hear and to determine the same, as in other Cases of Felony, shall suffer pains of Death without Benefit of the Clergy."[47]

Hunters and informers all started to claim the rewards for the discovery of Henry Avery, his men, and the *Fancy*. John Dann wanted £500 for informing the Duke of Shrewsbury that Avery's ship was at the island of Providence.[48] A petitioner and his mother who discovered goods and money belonging to Avery's pirates, and handed them over to Justice Pevon and Justice Baldwyn, sought £100.[49] William Philips and Edward Saville each wanted £50 for squealing on their fellow sailors.[50] In December 1700 Philip Middleton was paid £40 as a royal bounty out of Secret Service money.[51] Thomas Davis requested payment for his charges and fees for catching William May and William Bishop red-handed with foreign gold.

From September 1696 to May 1701, the East India Company paid out a stream of expenses: £56 to I. Davis for apprehending pirates, £66 to Captain South for the same, £319 to I. Bromwell and Company, and £341 to P. Drencour.[52] Still, making convictions stick was tough. Two more members of Avery's crew were indicted in July 1697, but Henry Adams escaped from jail before the hearing started and David Adams was found not guilty after a witness testified that Avery had forced him into a life of crime.[53]

When in December 1698 the Lords Justices of England offered the "assurance of our most gracious pardon" to all pirates to be let off the hook if they gave up the game, an offer that would be taken off the table on June 30, 1699, Henry Avery was excluded from the royal pardon.[54] The pirate king was still wanted, dead or alive.

PART THREE

PART THREE

His Majesty's Secret Service

Through the window of a Cornish tavern in Falmouth, Henry Avery watched the English Channel's waves crash onto the beach. These were familiar seas. He had sailed these waters since a child. He knew their moods, where they led, the damage their power could cause. Christmas Day 1700 was just two weeks away. No one had forgotten the pirate king, especially the government and chasing pack of bloodhounds.

With the new century, though, the world was looking forward, not back. No sighting of Avery had been reported in four long years, and the powers that be—outside the royal doors—started to admit that he was probably living his own royal rogue's life on the far side of the world. The best minds of the Admiralty and the Royal Navy had failed to track him down and bring him to justice. The pirate king was still vanished.

Avery put down his pen quill and cleared his head. Falmouth was a welcome town to lay low. It had a bit of everything. It may have been quiet, but it was far from sleepy. Avery, too, was fully awake and focused on big business, affairs of the state that could sink or swim Britain's fortunes. Avery ordered another pint from the counter in the Penny-come-quick alehouse on Green Bank and sipped heartily. The pub got its name from the old dame who counted her pennies running the ferry from here since 1600.[1] Avery was not a beer man, but he needed to blend in, pretend to be just another busy merchant sailor. Most of all, he needed to be faceless.

Shipping had come and gone through the Cornish haven of Falmouth, known as Falamua since 1403. There was little to show by way of a town, but nature had perfectly designed "a havyn very notable and famose, and in a manner the most principale of al Britayne."[2] Daniel Defoe knew it as "the fairest and best road for shipping that is in the whole isle of Britain."[3]

Life took an upturn in the second half of the seventeenth century when Sir Peter Killigrew, 2nd Baron of Arwenack, built a quay and persuaded the powers that be to move the customs house from Penryn to Falmouth. Killigrew lobbied the government favorably to grant him a patent to run a weekly market and two fairs at Falmouth and to manage the local ferry to Flushing, separated from the town center by the Carrick Roads water channel. The new borough of Falmouth was born and turned from a place of 10 houses before 1664 to 350 when Henry Avery rode into town.[4]

The Falmouth of 1700 may have felt well off the beaten track, being 66 miles from Plymouth and 295 miles from London, but it was now firmly on the world map. Avery had taken notes on the goods landed along its quays. There was timber, hemp, tallow, grain, and iron from northern England; wine, fruit and strong spirits from Spain, Portugal, and the Netherlands; and, of course, rum and sugar from the West Indies. Falmouth sent out to the world Cornish tin, copper, woolen goods, pilchards, oil, and mountains of cotton goods. All the trade was protected by the looming walls of Pendennis Castle, a daunting defense paid for by King Henry VIII.[5] Avery tried his best to give the castle a wide berth, just in case he ran into sparring partners from his old life.

Falmouth felt comfortable and familiar to Avery. It was a smaller version of Plymouth, his hometown, but with a much bigger harbor. The two competing coastal towns had long trumpeted their greater advantages. "Likewise as Plymouth vaunteth richer and fairer towns and greater plenty of fish than Falmouth, so Falmouth braggeth that a hundred sayle may anker within its circuit, and no one of them see the others' top, which Plymouth cannot," the antiquarian Richard Carew noted in 1603.[6] Strolling along the bay, Avery remembered his childhood in Plymouth, days of innocence that he sorely missed but could never recover.

Falmouth may have been much smaller than Plymouth, but you had to be on your guard at all times. The town was full of gossiping busybodies. Even sitting quietly in the corner of the Penny-come-quick with a look on his face that told people to stay away, the pub bustled with characters looking for a chat or friendly ear. Right now, one old Cornishman was sharing a story of how a doctor had just amputated his toes. He was covered in soil, having just buried them in the local churchyard, ready for the day of his resurrection. "I couldn't appear before the Lord with no toeses," he told anyone who would listen.[7]

Then there were the do-gooders, cap in hand, always asking for donations for fine causes of all kinds. Avery had been approached for cash for down at heel people formerly enslaved in Algiers and Turkey, to fix churches, to help Protestant fugitives flee from France. And there were always new shipwrecked sailors to help out.[8] Avery did not care to talk. How could he say no, though, to such charity when he had struck it so lucky? As long as he was careful to hand over local coins and not dip into his purse full of Arabian silver and Spanish pieces of eight he always traveled with. If anyone asked, the pirate king was no longer called Henry Avery. Now he was Whilest, Mr. Whilest.

Many locals would do anything for easy cash, as well. This was Cornwall, home of the wreckers, with a reputation equally as bad as the Bahamas but not as brutally efficient at rushing to the scene of a tragedy. When a Dutch ship laden with brandy and saffron ran aground near Falmouth, the wreckers moved in without caution and with their own calamity: "Some of those plunderers having drunk so much brandy, and being busy in the hole [hold] with a candle, they set fire to the bandy by which means the ship and cargo were destroyed and two of the ruffians perished in the flames."[9]

As much as he enjoyed Falmouth, the pirate king was not in town for fun. And the clock was ticking. Avery had based himself in the port town for one reason and one reason only: for the last twelve years the port had served as the home of England's new postal service. From here the *Ally-ance*, *Expedition*, and *Prince* sailed to and from Lisbon in Portugal.[10] More recently, postal ships started heading for the West Indies and Avery's own stomping ground where all his adventures began, the Groyne, La Coruna, in northern Spain.[11] Avery smirked at how the strange arc of life had swept him to this time and place, helping the most unexpected of power brokers. Between the arrival and departure of the world's post, very queer goings on were afoot in Falmouth.

Henry Avery was exhausted. His latest sea voyage had taken much out of him. He would push on. Avery wiped the black ink off his fingers, dipped his quill again, and signed his letter, "Pray present my humblest service. Your most humble servant, Whilest."[12] He lifted the paper close to his face and quickly reread the contents. The letter was a reply to another he received on December 10. Avery explained how he was meeting his contact that evening. Together they would "consult what is fitt to be done." He confirmed that he was working with the highest secrecy and that "there's noe suspicion upon any Account." Avery promised that his source "may expect to hear from me upon every mocion that's material." Avery thanked his contact for covering his last bill and explained the reason he had been indisposed. "I have been very much out of order since my coming ashore," he admitted. "I have not yet recover'd that fateague at sea."[13] Finally, a life not so much of hell-raising, but looking behind him constantly, was catching up with Avery.

The letter was punctual, familiar, and clear, yet obscure. Where Avery needed to make absolutely sure no outsider could read his lines, he swapped letters for numbers. In his weather-weary leather sea satchel he carried a small diary. Four pages were covered with numbers and the names and places the code stood for. Only a very small inner circle had access to the same codebook. Without it, the letters read as complete mumbo jumbo. Avery, for instance, had covered his tracks by writing, "I am not the least concerned for Tank 29 f B26 being out of the T9211597." Job done. The code was so good that its true meaning is still secret until today.[14] With one final flourish, by memory Henry Avery addressed his letter to "The Reverend Mr. James Richardson att the Liberary over against Orenge Street, St. Martins in ye. Fields, London."

Mr. Whilest would keep his head down and relax until Claude Guilot turned up. Then the men had some skulls to crack. Putting the fear of God into any man was Avery's specialty.

☠

By apparent coincidence, an old friend of Henry Avery's was in Cornwall that same winter. Daniel Defoe had spent most of the year 1700 incognito. The show-off who loved to talk and impress people had kept his mouth shut tight since the summer of 1699. Defoe's support from the powerbrokers Thomas Neale and Dalby Thomas may have been dead in the water, but the expert in spinning propaganda and rubbing shoulders with the good and great had a voracious hunger for influence. Defoe had gambled on going it alone, striking out to get the ear of King William.

Defoe had not been idle. Far from it. The ideas had poured off his pen. When the time was right, he would unleash his ideas for a better Britain, warts and all. In May 1699 his last poem, *An Encomium upon a Parliament*, continued the spirited fight for King William III's need for a large army. Defoe relentlessly swore that:

> Faile not our Freedom to Secure
> And all our Friends disband
> And send those Men to t'other Shore
> Who were such fools as to come o'er
> To help this grateful land.[15]

William heard the message and was suitably flattered. Defoe, soon to turn forty years old, entered the service of the king, everything the wit and merchant had dreamed. There was not a minute to spare. The Catholic menace was undimmed, and bold tongues were again attacking the king in the most xenophobic and hostile way, laughing at his expense. None more so than the radical journalist John Tutchin, who in 1700 lampooned the monarch's reputation in "The Foreigners":

> Mounted to Grandeur by the usual Course
> Of Whoring, Pimping, or a Crime that's worse;
> Of Foreign Birth, and undescended too,
> Yet he, like *Bentir,* mighty Feats can do.
> He robs our Treasure, to augment his State,
> And *Jewish* Nobles on his Fortunes wait:
> Our ravish'd Honours on his Shoulder wears,
> And Titles from our Antient Rolls he tears.[16]

Tutchin was arrested for seditious libel but the accusation did not stick. He escaped punishment. A fired-up Defoe hated the poem and set about washing away its message. Forget *Robinson Crusoe.* When *The True-Born Englishman* was published in 1701, it became Defoe's lifelong literary triumph. Twenty editions were printed in Daniel's lifetime of the vicious satire that attacked how

> when I see the town full of lampoons and invectives against Dutchmen, only because they are foreigners, and the king reproached and insulted by insolent pedants, and ballad-making poets, for employing foreigners, and for being a foreigner himself, I confess myself moved by it to remind our nation of their own original, thereby to let them see what a banter is put upon ourselves in it; since speaking of Englishmen *ab origine,* we are really all foreigners ourselves.[17]

Defoe wittily reminded the lords and ladies about town that if any of them peered far enough back in time, every British citizen had foreign blood cursing through their veins:

> These are the heroes that despise the Dutch,
> And rail at new-come foreigners so much;
> Forgetting that themselves are all derived
> From the most scoundrel race that ever lived;
> A horrid crowd of rambling thieves and drones
> Who ransack'd kingdoms, and dispeopled towns;
> The Pict and painted Briton, treach'rous Scot,
> By hunger, theft, and rapine, hither brought;
> Norwegian pirates, buccaneering Danes,
> Whose red-hair'd offspring everywhere remains;
> Who, join'd with Norman French, compound the breed
> From whence your true-born Englishmen proceed.[18]

The True-Born Englishman appeared to great fanfare in January 1701. Daniel Defoe was a household name. The poem had taken up most of his time in 1700, and Defoe took the boldest gamble of his life by presenting it personally to King William III before its publication.[19] The risk hoped to secure the king's favor. And that meant crossing the choppy waves of the North Sea to track down William in the Netherlands in the fall of 1700.

Defoe cashed in a big favor to get to his ruler by approaching William Carstares, the king's chaplain, close companion, and a trusted adviser. The men had met in the Netherlands when they were both exiled there during the reign of King James II after being defeated at the Battle of Sedgemoor in July 1685.[20] The cheek paid off. King William was even more deeply flattered and impressed by Defoe's hero-worshipping talent. The pair talked long into the night and found a string of personal and ideological similarities. As the weeks passed, the king started freely discussing matters that he did not even confide to his ministers.

When it was time for Defoe to return to England, the master asked his dog-like devotee what he wanted for his allegiance. Defoe bowed deeply and answered that his life's work was merely to serve His Majesty. Daniel Defoe, outsider, Dissenter, and criminal defrauder was now on His Majesty's Secret Service. The king had a new champion with a sharp mind, great influence over the national press, and a poison pen at the ready.

☠

The year 1700 was a powder keg. At the beginning of November, King William learned that Charles II of Spain had died. In his will his entire possessions were left to the sixteen-year-old Philippe, the Duke of Anjou, and younger son of the dauphin, the heir apparent of King Louis XIV of France. England's great fear was that King Philip V would fall under Spanish influence. So Defoe feared:

> If the French get the Spanish Crown, we are beaten out of the Field as to Trade, and are besieged in our own Island, and never let us flatter our selves with our Safety consisting so much in our Fleet . . . If the French get Spain, they get the greatest Trade in the World in their Hands; they that have the most Trade, will have the most Money, will have the most Ships, the best Fleet, and the best Armies; and if once the French master us at Sea, where are we then?[21]

Then, the worst nightmare came to pass. The Duke of Anjou became King Philip V of Spain. Spain and William and Defoe's greatest foe, France, were wed in what felt like a terrifying unholy Catholic alliance. Now England would have to watch out for two nations attacking its Narrow Seas. Europe is ruined, King William was heard to sigh.

Defoe was in the right place at the right time. After November 1700 a new wave of potent pamphlets flew off his pen, most anonymous, to spin the king's interests. In November Defoe released his long-winded *The Two Great Questions Consider'd. I. What the French King Will Do, with Respect to the Spanish Monarchy. II. What Measures the English Ought to Take.* At the same time, Defoe advised the king to be sure to keep his friends close and his enemies in parliament closer. "Your Majtie Must Face About, Oblige your Friends to be Content to be Laid by, and Put in your Enemyes, Put them into Those Posts in which They may Seem to be Employ'd, and Thereby Take off the Edge and Divide the Party."[22] Defoe the spy was in full flow.

Daniel Defoe was not just stuck with his feet under a desk. He wrote while on the move. A new government would be sworn into office in February 1701 and William wanted to take the pulse of the nation. What was the man in the tavern thinking? How could he turn the nation's anti-foreigner mood? Defoe became the king's eyes and ears. The tradesman had traveled widely at home and abroad. He was an expert in history's ebb and flow. Crucially, for the overseas King William, Defoe knew the mind of the man drinking in the coffeehouses.

In 1700 Daniel Defoe became a man of greater surprise and mystery than any plot line in one of his famous novels. He was always coming and going at the strangest of times, so that "his own Coachman knew not where he lodg'd."[23] Prizing secrets out of informers was a world where Defoe excelled. Dissenters knew how to keep secrets and listen. Many a loose tongue had spilled secrets in the taverns and coffeehouses, so much so that King Charles II had even tried to close them down in 1675, fearful that they "produced very evil and dangerous effects."[24] The ban was lifted after just eleven days when caffeine-deprived Londoners threatened to riot.

These were the years when Defoe developed his contacts and spycraft. He traveled the land in disguise, sometimes under the name of Alexander Goldsmith, among a hundred other pseudonyms.[25] When it was needed, he disguised himself in women's clothes. Defoe wrote reports left-handed to obscure his handwriting and invented a 247-word numeric code for sending letters in case the enemy intercepted them. The French king was 131, invasion 157, and Secret Service 249.[26]

Defoe's decades sweating as a merchant meant that he knew England inside out and could call on useful contacts wearing his tradesman's hat. Normally he rode five to seven hours a day on horseback and spent the afternoons and evenings in town, talking politics in the coffeehouses and visiting traders and clergymen.[27] London's spy masters fed him information to barter for news and intelligence.

Even if he got a kick out of the trappings of spying, Defoe took his job extremely seriously. "Intelligence is the Soul of all Publick bussiness," he wrote.[28] For military and political reasons. England was still threatened by invasion by foreign powers. Defoe even wanted his paymasters to list people's allegiances in a Big Brother database.[29]

All the while, Daniel peered across the English Channel at the threat of invasion. At home and abroad he still lived in fear, writing in rhyme of "Pride, Plenty's Hand-maid, deeply taints their Blood, And Seeds of Faction mix the Crimson Flood. Eternal Discords brood upon the Soil, And universal Strifes the State embroil."[30] Whatever it took to keep the Catholics off the throne, and France locked south of the Narrow Seas, Daniel Defoe was all in.

In the winter of 1700, Defoe started making his way into southwest England to take the nation's pulse. He had the perfect cover. Once more he was dreaming of the good life. His Secret Service salary was a terrific bonanza. By his own words, he was "beyond my merit bountifully rewarded."[31] The brick and tile factory in the Tilbury marshes was still delivering healthy profits.

"I began to live, Took a Good House, bought me a Coach and horses a Second Time," he later wrote. "I paid large Debts gradually, small Ones wholly, and Many a Creditor after composition whom I found poor and Decay'd I sent for and Paid the Remainder to tho' Actually

Discharged."[32] The crippling debts had been cut from £17,000 to just over £5,000.[33] Defoe could see the light at the end of the tunnel, a day when he could walk the streets a free man without always looking over his shoulder.

Defoe had not given up on his dream of shipwrecked treasure and as he rode to Cornwall, a ship was transporting the latest contraption designed to dive for plunder. Robert Davis, Defoe's brother-in-law, was his closest and most trusted friend. Davis was a shipwright who earned great experience working in Chatham and Portsmouth dockyards. The spy had challenged him to invent a diving engine and Davis duly won the bet.[34] To the outside world, the travelers were "projectors," speculators on their way to the Lizard to try their luck fishing for silver.

Defoe and Davis rode through Dorset and Devon, passing Christchurch and Wimborne over sandy, wild, and barren countryside to Poole. In Weymouth they followed the shore, watching men fishing for mackerel in Bridport that were so plentiful that the locals could buy fish cheap enough to use them to manure their fields. Eventually they reached the Lizard. Davis dived in his engine in Polpeor Cove—the scene of Defoe's great failure in 1692. He plunged several leagues underwater and proved the machine's merits by belting out the Hundredth Psalm.[35] The lines could have been written about Daniel Defoe and King William's own intimate rapport:

> You faithful servants of the Lord,
>   sing out his praise with one accord,
>   while serving him with all your might
>   and keeping vigil through the night.

The dive engine worked. The two friends then headed to the Bumble Rock. Defoe did not make the same mistake as before in 1692. The cold autumnal weather put off any sane would-be treasure hunters. The wreck was hauntingly isolated and this time the friends salvaged "several bars or pigs of silver."[36] Daniel Defoe could add adventurer in the grand footsteps of Sir William Phips to his resume.

All the while Defoe was plotting and planning. Diving for treasure was just a front. The winter of 1700 was the crucial time to shore up the monarchy's power in the newly coming Parliament. The royal purse was opened. Out poured funds for bribes, henchmen, and intelligence.

☠

Mr. Whilest, Henry Avery the pirate king, was wiling away his time in the Penny-come-quick alehouse, quietly drinking slow and keeping a low profile. He was obscured by billows of Virginia tobacco smoke bellowing out of his pipe and the latest copy of the *Post Boy*. That morning he had dropped into the post office and stuffed a bundle of letters in his leather bag, ready to go through them with Claude Guilot.

The sun had gone down and Avery was thinking about heading out for a spot of dinner. The distant lights of traders heading into port from the far-off Indies took the pirate king back to what had started to feel like another age, a time that was buried, if not dead. Henry Avery, against the odds and against anything he could have ever imagined while cutting up the high seas, had been handed a lifeline on a plate.

Just then the inn door swung open, creaking on hinges badly needing oiling. In walked a travel-weary Daniel Defoe.

"Ah, Mr. Guilot, I've been expecting you," Mr. Whilest said, standing up to give his old friend and savior the warmest of bear hugs.

To the outside world, Daniel Defoe and Henry Avery looked like traveling merchants letting off steam. No one knew what Avery looked like. There were no MOST WANTED posters tacked to the inn's door to betray him, and Defoe's creditors would never catch him so far from London.

The undercover agents had lots to discuss. The king had dissolved Parliament on December 19 and had called for a new government to be formed on February 16 "in respect of some matters of the highest importance to our kingdom,"[37] Defoe and Avery had read in the latest post. The spies did not have long to help influence the next administration. King William needed to know who to trust and who was a fox. Enemies raking mud needed leaning on and persuading to back off, if they knew what was good for them.

All the while, Catholic Jacobites continued plotting to destroy the king. Just at the start of the month, "treasonable papers" had been seized in Exeter on December 3 by Hugh Speke writing to a Mr. Macky. They discussed a troublemaker called Maxwell coming from France by way of Flanders, "upon an ill design." The king was expected to command that the communications "direct be sent to attorney-general with view to prosecution."[38] In Dublin, so Defoe and Avery had read, seven "very credible persons" had been arrested for a former attempted assassination of the king. A fellow spy who had infiltrated their ring was warned from London, "For your life, do not frequent them; and let them be dispersed, so as not to be found out by any of the Jacobites."[39]

Not much got passed the shrewd captain, but Henry Avery would need to be extra cautious until the new Parliament was sworn in. These were dangerous times. Sedition was in the air and high treason being planned. Which was exactly why the pirate king was in Falmouth: to stamp out opposition to William and keep his ear to the keel, not just the ground, for any whisper of would-be murderers crossing the English Channel—or worse, a French invasion.

Falmouth was the only place in Britain to carry out his undercover mission. This was where all the country's post arrived and left for Europe and the world. Word of Avery's pillage of the Mughal emperor's treasure ship the *Gunsway* landed here. The royal proclamations calling for Avery's head sailed out from these same shores.

The English Post Office opened the Falmouth Packet Service in 1688 with a direct crossing to Spain,[40] irony of ironies La Coruna—the very port where Henry Avery spirited away the *Charles II* frigate, renamed it the *Fancy*, and went on the pirate account. The waterway leading into

Falmouth was secure, wide, deep, and calm for sailing ships and the port boasted a well-protected harbor in bad weather. At the extreme southwest of Britain, Falmouth was the first suitable port reached by ships returning home.

The Falmouth Packet Service sounded dull and that was just what King William's supporters wanted the country to think. But it played a key role in defending the realm as a cog of the General Post Office's Secret Office. Henry Avery's mission was to watch the sailing traffic and people coming and going, gather strategic intelligence, and intercept dubious mail for covert scrutiny. Avery's counterintelligence protected government dispatches from falling into enemy hands before and during sea voyages too. William wanted "accounts of all that passes in those parts."[41] Avery kept a beady eye on every passenger and, when called for, secured them for interrogation.

Letters like the one Avery had just written in the Penny-come-quick alehouse flew between Falmouth and London by boat for the eyes only of Secretary of State James Vernon, and then for the king himself. In recent mail the pirate king had shared the report of Commander Captain John Cranbey of HMS *Poole*, who learned from a fishing boat near Brest that seven French men-of-war had sailed with the new viceroy to join forces with Spain in a push to conquer the riches of the West Indies. Seven more great ships were ready to sail from Brest as well. "I believe I could with less suspicion obtain a more certain account of the naval preparations of France than any ship wearing the king's colour," Avery wrote to his paymasters.[42] Another source warned that a mail packet boat flying the king's English colors had been attacked without warning by a French warship of forty guns and chased for three quarters of an hour.[43]

Claude Guilot was exhausted from his travels but did not believe in wasting time sleeping. He and Mr. Whilest stayed up most of the night talking affairs of the state and plotting the king's safety. Defoe was disappointed that there was no clear noise of a French invasion to scare the king's enemies and decided, nevertheless, to ramp up project fear to bend

Westminster to William's way. What if London was instructed that the word on the coast was that the French fleet was planning to put to sea and land on this very shore? All it would take was a little sleight of hand.

Defoe and Avery put their mind and humor to a few choice lines while the ale flowed. "There is no doubt but this [French] fleet will be master of the sea for some time, if not all the summer," they wrote, "because the Dutch dare not stir till the English be ready, and they have long debates yet before they can be in a condition to act, if they have the will; and it is a question whether they will have it at all."[44] If Parliament refused to vote William more troops, France could not be stopped, their message explained. It was good but not enough. On the spot, Defoe, grinning mischievously, dipped his quill and began a new document, *The Apparent Danger of an Invasion. Briefly Represented in a Letter to a Minister of State.* He could hardly put his own name on it, so signed it as by "a Kentish Gentleman."

Scribbling furiously, and speaking the words aloud as they poured out of his mind, so Avery could share the fun, he wrote:

> The City Militia, I believe is our best; but what Discipline can Men have, who appear in Arms but once a year, march into the Artillery Ground, and there wisely spend the Day in Eating, Drinking and smoking, in Storming half a Score Sir-Loins of Beef, and Vennison Pasties and having given their Officers a Volley or two, and like so many Iddle Boys with Snowballs, fooll'd away a little Gun Powder, return Home again as ignorant as they went out, and as fit to Fight the French at *Black Heath*, as one of our little *Yatches* is to engage the *Brittania*.[45]

It was dynamite. Even Henry Avery, who had seen it all, was impressed. These days, most of Defoe's actions impressed him. Daniel Defoe, who had slurred drunkenly when they met by chance in his own tavern, the World's End, in 1696, about wanting to help his old friend had come good. Avery was shocked when he received a verbal pardon from the king himself in return for a financial contribution and, more importantly, an oath to serve William to the end of his days. The king needed a strongman and none came stronger than the pirate king, a master strategist who had managed to escape the law for more than five years and could talk most men round to his way of thinking or otherwise turn to pistol and cutlass. Now Daniel Defoe was not just a great friend, he was his spymaster. Henry Avery was back from the dead. The pirate king had come in from the cold.

Defoe and Avery still had to step extremely carefully. No one could know about their work on His Majesty's Secret Service. And, on paper, the pirate menace had not gone away. It was hardly going to win any political favor for King William, either at home or abroad. Powerful men were still furiously hunting the seven seas for the pirate king. That very day, Vernon had written to the Admiralty. HMS *Dolphin* had just docked from Jamaica with one Bolton, an ally of Captain Kidd, who had hid "much of Kidd's goods, to a great value."[46] Closer to the scene of the crime, Sir William Beeston, the governor of Jamaica, had sent the *Germoon* cruising after pirates.[47] And there was still a warrant out for Avery's arrest. Henry Avery, alias Bridgeman, was still exempt from the general pardon for pirates wanting to go clean and would stay so into 1701 and beyond.[48]

Yet the newly minted spy had pressing work that would not stop until Parliament was sworn in the coming February. Every day the man who no one knew was the pirate king went to the office of Falmouth's postmaster to pick up intelligence, post, and instructions from Secretary of State Vernon marked KING'S SPECIAL SERVICE, dispatched to him by flying packets, the fastest boats on the water.[49]

The next day Henry Avery would add a valuable letter to the fast packet returning from Falmouth to London. Only it was not for the eyes of the king. This letter, written in code, was addressed to the Reverend James Richardson at the library in London's St Martin's-in-the-Field. "God's speed," Avery whispered as he dropped it into the special Falmouth mail.

Spy Factory

A *mo, amas, amat, amamus, amatis, amant* (I love, you love, he loves, we love, you love, they love). The postman stopped to listen to the words singing out of the school windows and knocked softly on the front door. They all sounded Greek to him.

The Reverend James Richardson was engrossed teaching the latest crop of students the classics. Today was time to mug up on Latin. So far, so good. Richardson did not like being interrupted, especially mid-flow. The man in the gold-braided scarlet coat with blue lapels and a black hat with a gold band was the royal courier who serviced the Falmouth packet boats. The reverend had been told to keep a close eye out for him. Richardson dutifully nodded, took a single letter without uttering a word of thanks, and marched upstairs to the darkest corner of Archbishop Tenison's Library and School in London.

To his students, Mr. Richardson was a figure of authority. Little did they know he was just a pawn, well-paid to keep the London school and library running, who topped up his salary with another £20 a year for reading the six o'clock nightly prayers at St Martin-in-the-Fields Church,[1] just around the corner from the Crown Stables. There the king's horses were kept, as well as the royal hawks. Richardson knew exactly who his own lord and master was.

Archbishop Thomas Tenison was bent over a strange contraption surrounded by letters and a steaming bowl of water in the first-floor library
on Orange Street in the parish of St Martin-in-the-Fields. Richardson
knew better than to ask questions. He was paid to be the soul of discre-
tion. When the archbishop, absorbed in his work, failed to notice him,
the schoolteacher coughed sharply. A hand reached out, took the new
post, and waved the reverend away. Dismissed. Time to get back to Latin
conjugation. The passing of letters never happened.

The man who Jonathan Swift, the wordsmith who wrote *Gulliver's
Travels*, called "the dullest good for nothing man I ever knew"[2] was certainly up to no good and it was far from dull. Tenison pursed his narrow
lips set above a weak double chin and stroked his wavy gray hair. *What
mischief was afoot in the land now?*, he thought. Inside the Falmouth post
he scanned a letter signed by Whilest 2—Henry Avery, keeping busy
on the king's business.

The archbishop had had serious misgivings about bringing the pirate
king into the doors of inner power. Pirates were unhinged madmen,
capable of anything. Daniel Defoe, though, had sworn for the man and
promised to run him. The cause needed all the bright minds it could get.
A fearsome henchman, sad but true, came in useful from time to time.
If it was God's will, so be it.

Thomas Tenison, at the time the local vicar in St Martin-in-the-Fields,
came up with the idea for a library in his parish in 1683. The place of
learning would enlighten the flock, serve the greater good, and give Tenison a place to house his ever-growing book collection. So his good friend,
the landscape gardener John Evelyn, reported hearing the archbishop say:

> He told me there were 30 or 40 Young men in Orders in his
> Parish, either, as Governors to young Gent: or Chaplians to

Noble-men, who being reprov'd by him upon occasion, for fre-
quenting Taverns or Coffè-houses, told him, they would study
& employ their time better, if they had books: This put the
pious Doctor upon this designe, which I could not but approve
of, & indeede a great reproach it is, that so great a Citty as
Lond: should have never a publique Library becoming it.[3]

The library opened in December 1684, a design of another of Tenison's
great friends, Sir Christopher Wren, England's brilliant architect who
resurrected London after the Great Fire gutted the medieval city in 1666.
Wren single-handedly designed fifty-one new churches. His triumph
was the new St Paul's Cathedral. Now he had agreed to put his skills to
Tenison's scheming. Both men were at the new school and library—all
smiles and handshakes—when they were endowed in 1697.[4] Little did
Wren know to what use the quiet bookshelves would soon be turned.

Forty boys attended Archbishop Tenison's School. Foundation pupils
were taught for free; the less advantaged paid twelve shillings and sixpence every quarter of a year. The library was "a noble structure, extremely
well contrived for the placing of the books and lights, and furnished with
the best modern books in most faculties: the best of its kind in England."[5]
A long, narrow window ran up the entire height of the first-floor room,
throwing much-needed light over the stacked shelves.[6]

London's impressive first public library, sixty-eight feet long and
straddling a colonnade, meant well, and was well stocked with four
thousand choice books. In truth, the collection of fine medieval and later
manuscripts and the works of Geoffrey Chaucer were too rarefied to pull
in the public.[7] Its volumes were little thumbed. Being surrounded by a
workhouse, the building appeared isolated, just as Tenison intended it
to look to the outside world. Thankfully, the public, and even the archbishop's wayward parishioners, never bothered using its services.

For a man of the cloth in such a position of public power, Thomas
Tenison was a contradiction of dark secrets. His great opposition to the

threat of the Catholic Church was not one of them. Tenison fiercely criticized the inhumanity of the French against the Protestants. To Dissenters like Daniel Defoe, he offered the church's hand of peace and a welcome right to worship. He made the writer-spy's world safe—as long as they joined forces to fight the Popish threat. Defoe and Tenison shared the same mind-set.

Like Defoe, Tenison saw threats everywhere. "The Romanists are a mighty body of Men," he believed. "They are favoured in many places by great men . . . they have the Nerves of Worldy Power, that is, banks of Money, and a large Revenue."[8] It was a special responsibility, and a godly one, to keep a close watch over Catholics and what they got up to.

Tenison supported the Dissenters' right to free worship. His church at St Martin-in-the-Fields was a rallying ground for the Protestant national cause and for ruthless foes of the Catholics to meet and grind their teeth. So much so that a Roman priest was caught planning to "take some course with him [Tenison] . . . if they met with him in the night, or could get him out under pretence of visiting some sick person." The archbishop was easily spooked. When he heard word in August 1697 of a plot to seize Dover Castle with fifty men and hang out "a flag next day which would be a sign for the French to land," he led the investigation into the would-be invasion that turned out to be invented scaremongering.[9]

Tenison supported the House of Commons' big ticket Act for the Further Preventing the Growth of Popery, which banished all Roman Catholic priests, and offered a £100 reward for information that convicted illegal worship. More widely, the Catholic community was banned from buying, inheriting, or owning estates. The archbishop encouraged Catholics to convert to the Church of England.[10] The form he drafted to make conversions from the Church of Rome legal stayed in use as late as 1827.[11] Not content with stifling worship at home, Tenison extended his thought police overseas when, in 1701, he became the founder and first president of the Society for the Propagation of the Gospel to promote the modern idea of missionary work. All in all, so the archbishop preached:

Popery is ye mother of a numerous offspring of Evills of an high nature, I have not bin wanting in giving discouragement ever to ye Appearances of it . . . I should be a very negligent watchman, if I should not give you warning of ye perill & exhort you not to listen to ye directions of blind and Crafty Guides who would lead you into ye pit of destruction. You would say perhaps, that ys would have bin seasonable Admonition whilst we had over us two Popish Kings; but that now we have a Protestant Head over a Protestant Body, it may seem a fals alarm; I believe ye Contrary.[12]

Just how severely Tenison was willing to stamp out Popish ways was guarded by a small group of powerbrokers united in doing whatever it took to defend the realm. While King William kept the Catholic threat under a spotlight, the archbishop took his own astonishing private steps to neutralize its faithful. Tenison's agents had infiltrated the General Post Office, where they secretly intercepted letters passing between Catholics at home and abroad for the archbishop to inspect. Thomas Tenison, like Daniel Defoe and Henry Avery, was willing to get his hands dirty for the good of the country.[13]

When the Reverend James Richardson disturbed his master in the library, he was busy reading letters that Henry Avery had "borrowed" from the postal service in Falmouth. Hidden away in the library, Tenison kept the trappings for opening and closing letters without anyone realizing and to write correspondence that hid the true author's handwriting. Once, when the Earl of Shrewsbury dropped into the library unannounced, he disturbed the archbishop working on two intercepted letters and next to them a "store with tools for that business and well skilled in it; but neither he nor I having very fine fingers, he has promised to engage one whose fidelity he can be answerable for, and who is already adroit, but he will assist him in his skill." Shrewsbury added that the Archbishop knows how to set up the engine for imitating hands, but thinks it so dangerous an art that, unless his Majesty commands him, I perceive he is desirous it should be discovered to nobody, but die with him, being confident that he is now the only person alive that is perfectly master of that secret.[14]

Setting up a secret office so "a Correspondence may be Effectually Settled with Every Part of England, and all the World beside, and yet the Very Clarks Employ'd Not kno' what Thay are a doeing" was exactly what Defoe schemed to set up. The plan would set "the foundation of Such an Intelligence as Never was in England."[15]

The Earl of Shrewsbury's letter was addressed to William Bentinck, the Earl of Portland, a friend and supporter of the archbishop. They shared many heartaches. When Queen Mary fell ill with smallpox and died in December 1694, Tenison and Lord Portland together carried the collapsed King William out of the room. In these years, Portland was the heart of the king's intelligence network. His agents gathered information for counterespionage in Paris, Berlin, Amsterdam, Vienna, and Madrid.[16]

The Earl of Portland first set up a royal intelligence network for William in 1687. Letters were partly written in invisible ink, encrypted, and posted, as part of the Prince of Orange's very real need for a constant update of threats in England and any heading his way across the seas.[17] The archbishop of Canterbury, Daniel Defoe, and Henry Avery were co-conspirators in the most surprising unholy trinity. In 1700, when Avery and Defoe were in deepest Cornwall, both men were in the employ of the Earl of Portland.

Snickering Londoners also set the salons and coffeehouses alight with gossip of another reason for the close friendship between the king, Portland, and Defoe. William and Bentinck were especially close. When the king was on his deathbed on March 8, 1702, with his dying breaths he beckoned for the earl. Unable to speak, the stricken William "grasped

his hand, and laid it to his heart, with marks of the most tender affection."
Also in the room that day giving the dying monarch spiritual guidance
was Archbishop Thomas Tenison.[18]

Calling for the Earl of Portland was no surprise. Bentinck, a Dutch
aristocrat, was just one year older than William. He entered his service
aged sixteen and was the Prince of Orange's closest friend, advisor, and
most trusted intimate political ally for three decades. Was there more
to the relationship? Even the king's friend and defender Bishop Gilbert
Burnet admitted that "he had no vice, but of one sort, in which he was
very cautious and secret." Another writer put it less subtly: "If a wily
Dutch boor for the rape on a girl, Was hanged by the law's approbation,
then what does he merit that buggers an Earl."[19]

The men's close ally, Daniel Defoe, was having none of it, and as ever
defended the Earl of Portland to the hilt in *The True-Born Englishman*:

> Ten Years in English Service he appear'd
> And gain'd his Master's and the World's Regard
> But 'tis not England's custom to reward.

Did Defoe protest too much? Some contemporaries saw the propaganda writer with the inside line to the king as a cross-dressing bisexual.[20]
King William III, the Earl of Portland, and Daniel Defoe were definitely
an uncommonly tight group of secret spies. As the Cambridge Five spy
ring—which passed information to the Soviet Union in World War II
and during the Cold War—shows, homosexual spies were not unheard
of.[21] The real truth may never come out.

Henry Avery's letter to "The Reverend Mr. James Richardson att the
Liberary over against Orenge Street, St. Martins in ye. Fields, London"
was not just stunning for showing that the pirate king was alive and
kicking four years after vanishing—it was amazing for revealing the true
nature of those sleepy bookshelves. Even the location had been carefully
chosen. Orange Street was built on the site of the former stables of the

Duke of Monmouth,[22] the great hope of Defoe and his friends to oust King James the Catholic king of England. Defoe had even gone into exile after fighting with Monmouth at the doomed Battle of Sedgemoor in 1685. It was Sedgemoor, and the hanging of his old school friends and fellow soldiers, that persuaded Defoe that any success against a foe needed reliable intelligence.

Orange Street was a place of strong sympathies for the anti-Popish cause. The street's history appealed to King William's spies. When Tenison, Portland, Avery, or Defoe visited the library, no eyes were peeping out of hostile windows.

Orange Street was more than a dead drop—it was a spy factory. In the quiet upper room, to the backdrop of school students practicing Latin verbs in the school below, intercepted letters were peeled open, intelligence assessed, and communications written in manipulated handwriting. One of those spies was the new boy, Henry Avery, the team's brawn and brains, not that anyone would call him that to his face.

Henry Avery, the pirate king, in Charles Johnson's *General History of the Pyrates* of 1724. *Credit: Science History Images, Alamy Stock.*

The port town of Plymouth in Devon where Henry Avery was brought up. By Hendrik Danckerts, 1673. *Credit: Yale Centre for British Art, Creative Commons.*

Mⁱ: Daniel De Foe

Author of the True born Englishman

LEFT: An engraving of the spy and writer Daniel Defoe in 1706 by M. van der Gucht. *Credit: Wellcome Collection, 2425i.* BELOW: Daniel Defoe in the pillory stocks on July 31, 1703, as the crowd throws flowers at him in sympathy. *Credit: Wellcome Collection, 43309i.*

The port of Coruna in northern Spain by Mariano Sánchez, 1792. Henry Avery arrived in Coruna in 1694 as chief mate of the *Dove*, ready to salvage Spanish ships in the Americas. *Credit: Creative Commons.*

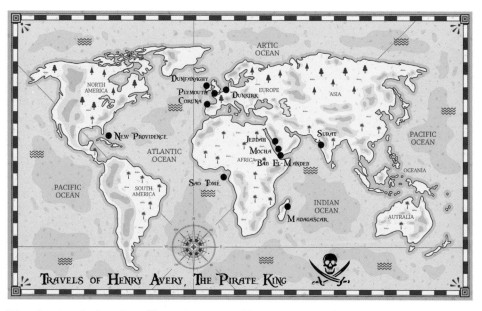

Map showing the key places Henry Avery visited between 1693 and 1700. *Map template designed by pikisuperstar, Freepik.*

ABOVE: Sainte-Marie Island off east Madagascar, a supply base for pirates heading for the Indies. Henry Avery stopped there in the summer of 1695 on the way to the Red Sea. *Credit: Creative Commons.* BELOW: Traditional huts on Sainte-Marie Island in Madagascar give a feel of how pirates lived there in the 1690s. *Credit: Marco Cazzato (marcoduezeta), Alamy Stock Photo.*

RIGHT: The Mughal Emperor Aurangzeb around 1655, the wealthiest man in the world. Henry Avery plundered his treasure ship, the *Gunsway*, in September 1695. *Credit: Metropolitan Museum of Art, 2022.182, Creative Commons.*

BELOW: The harbor of Surat, base of the English East India Company in India. The home port of the *Gunsway* treasure ship looted by Henry Avery in 1695. *Credit: Rijksmusuem, SK-A-4778.*

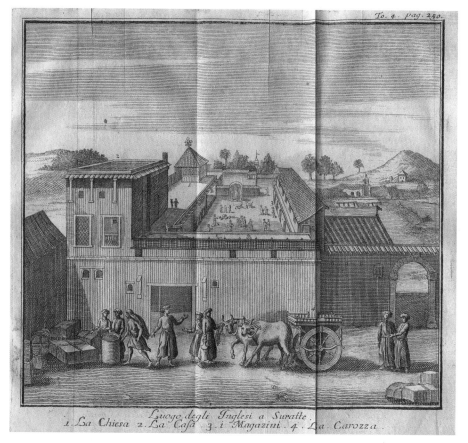

ABOVE: The English East India Company factory compound in Surat, India, was locked down for 11 months after Avery seized the *Gunsway* in September 1695. Engraving by Thomas Salmon, 1751. *Credit: Columbia University, Creative Commons.* BELOW: The Red Sea port of Mocha in Yemen. Pirates attacked Mughal and European ships visiting the harbor to trade and transport pilgrims on the hajj to Jeddah. Engraving by Jacques Peeters, 1690. *Credit: Creative Commons.*

The closest surviving likeness of Henry Avery the pirate king. Avery and his crew on the *Fancy* (right) attack the *Gunsway* treasure ship (left). Late 1690s engraving by W. Pritchard after William Fett. *Credit: Lebrecht Music & Arts, Alamy Stock.*

LEFT: The lost treasure chest of the pirate Thomas Tew shows how riches were shipped and stored. Tew died in the raid on the Mughal fleet led by Henry Avery in the fall of 1695. *Credit: St. Augustine Pirate & Treasure Museum.* CENTER: A gold coin minted in Surat, India, in the reign of Aurangzeb, emperor of the Mughal Empire. Some of the plunder seized by Henry Avery would have been coins like this. *Courtesy of Baldwin's, London.*

RIGHT: Henry Avery finds the grand-daughter of the Mughal Emperor Aurangzeb sailing home to India on the *Gunsway* after going on the hajj to Mecca. *From The Works of Daniel Defoe by John Dunsmore.*

ABOVE: In April 1696 Henry Avery changed his name to Henry Bridgeman and began his getaway in New Providence in the Bahamas, pretending the *Fancy* was a slave trader. *Photo by Sean Kingsley.* BELOW: The entrance to the harbor of Nassau, New Providence, in the Bahamas, passing Hog Island. *Photo by Sean Kingsley.*

ABOVE: Reconstruction of the pirate shanty town of New Providence in the Bahamas in the Pirates of Nassau exhibit. *Photo by Sean Kingsley.* BELOW: Tilbury in the Essex marshes seen from the River Thames, where Daniel Defoe ran his tile factory. Painting by Clarkson Stanfield, 1853. *Credit: Creative Commons.*

LEFT: Before turning spy, Daniel Defoe hid from creditors in Tilbury in the Essex marshes while running his successful tile factory. *Credit: Stephen Craven, Creative Commons.*

CENTER: Henry Avery landed home from his adventures in June 1696 in Dunfanaghy in remote northern Ireland before vanishing off the map. *Credit: Creative Commons.* RIGHT: Five of Henry Avery's pirate crew were caught and hanged at Execution Dock in Wapping, London, in November 1696. From *The Pirates Own Book . . .* (Salem, Mass., 1924). *Credit: North Wind Picture Archives, Alamy Stock Photo.*

✝ Villany Rewarded;

OR, THE

PIRATES Laſt Farewel

To the VVorld:

Who was Executed at Execution-Dock, on *Weaneſday* the 25th. of *November*, 1696.
Being of *Every's* Crew. Together with their free Confeſſion of their moſt Horrid Crimes,
To the Tune of, *Ruſſels Farewel.*

VVEll may the World againſt us cry,
  for theſe our Deeds moſt baſe,
For which, alas! we now muſt dye,
  Death looks us in the face ;
Which is no more than what's our due,
  ſince we ſo wicked were,
As here ſhall be declar'd to you,
  let Pyrates then take care.

We with our Comrades, not yet ta'en,
  together did agree,
And ſtole a Ship out from the Groyne,
  to Roam upon the Sea :
With which we Robb'd, and Plunder'd too,
  no Ship that we did ſpare,

This many a one we did undo,
  let Pyrates then take care.

Our Ship being well ſtored then
  for this our Enterpriſe,
One Hundred and Eighty Men
  there was in her likewiſe :
We Pillag'd all we could come nigh,
  no Nation we did ſpare,
For which a ſhameful death we dye,
  let Pirates then take care.

We Robb'd a Ship upon the Seas,
  the Gunſway call'd by name,
Which we met near the Eaſt-Indias,
  and Riſled the ſame ;

The ballad *Villany Rewarded; or the Pirates Last Farewel* commemorated the hanging of five of Henry Avery's crew in London in November 1696. *By permission of the Pepys Library, Magdalene College, Cambridge.*

at that time, if in a strange place — & hope your Lady
is in a way of recovery — May present my humb. Service
and accept if same your self from

Sir

   I have been very much out
of order since my coming a shore
I have not yet recover'd that fetague
at sea, I hope itt will make amends
for all.

Your most humb Servant

Whilest 2

Addressed
to

The Reverend Mr. James Richardson
the Liberary over against Orenge street
St. Martins in ye. feilds
London. —

Note annexed to the Letter.

1 Chest. Seabarwood Two foot long and one Square, in itt pretious
stons in Gerdles & Brasletts, and large Rubyes, Saphirs, Emerolds,
Topaces & Diaments, & Jewells all sett with pretiouse stones
of severall sorts and couleres, theire vallue unknowne. —

2.°   The Second Chest almost the same size and make as ye
first

The second page of the "Avery the Pirate" letter, addressed to a Library in Orange Street, London.
Used with permission of the National Records of Scotland, GD152/160.

first stufft of some peeces of the right Indean Brochadors.
120 Ingotts of Gould
40 thick flatt peeces of Gould as lang as a round Tobacco Box w.th variouse Carreters on some of them
25 Barrs of Gould some 4 & 5 Inches long. —
3.o — The 3 has 3000 peeces of 8 besids Bullian not wayed itt being cramed in with the Peeces of Brochadores. —

The third page of the "Avery the Pirate" letter, listing the pirate king's treasure. *Used with permission of the National Records of Scotland, GD152/160.*

CENTER: Falmouth harbor in 1678 by Hendrick Danckerts, the town that handled England's overseas post. The pirate Henry Avery was in town in December 1700. *Credit: Royal Museums Greenwich, BHC4166, Creative Commons.* RIGHT: Thomas Tenison, the Archbishop of Canterbury, by Simon Du Bois in 1694. Tenison owned the library and school in London where Avery the pirate sent his letter in 1700. *Credit: Lambeth Palace, Creative Commons.*

Archbishop Tenison's library and grammar school in London where Henry Avery sent his letter in 1700. By Thomas Hosmer Shepherd, 1850. © *The Trustees of the British Museum.*

Henry Avery selling his plundered jewels. From Howard Pyle's "Buccaneers and Marooners of the Spanish Main" in *Harper's Magazine*, 1887. *Credit: Creative Commons.*

Even today, Henry Avery's lost pirate treasure is still said to be buried somewhere off the Lizard in Cornwall. *Credit: Shutterstock.*

State of the Union

T he villain in the smart jacket screwed up his eyes and waited for the inevitable—rotten turnips and tomatoes to pelt his face if he was lucky; rocks and rubbish if the mob was in a sour mood. Assaulting miscreants locked in the pillory—wooden stocks—was traditional fair game for London's baying mob, all part and parcel of the public humiliation. Mockery, shouting abuse, and physical punishment were commonplace. Yet again, Daniel Defoe, the man of many faces, was in serious hot water.

Just when the king's agent thought he had climbed the mountaintop to reach the summit of ambition, his carefully built house lay in ruins. No surprise, the chaos was all of his making. The year 1701 had been a catastrophe, and 1702 and the start of 1703 were looking even worse. This time it could be curtains.

☠

The election of February 1701 that Defoe and Henry Avery had worked underground to influence in deepest Cornwall the December before ended going the wrong way with a win for the Tory opposition. On the positive side, though, King William's battle to arm England with a large army found a champion in the most unexpected place.

Public opinion rescued the king when the freeholder landowners of Kent signed a petition to the House of Commons that May promising to give William the troops he wanted to fight off France and Spain. No sooner was the petition presented to the government than five of its envoys were thrown in prison by the Tory House of Commons. A livid Defoe reacted by dashing off *Legion's Memorial*, which reminded Parliament of their conduct. "Englishmen are no more to be slaves to Parliaments than to a King," he wrote. Defoe wrote the ink missile concealed "in a hand that stood the wrong way"[1] and presented his pamphlet in person to Speaker of the House of Commons Robert Harley, some say disguised in women's clothes. Harley got the biblical message. The document was named after a passage in the Book of Mark, which warned that "my name is Legion: for we are many." The good men of Kent were set free. Defoe's stock was on the rise, but not for long.

On February 21, 1702, Daniel Defoe's world collapsed when King William III was riding near Hampton Court when his horse, Sorrel, stumbled over a molehill. William fell heavily and broke his collarbone. The weak king died from complications on March 9. Daniel Defoe and Henry Avery had lost their champion and compass. Queen Anne, the new monarch, was quick to throw the Whigs out of the Privy Council. The keys of state now rested in the hands of the enemy Tories. Defoe's powerful allies were swept out of power and with it went his financial security.

All that Defoe feared in his life erupted in dread in 1702. On May 4 England declared war on France. Then, reeling from the death of his savior, Defoe's creditors came knocking in the same month. Daniel still owed £5,000 to various investors. When he pleaded poverty, he was locked up in Fleet Prison, a familiar tight spot for the serial debtor.[2] The mischievous wordsmith then made the worst decision of his life. The start of Queen Anne's reign saw a backlash against "others," including the Dissenters to which Defoe's family belonged and King William had favored. Now the Church of England was trying to end the land's religious tolerance and block Dissenters holding positions of power. With cruel irony, Defoe was about to be reduced to the level of a Catholic outsider.

The writer responded by penning an anonymous hoax written in the pompous style of the High Church. *The Shortest Way with the Dissenters*, imitating the language of fanatical churchmen, appeared in December 1702. "Now let us Crucifie the Thieves [the Dissenters]. Let her Foundations [the Church] be establishd upon the Destruction of her Enemies: The Doors of Mercy being always open to the returning Part of the deluded People: Let the Obstinate be rul'd with the Rod of Iron," Defoe mocked.[3]

Only no one got the joke. The public bought into the words hook, line, and sinker, while the government denounced the pamphlet as seditious libel. Its author was to be hunted down and arrested under the order of Daniel "Dismal" Finch, the Earl of Nottingham and secretary of state. Defoe's printer was arrested and copies of *The Shortest Way* ordered to be burnt by the "common hangman." Advertisements offered a £50 reward for information leading to Defoe's arrest.[4] An advert in the *London Gazette* described the villain:

> He is a middle Sized Spare Man about 40 years old, of a brown Complexion, and dark brown coloured Hair wears a Wig, a hooked Nose, a sharp Chin, grey Eyes, and a large Mould [mole] near his Mouth, was born in London, and for many years was a Hose Factor in Freeeman's-yard in Corn hill, and now is Owner of the Brick and Pantile Works near Tilbury-Fort in Essex.[5]

In his own time-honored fashion, Defoe went into hiding, this time north of the border in Scotland—safe from English law—under one of his many pseudonyms. He could not bear the thought of another day back in prison. He would rather die in battle or in a noble cause. "My Lord a

Body Unfitt to bear the hardships of a Prison, and a Mind Impatient of Confinement," Defoe pleaded to the authorities, "have been the Onely Reasons of withdrawing My Self: And My Lord The Cries of a Numerous Ruin'd Family, The Prospect of a Long Banishment from my Native Country, and the hopes of her Majties Mercy, Moves me to Thro' my Self at her Majties Feet, and To Intreat your Lordship's Intercession."[6] The masterless spy was desperate.

In the end the secret agent was turned in by an informer chasing the bounty in May 1703. Daniel Defoe was arrested in the house of a French weaver in Spitalfields, London.[7] Yet even when harshly interrogated, Defoe showed his metal by refusing to betray his accomplices who helped him publish and print *The Shortest Way*. "Dismal" Daniel had him locked up in the stink hole of Newgate Prison until he squealed. It was a new low point in the author's life.

After being released for the extremely high bail of £1,500 on June 5, Defoe stood trial a month later at the Justice Hall in the Old Bailey, where Henry Avery's crew had been tried seven years earlier, and was convicted of seditious libel and sentenced severely to be locked up in the pillory three times over three days at the Royal Exchange in Cornhill, near the Conduit in Cheapside, and by Temple Bar in Fleet Street, to pay a fine of £135, and to be again imprisoned in Newgate until he could "find good sureties to be of good behaviour for the space of seven years from thence next ensuing."[8] Now Defoe could not even keep his tile factory in Tilbury running. By refusing to appear in front of the law, Defoe became an outlaw, and outlaws were not allowed to own property. His factory and fate lay in ruins. Bad decisions cost the spy losses of £3,000 in 1702 and 1703.

Newgate was a living nightmare of a prison. In Defoe's own words:

> My very Blood chills at the mention of its Name . . . 'tis
> impossible to describe the terrors of my mind, when I was first
> brought in, and when I look'd round upon all the horrors of

that dismal Place. I look'd upon myself as lost, and that I had nothing to think of, but of going out of the World, and that with the utmost Infamy: the hellish Noise, the Roaring, Swearing and Clamour, the Stench and Nastiness, and all the dreadful croud of Afflicting things I saw there; joyn'd to make the Place seem an Emblem of Hell itself, and a kind of Entrance into it.[9]

All the while the catastrophes piled up, Defoe struggled to find a way out, to seek mercy from "discovering parties"—anyone who would save him from a fate he felt dramatically was worse than death. It took Defoe many favors to reach the ear of the queen. The courtier and politician Francis Godolphin, 2nd Earl of Godolphin, eventually intervened by sending Queen Anne a note.[10] The court knew all about Defoe's double life, unique skills, and also his loyalty to whoever paid the right cash and kept his wolf creditors at bay.

The man who the queen asked to deal with Defoe was Speaker of the House of Commons Robert Harley, the most feared man in the lower Parliament. When Harley asked the criminal what he wanted, Defoe replied in typical biblical fashion, "Lord, that I may receive my sight."[11] Behind the flattery, Defoe made bold promises. He would no less set up "a scheme of an Office For Secret Intelligence at home and Abroad" to be "Most Serviceable to the Queen."[12] Harley, the "Principall Agent of this Miracle," paid Defoe's fine and set him free. The survivor swapped one royal champion for another. So began the next chapter in an extraordinary stage of life that took Defoe to new heights as a royal spy.

Defoe had spent four months rotting in Newgate Prison. Now the royal court owned him. From the end of 1703 until Harley's fall from power in 1714, Defoe's life was entwined with this cunning politician wherever it took him. Harley and Defoe could work together. They were the same age and both came from Puritan families. Both loved a good bottle of wine, and Harley's collection of books and manuscripts included Defoe's works. The men got a kick out of secrecy and mystery.

☠

By the time Daniel Defoe was freed from Newgate Prison, he was a broken man. His finances were desperate, his brick-and-tile business ruined, and his debts soaring. At his lowest ebb, the Crown had him eating out of its hand. As the embers of the summer of 1704 burned out, Robert Harley started making use of his new agent, dispatching Defoe to England's West Country to harvest political intelligence as another national election loomed.

By late August 1705, Defoe with "one Friend, and his Friend's Servant, being in the Western Counties of England, on a Journey," was dropping off for his spy network "Things written Darke and Unintelligible."[13] Prominent and influential men were leant on and turned for the greater good, persuaded it was in their interests to keep Defoe and Avery informed of local happenings and how people were reacting to national news, and to hand out the spies' propaganda. The men would "Caress The Fools." When it came to people of influence, "Such a Man Can Not be bought too Dear," Defoe told Harley.[14]

The spy ring had to keep their wits about them, especially when they rode into Barnstable in Devon, where the local justice got wind of "Severall Seditious persons Come Down into the Country spreading Libells &ca and Embroiling the people, and advises the Justices to Apprehend them."[15]

Defoe pushed deeper into the West Country, the land where Henry Avery was born and so many sailors of the golden age of piracy started out. The end of the line was the Lizard, where Avery had run the coastal intelligence in and out of England. Perhaps the pirate king was lying low in Bideford in Devon, where his family came from. When Defoe visited the town, he was forced to flash Harley's secret pass to avoid being arrested.[16] Not only was a warrant out for his arrest for sedition, but the creditors from a recent bankruptcy in London had filed fresh lawsuits against him. Defoe rarely enjoyed a week of peace. The walls were starting to cave in again.

Still, the spy bragged to Harley that everything was under control as he traveled in total secrecy like a hero in one of his novels. "I have Visited Every Town So securely by being lodg'd among friends that I am Now under the Nose of the Justices Concern'd in the Enclos'd warrant and yet Out of their Danger," he crowed.[17] Defoe was up to no good for the good of queen and country.

☠

Intelligence gathering was small fry compared to what came next: a task on Her Majesty's Secret Service that would go down as the most important in Daniel Defoe and Henry Avery's careers. In September 1706 the spies were at the far northern end of the British Isles in Scotland. Defoe had the perfect cover: fleeing from the political cutthroats and creditors that everyone knew wanted his neck. Avery acted as his merchant partner. Scotland would be a fresh start.

The mission, dangerous and thick with adventure, was crucial to England's very future. England and Scotland may have been wedged into the same British Isles but the fiercely independent Scots enjoyed their own constitution, laws, and national church. Defoe and Avery were charged with promoting the union between both countries, trying to stop hostile Scotland from breaking away from England and becoming a hotbed of French and Jacobite support.

Harley had issued orders for them to operate in secrecy at all times. "You are to use the utmost caution that it may not be supposed you are employed by any person in England," he told them, "but that you came there upon your own business, & out of love to the Country."[18] Defoe and Avery quickly settled in Edinburgh, a familiar city. The men took on whichever roles the day needed. They were all things to all men. As Defoe told Harley in November 1706:

> I have Compass't my First and Main step happily Enough, in That I am Perfectly Unsuspectd as Corresponding with anybody in England. I Converse with Presbyterian, Episco-pall-Dissenter, papist and Non Juror, and I hope with Equall Circumspection. I flatter my Self you will have no Complaints of my Conduct. I have faithfull Emissaries in Every Company. And I Talk to Everybody in Their Own way. To the Merchants I am about to Settle here in Trade, Building ships &c. With the Lawyers I Want to purchase a House and Land to bring my family & live Upon it (God knows where the Money is to pay for it). To day I am Goeing into Partnership with a Membr of parliamt in a Glass house, tomorrow with Another in a Salt work. With the Glasgow Mutineers I am to be a fish Merchant, with the Aberdeen Men a woolen and with the Perth and western men a Linen Manufacturer, and still at the end of all Discourse the Union is the Essential and I am all to Every one that I may Gain some.[19]

The cover was not all lies. Always eyeing an opportunity to turn a quid, Defoe took the chance to trade in wine, to talk about dabbling in ventures in linen, brass, salt, and wool. Defoe and Avery sold horses to the garrison in Edinburgh Castle and the Earl of Hyndford, commander of the queen's forces in Scotland.[20]

While Defoe could never turn his back on a little wheeling and dealing, his chief concern was a fifteen-month tour of duty intended to use propaganda to persuade the public, Parliament, and Scottish church of the benefits of staying in a union between the two kingdoms, and "the Eyes of the People . . . a little to open.[21] Defoe and Avery were a force of nature. They quickly got the ear of the powerful Church of Scotland, joining their debates and dinner parties in Edinburgh. In the halls of commerce, they befriended merchants, factory owners, and lawyers of the Society for the Reformation of Manners. In a stunning coup, Defoe got access to Scotland's registers and parliamentary minute books by pretending he was writing a history of Scotland. He was able to expose to London the complicated family and financial alliances among the Scots with his own ideas about how to control them. Bribes were siphoned north of the border to buy new partners. Defoe's reports were dispatched to Harley and then onto the courtier Francis Godol-phin and finally Queen Anne herself.[22]

Talking, meeting, and greeting was just half of Defoe and Avery's strategy. These were epoch-changing times when energy was shifting from courting the small fraction of the population allowed to vote to controlling public approval. The rise of the coffeehouses and newspapers created "the Dawn of Politicks among the Common People." On the streets, lower-class men and serving maids gossiped about and debated the weighty matters of the day. No one in Britain was as expert as Daniel Defoe in manipulating public opinion. "Generally Speaking the Common People have been Allwayes in the Right," he understood before most.[23]

To control and misdirect public opinion across Scotland, that "Fer-mented and Implacable Nation,"[24] Defoe and Avery cranked up their charm offensive, supported by a suitcase of hush money. Defoe showed his hand as a lover of culture north of the border, all the while softening opposition to the union, by publishing his *Essays at Removing National Prejudice* and *A Poem in Honour of Scotland and the Scots Nation*. The spies weaseled their way into the friendship of the printer Agnes Campbell Anderson, who enjoyed a near monopoly printing papers in Edin-burgh.[25] Defoe and Avery got to read freshly submitted manuscripts, parts of which were scribbled down and sent south for Harley's eyes.

At other times, Defoe delayed or changed damaging publications. And then the spies started pushing out the opposition in the Scottish press by buying up the *Scots Postman* and taking over the *Edinburgh*

Courant.[26] To control Scottish minds more closely, Daniel set up his own *Review* to push whatever agenda he pleased. Within months of reaching Edinburgh, Defoe and Avery controlled much of the press.

Defoe's strategy—suppressing favorable news and stamping out resistance—was the work of a very modern spin doctor and it worked liked a charm. The spy gloated to Harley:

> In my Management here I am a perfect Emissary. I act the Old part of Cardinall Richlieu. I have my spyes and my Pensioners In Every place, and I Confess tis the Easyest thing in the World to hire people here to betray their friends. I have spies in the Commission, in the parliament, and in the assembly, and Undr pretence of writeing my hystory I have Every Thing told me. I am in Dayly Conferences with the Ministers.[27]

For once, Defoe was not pompously exaggerating or being overdramatic when he described the work's dangers. On October 24, 1706, he was relieved to have the muscled experience of the pirate king when he "found the wholl City in a Most Dreadful Uproar and the high street Full of the Rabble."[28] Another time, from his lodgings Defoe

> heard a Great Noise and looking Out saw a Terrible Multitude Come up the High street with A Drum at the head of Them shouting and swearing and Cryeing Out all Scotland would stand together, No Union, No Union, English Dogs, and the like . . . This Mob fell upon a Gentleman who had Discretion little Enough to say something that Displeased them just Undr my Window.[29]

Several times, Defoe barely escaped the Edinburgh mob. When some agitators discovered the English scum in town, they set a watch out to find where he was staying and broke the wrong windows of the chambers where he was living. Only "by the prudence of his friends, the shortness of its continuance, and God's Providence" did he escape.[30] Avery served as an enforcer and the eyes in the back of Defoe's head, letting him focus on the queen's business.

Just when London started to get confident that Defoe and Avery could swing the vote for Scotland to stick to the union, a Catholic Jacobite attempt to take control of Edinburgh almost derailed their fine work. At the end of 1706, the city was flooded with men with "secret designs," and Defoe watched aghast:

> Unusual concourse of strangers and Highlanders are resorted to town in these few weeks. At the ferries of Leith and Queen's Ferry unusual numbers of men armed and horses have been seen to come over, and some circular letters have been discovered sent privately about. This makes honest people here very uneasy, and I must own I am not without just apprehensions.[31]

It was all too late. Defoe and Avery weathered the storm. The master manipulators had already made the hay. On May 1, 1707, the Act of Union passed into law. Scotland and England were "United into One Kingdom by the Name of Great Britain." Daniel Defoe and Henry Avery had kept their secret hidden and pulled off a spectacular political coup. England could sleep more comfortably without forever looking north of the border or across the waves at Popish Scots helping France invade and supplant the throne with a Catholic king.

Daniel Defoe, in the pillory stocks of London, winced in anticipation of the eggs, rotten fruit, and vegetables about to be hurled at his face. Tradition willed a very public humiliation:

Where elevated o'er the gaping Croud,
Clasp'd in the Board the perjur'd Head is bow'd,
Betimes retreat; here, thick as Hail-stones pour,
Turnips, and half-hatch'd Eggs, (a mingled Show'r)
Among the Rabble rain: Some random Throw
May with the trickling Yolk thy Cheek o'erflow.[32]

On Thursday, July 29, 1703, Defoe had been led from Newgate Prison and locked into the stocks in Cornhill, just around the corner from Freeman's Yard in London, where he once ran his hosiery factory. It was beyond embarrassing.[33] The writer was at an all-time low. The future looked ruined. Little could the once and future spy dream of the success just around the corner, the £300–£400 he would reap from the Secret Service for many years to come.[34] It was time to literally take his punishment on the chin.

The first missile struck. Only it did not smell rotten but wonderfully fresh. Through the corner of one eye, Daniel chanced peering out at the mob. The rough crazies had scattered. In their wake, men and women were throwing flowers at their hero. And then the lines of the poem that he had written in a fit of despair in Newgate, "A Hymn to the Pillory," sang out across the streets:

Thou like a True Born *English* Tool,
Hast from their Composition stole,
And now art like to smart for being a Fool:
And as of *English* men, 'twas always meant,
They'r better to Improve than to Invent;
Upon their Model thou hast made
A Monster makes the world afraid.[35]

Defoe still had a few friends in high and low places. His enemies had been scared off, complaining bitterly "that dirt themselves protected him from Filth."[36]

At the head of the "flower men" was one of the world's great enforcers, still loyally back from the dead—the pirate king, sword in hand, and two pistols sticking out of his belt.

Smoke Screens

The crowd had headed home chuckling long ago through London's evening fog when three men, one by one, crept out of the Theatre Royal on Drury Lane. They stopped to chat on the bottom steps of the entrance. To any nosy observer, the meeting looked like a happy coincidence. Thomas Tenison, Daniel Defoe, and a weather-beaten man with a round face and eagle eyes—Henry Avery—all just happening to go to the theater on the same day, November 7, 1712, to watch Charles Johnson's *The Successful Pyrate*. The play had not quite been a sell-out, but good enough. As fun as anything staged since the King's Playhouse opened its doors in 1663.

In the days of Queen Anne and then King George I, pirates were all the rage. A few critics were outraged by Johnson crossing "a bridge too far" by making romantic heroes of the enemies of all mankind.[1] No matter. The public lapped up their adventures. Who cared what was true and fantasy. As long as the money came in, no harm done. It was all rollicking good fun.

The three men talked in low whispers about the cast and plot. The hero of the play was the pirate and royal outlaw Arviragus, who had built an empire, the city of St. Laurence, on the island of Madagascar. In his seaside haven he lived in a tropical paradise with his captive bride, Zaida, the Mughal emperor's granddaughter—"the Brightest Jewel of his East"—he clapped eyes on when he captured the treasure ships the *Gunsway*. London society knew perfectly well that Arviragus was a play on words for Henry Avery the pirate king.

Johnson's Avery came across on the stage of Drury Lane as a "worthy Mind." Experience had taught the former sea rogue "by Various Fate To Use my Power with Mercy; here no Slaves In Barb'rous Triumph grace the Victor's Wheel . . . if there be a Mirror in the World Worthy to hold Men's Eyes, 'tis our Laurentia."[2] Life, though, was far from trouble-free on this paradise island when Arviragus's second-in-command plotted to steal his king's power and his wife, Zaida. Greed and corruption, the real Henry Avery's eternal enemies, raised their ugly head.

With one day blurring into another, Avery dreamed of returning home to a land that "holds the equal Balance of the Globe." And so Arviragus, "weary of Rule . . . resolv'd to quit Imperial Sway, and die a private Man, As I was born—and well I hop'd in Britain, Such strong Desires mov'd me to taste again The Sweets of native Air." The outlaw would buy a pardon with "Gold (the World's Mistress) to attone my Crimes, And buy off with the Prize the Penalty." Only it never happened because Arviragus' "trembling Guilt dares not approach her [Queen Anne's] Throne."[3] The pirate king with everything and nothing was forced to live out his days in the rotting paradise he created.

Thomas Tenison, Daniel Defoe, and Henry Avery were confident that even though the play was entertainment, not just London but the world really did believe that the pirate king and his crew were spirited away on the far side of the globe on a mysterious African island where the drums beat all day long. They had no clue that Henry Avery was very much alive, walking the streets of the great city of London, and had taken a silent bow that very night in the shadows of the Theatre Royal. Or that the cunning trio of late leavers had masterminded *The Successful*

Pyrate, and smoke screen upon smoke screen, to keep Avery hidden from would-be trackers and daggers still keen on cashing in the bounty on his head. And this play was just the beginning of other entertainments based on Avery's life.

The Adventures of Henry Avery, the Pirate King

1694: *A Copy of Verses Composed by Captain Henry Every, Lately Gone to Sea to Seek His Fortune* (London).

1696: *Villany Rewarded; Or, the Pirates Last Farewel to the World: Who was Executed at Execution Dock, on Wednesday the 25th of November, 1696. Being of Every's Crew. Together with their Free Confession of their Most Horrid Crimes* (London: Charles Barnet).

1708: *Some Memoirs Concerning that Famous Pyrate Capt. Avery* (Memoirs for the Curious).

1709: Adrian van Broeck, *The Life and Adventures of Capt. John Avery, the Famous English Pirate, (Rais'd from a Cabbin-Boy, to a King) Now in Possession of Madagascar* (London).

1712: Charles Johnson, *The Successful Pyrate* (Theatre Royal, Drury Lane).

1719: John Avery, *The King of Pirates: Being an Account of the Famous Enterprises of Captain Avery, the Mock King of Madagascar* (London).

1720: Daniel Defoe, *The Life, Adventures and Piracies of the Famous Captain Singleton* (London).

1724: Captain Charles Johnson, *A General History of the Pyrates* (London: T. Warner).

Even late at night, Covent Garden was heaving with wags, wits, drunkards, and informers. Tenison's polite offer to share a cup of hot chocolate with Defoe and Avery was a good idea. The archbishop's library, just a few minutes away, seemed a dusty way to end such a bright evening. The spies headed south from Drury Lane to St. James's. Men wanting privacy could escape in any one of the five hundred coffeehouses that dotted London. The conspirators were too well-known to prop up a table in Covent Garden, a hive of politicians and newsmongers.

The likes of Button's Coffee House, just opened in 1712, and frequented by the stars of literary London, were too dangerous. A marble lion's head with a gaping mouth, razor-sharp jaws, and whiskers graced the entrance. There the public posted to the owner, the playwright Joseph Addison, letters, limericks, and stories and dreamed of fame and fortune: the best work was published in the *Guardian*, which just so happened to be edited inside the coffeehouse.[4]

Tenison, Defoe, and Avery needed a den of iniquity more like the taverns where the crew of the *Fancy* liked to raise hell. The pirate king suggested the discrete, drunken walls of White's Chocolate House, a temple of Venus where money talked and no one cared about your name or line of business. In White's, highwaymen drank chocolate before riding down Piccadilly for leafy Bagshot in search of innocent prey. Or rakes gambled away entire estates and bet on how long customers had left to live, a dark entertainment that evolved into London's life insurance industry.[5] No one batted an eyelid when the three cloaked men sat down in White's most shadowed corner and one of them ordered a shot of rum to add to his chocolate, a cheer-me-up he had picked up in his Caribbean days.

Tenison and Defoe were two years into concocting a cover for the pirate king. Avery had started the merry dance by leaving authorities bear traps everywhere he went. He had paid some of the crew of the *Fancy* to charade as Long Ben—so Henry Avery was known to his crew—and deliberately spread false trails. As well as John Dann caught in Rochester with £500 of treasure in his pockets, sightings of Avery spouted up in Chester, Dublin, Exeter, and Plymouth. Other collared crewmen were convinced he was living in London, where he had headed into the arms of his wife the wigmaker in Ratcliffe Highway. Another story reckoned he had done the dirty and run off with Mrs. Adams, wife of the *Fancy*'s quartermaster.

Truth be told, no one could even agree what Henry Avery looked like. Was he the very tall man with a fresh complexion, aged about forty-five, whose body was of an "indifferent proportion"?[6] Or the rogue described as fat and of a "gay jolly Complexion"?[7] If no one had a clue what the pirate king looked like, how could they hope to catch him?

Once Avery had been turned, Defoe and Tension started getting creative in public. The romantic idea that the pirate king cast himself away on a remote island first reached the world's ears in 1708, the year before *The Successful Pyrate* opened in London.[8] *Some Memoirs Concerning That Famous Pyrate Capt. Avery* was conveniently anonymous but revealed on authority how he decided to retreat to a place of safety to enjoy his £100,000 plunder of silver. Avery reckoned that with such wealth he would always fear someone doing a Brutus and stabbing him in his back on any mainland.

After hitting the big time, *Some Memoirs Concerning That Famous Pyrate Capt. Avery* saw Avery head to a bay in eastern Madagascar sheltered from the worst storms. There, the *Fancy*'s booty was split fairly "according to the Law of Pyrates" who "observe the severest Laws of Justice."[9] To Avery, Madagascar was at first a perfect retreat. It had it all: a fine natural harbor, nearby islands rich in wood, fish, oxen, sheep, buffalo, wild fowl, deer, spices, fruit, not to mention civil inhabitants. Best of all, the huge island—two and a half times the size of the British Isles—lay a long way from Europe's vengeful knives. The captain would build a colony here, safe from any worries the universe could throw at him.

The pirate king and his crew built a fort defending Henry Avery's colony with great guns. New laws and customs were voted in and Avery chosen as chief of the new state, "with such Power as the Dukes of Venice of the Doge of Genoa." A cargo of ladies was shipped in for the sake of harmony. The men of the *Fancy* had everything their hearts desired. As time went by, more pirates from all nations joined the colony. Passing shipping was sold refreshments, provisions, and naval stores at crazy rates, making Avery even more "prodigiously Rich by the Hazards of others." The author of the pirate king's memoirs had heard that Avery offered great sums of money in exchange for a pardon (though not his forgiveness) but without success. And so he stayed all his days in his "Petty Kingdom, which the Sun gilds with his constant Rays, and where the Water is perfectly good."[10]

Just as no Charles Johnson, playwright of *The Successful Pyrate*, is known to have written scripts in London, Adrian van Broeck, author of *The Life and Adventures of Capt. John Avery*, published next in the capital in 1709, was an invention too. Van Broeck claimed his sixty-four-page pamphlet, which sold for sixpence, drew on a real journal he kept after being captured by Avery. No written record lists a sailor by this name gracing the decks of the *Fancy*. Tenison and Defoe were among the few who knew the truth.

Whichever mischievous mind was behind *The Life and Adventures of Capt. John Avery*, it shamelessly borrowed from *Some Memoirs Concerning That Famous Pyrate Capt. Avery* a year earlier. As in former accounts, the pirate king set down roots in Madagascar after paying his respects to the local ruler. The two power brokers from completely different walks of life then reached a "perpetual Alliance . . . and regal'd themselves after an extraordinary Manner."[11] Fort Avery was armed with forty-eight guns seized from an East India Company ship. A "Republic of Pirates" was born, where Avery had a son with the granddaughter of the Mughal emperor. Life on the island brought out the pirate king's true character, a "good Genius" that was "superior to his evil."[12]

Henry Avery's Madagascar was greater than anything described before. "Towns were built, Communities establish'd, Fortifications built, and Entrenchments flung up, as render'd his Dominions impregnable and inaccessible by Sea and Land," van Broeck wrote.[13] The colony was protected by a fort manned with one hundred cannon, a fifteen-thousand-strong army, and more than forty warships primed with thirty-six to seventy guns. A six- to seven-feet-deep dry moat was dug around the town. Again, Avery's wealth grew and grew after he seized from the East India Company the port of Sainte-Marie Island off the east coast of Madagascar, "with upwards of two Million in Plate, Jewels and other valuable Commodities."[14] The island was blessed with the best and purest water in the world, fruit, nuts, oil, honey, white pepper, and sugarcane. As well as very fine tobacco, the locals liked to chew hemp, which "makes them fall asleep, and afterwards renders them extraordinary chearful, but such as are not accostom'd to it, it makes mad for three or four Days."[15]

As the years went by, Avery's mind wandered to memories of home until he wrote to the governor of Fort St. George in India, offering a deal, whereby:

> Whatever my Demenour has been to other Nations, you may always rest assur'd of my particular Deference to my own. Nothing lies more at Heart on my side that I have given Occasion for her Majesty's Subjects formerly to complain of me, but as I have it in my Power to make Amends, so I am now ready to do it after what manner shall be thought convenient, provided I may be suffer'd to return Home to my own Country in Safety . . . The Necessities of the War, in all Probability, may make a proposal of some Millions of Money, not altogether unacceptable.[16]

Avery added that he disliked "things that are Unjust" and cryptically shared his "Inclination to do my own Country Service."[17] For whatever reason, his letter went unanswered, and he stayed put in Madagascar.[18] The pub owner Ned Ward, author of *The London Spy*, would write elsewhere of Henry Avery:

What 'tho, by your Consent, I share a Throne,
I'm still a Prisoner in a Land unknown?
Fetter'd amidst the Pomps and joys of life,
And but a Slave, although a lawful Wife . . .

Debar'd of Friends, and from the Native Soil
Chain'd for my life, within a barb'rous Isle.
How then can I subsist without remorse,
Since all my Joys are the effects of Force?[19]

Mystifying the world about Henry Avery's whereabouts was a major conspiracy planned to keep everyone guessing wrong. Supposedly frustrated by "former ridiculous and extravagant Accounts,"[20] in 1719 two letters were published from Paternoster Row, next to St Paul's Cathedral in London, under Avery's name. The real author was none other than Daniel Defoe.[21] In *The King of Pirates: Being an Account of the Famous Enterprises of Captain Avery, the Mock King of Madagascar*, Avery set out to correct the "scandalous and unjust Manner in which others have already treated me."[22] The pirates once more used Madagascar as a raiding base, where over eight months:

We built us a little Town, and fortify'd it by the Direction
of one of our Gunners, who was a very good Engineer, in a
very clever and regular Manner, placing a very strong double
Palisado round the Foot of our Works, and a very large Ditch
without our Palisado, and a third Palisado beyond the Ditch,
like a Counterscarp or Cover'd-way; besides this, we rais'd a
large Battery next to the Sea, with a Line of 24 Guns plac'd
before it, and thus we thought ourselves in a Condition to
defend ourselves against any Force that could attempt us in
that Part of the World.[23]

Weighed down with wealth that he could buy little with, eventually Avery resolved to head home. In New England, he turned his cash into gold, bought a cargo of molasses, and dressed up as the master of a ketch. The disguised pirate king took passage on a ship owned by a merchant from Hackney in London. In a nod and wink by the pamphlet's real authors, the owner was called Mr. Johnson.

In *The King of Pirates*, an unsettled Henry Avery returned to Madagascar after three years, not least to retrieve the rest of his loot. The idea of returning to England did not appeal to the pirate king or his crew because Avery "had now made myself too publick to think any more of England, had given over all Views that Way, and began to cast about for farther Adventures." The pirates were ready for fresh shannanigans. Avery himself "abhorr'd lying still, and burying my self alive, as I call'd it, among Savages and Barbarians."[24]

Avery's capture of the Emperor Aurangzeb's ship, carrying his granddaughter, with all her retinue, jewels, and wealth, is shifted in *The King of Pirates* from India to Sumatra in Indonesia. After the crew went on a drunken bender for a fortnight, until six or seven killed themselves, the rogues headed back to Madagascar. When the hangovers lifted, in the cold light of the day, Avery yet again felt the pull of home, of England. The pirates privately believed that Queen Anne's War of 1702–1713 had left Britain in desperate need of money, and the pirate king had stacks of cash. The men would "not grudge to advance five or six Millions of Ducats to the Government, to give them Leave to return in Peace to England, and sit down quietly with the rest."[25]

By now looking like "Hell-hounds and Vagabonds," Avery decided to give his companions the slip, buy European goods, dress in vests and long gowns, and travel by camel with a friend as Armenian merchants through Baghdad and Persia to the Caspian Sea, down to Aleppo in Syria, onto Constantinople, capital of the Ottoman Empire, and finally any part of Christendom. The end of the line was Marseille, "from whence I intend to go and live in some inland Town, where, as they have, perhaps, no Notion of the Sea, so they will not be inquisitive after us." Avery's letters closed with him wondering across the fringes of the Mediterranean world.[26]

The scandal that would erupt if the true fate of Henry Avery ever came to light—the pirate who came in from the cold to serve kings and queens on Their Majesties Secret Service—forced Thomas Tenison and Daniel Defoe to keep the smoke screens swirling for almost fifteen years. For Tenison, the plot was deadly serious. To Defoe, it was also sport. When *A General History of the Pyrates* was printed in 1724, the sea rogues of the golden age were immortalized for all time. The greatest pirate princes—Edward Thatch (aka Blackbeard), Edward England, Charles Vane, John Rackham (aka Calico Jack), Bartholomew Roberts, George Lowther, and Edward "Ned" Low, as well as the women pirates Mary Read and Anne Bonny—became household names and the book a global blockbuster.

Henry Avery was given the honor of becoming the first pirate whose life story was shared in *A General History of the Pyrates*. In the book, life did not turn out so glossy for the people's hero who made such a "great a Noise in the World" and "raised himself to the Dignity of a King, and was likely to be the Founder of a new Monarchy." The truth, the author claimed, was that "while it was said, he was aspiring at a Crown, he wanted a Shilling; and at the same Time it was given out he was in Possession of such prodigious Wealth in *Madagascar*, he was starving in *England*."[27]

So the final story to bamboozle the public declared, the yearning for home eventually got too strong. Henry Avery headed by sea to England with the diamonds he had hidden from his crew. Eighteen of the *Fancy*'s crewmen secured a royal pardon, but Avery went to ground. Through friends, and going by the pseudonym Bridgeman, the pirate king arranged for Bristol merchants to fence his diamonds and gold, only to be stitched up when "they silenced him by threatening to discover him, so that our Merchants were as good Pyrates at Land as he was at Sea." The legend of the pirate king concluded with Henry Avery forced to beg.

His life finished where it began, home in Bideford, Devon, where he fell sick and died, "not being worth as much as would buy him a Coffin."[28] Captain Henry Avery was killed off, once and for all.

Finishing up their chocolate in White's, Defoe and Tenison were confident that no bloodhound hoping to find the pirate king would discover a sensible pattern in the bookshelf of memoirs, ballads, and books published in London since 1694. The fate of Henry Avery, skipper of the *Fancy*, was as clear as mud. Was he spirited away in Madagascar, sipping wine in the hills above Marseille, or dead and buried in an unmarked grave in Devon? Only one thing was certain: all that remained was a legend.

Since the ringleader was invisible in Britain, perhaps the Madagascar theory checked out after all. In February 1697 the Lords of the Admiralty sent two fourth-rates and a sixth-rate warship to the East Indies and Madagascar in search of Henry Avery, to suppress pirates, destroy their settlement, or persuade them to take the mercy of a royal pardon.[29] The commander of HMS *Windsor*, Captain Thomas Warren, reported to the East India Company in late November 1697 that

> There is a small island called Santa Maria at the north-east part of Madagascar, where the pirates have a very commodious harbour to which they resort and clean their ships. Here they have built a regular fortification of forty or fifty guns. They have about 1,500 men, with seventeen sail of vessels, sloops and ships, some of which carry forty guns. They are furnished from New York, New England and the West Indies with stores and other necessaries. I was informed that if they could obtain pardons they would leave that villainous way of living.[30]

Captain Warren had found six or seven pirate ships anchored in Madagascar when he arrived, armed with twenty-four to forty-two guns. Henry Avery and the *Fancy* were not among the rogues laying low on the island. The frustrated British government decided to update the ancient anti-piracy law passed more than 140 years before by King Henry VIII with a new Act for the More Effectuall Suppression of Piracy. Now it would be easier to arrest, try, and sentence villains like Avery.

On his deathbed in 1731, Daniel Defoe would look back at his many failures and successes. Keeping England safe from Catholic France made him most proud. And that had meant serving his monarch as a spy. As much a genius in writing, intelligence, and strategy as Defoe was, he was no one-man band. Henry Avery, the pirate king and lifelong friend, was a crucial part of his ring, the enforcer behind the Crown. And keeping Avery's secret existence hidden for so long was a masterstroke that filled Defoe with pride.

The idea of dreaming of a royal pardon, which never arrived, weaved its way through many accounts of the pirate king's fate. If anyone knew the truth—that King William really did accept a handsome payout to his war effort in return for Henry Avery's lifelong loyalty and liberty—the reputation of the Crown would have never recovered.

As his life ebbed away, Daniel Defoe would grin when he remembered the propaganda he published in his own magazine, the *Review*, yet another thick fog to blow over the smoke screen. In a whirl of passion, Defoe explained in 1707 how the pirates of Madagascar, that republic of sea rogues founded by Henry Avery, could never be defeated. Europe could never take them by force. Rather, he aired the scandalous notion that "if you will capitulate with them, and pardon them, you may have both them and their Wealth."[31] Defoe added his belief that:

> We are told, whether true or false, I do not determine; that some of the richest of these Pyrates, who are English, have made Proposals, that if they may have their Pardon, they will

return to their own Country, live quietly at home, and ceasing
their old roving Trade, become honest Freeholders, as others
of our West-India Pyrates, Merchants I should have said, have
done before them. I hope, the Gentlemen won't be offended,
that by a Slip, I had like to have given some of them their true
Names; I am not about to point them out, nor paint them out;
it would make a sad Chasm on the Exchange of London, if all
the Pyrates should be taken away from among the Merchants
there, whether we be understood to speak of your Litteral or
Allegorical Pyrates.

Defoe also let slip that for three or four million pounds languishing
on Madagascar, "Who would not be a Thief at that Price, that could
live in all Manner of Luxury and Wealth for a Time and then having
gotten Money enough to buy his Pardon, turn honest Fellow again." The
true-born Englishman was an unfettered fan of pirates and ended his
"most scandalous Piece of Meanness, and prostituting general justice to
the Bribe of a Sum of Money" by endorsing swapping ill-gotten gains
for royal pardons:

> Let them offer their Ill-gotten Money, then I am clear, it will
> be well gotten Money to us; I wish the Parliament had it,
> and their Ways and Means would be finely shortened for this
> Session, which otherwise I doubt will be difficult enough.[32]

The smoke screen hiding the true fate of Henry Avery the pirate
king was designed by Daniel Defoe, who personally wrote and managed much of the literary mischief sang about, watched, and read from
London to New York. The terror of the print world was obsessed with
his friend, even writing him a cameo in his novel *Captain Singleton* in
1720 and basing Captain Bob on the pirate king.[33] Here and there,
always thinking he was smarter than anyone else, Defoe risked flying

too close to the sun. He could not help having a laugh at the expense of the sponge-like public. How did anyone really buy into the Johnsons, who supposedly wrote *The Successful Pyrate* in 1712 and *A General History of the Pyrates*? The same name: a son of John. What could be more obviously make-believe?

Everything Defoe and his circle, signed off by Archbishop Thomas Tenison, wrote about Avery was invented, too. All the while the public lapped up the ballads and stories of the pirate king, the ghost was silently walking among them in the streets of London and riding across the roads of England, very much alive and kicking.

Hunting Treasure

The legend of Henry Avery haunted the British government, the Mughal emperor, his royal court, and the British public imagination. Yet even after the manhunt was given up, Avery went about his business in the shadows on His Majesty's Secret Service.

Since his new line of work was only known to a handful of people, most in the government and wider public felt that the next best hope was to track down and return his plundered treasure to Emperor Aurangzeb. The slicing up of the main haul into over a hundred parcels scattered with the crew of the *Fancy* between Africa, the Americas, and Britain did not stop diehard treasure hunters from going after the pirate king's ill-gotten riches. Loot was seized in Ireland, Rochester, Bristol, and London. Other plunder was being laundered fast: in August 1696, three notorious coiners—Charnock, Pritchard, and Jones—were taken into custody for turning Indian and Arabian silver into English currency.[1]

The investigations into the landing of Avery's two sloops in Ireland give a flavor of part of the treasure that made its way to England. There was Indian and Arabian gold bullion; cut-up silver bars; Spanish silver pieces of eight; gold sequins; gold guineas; fine Indian, and perhaps Chinese, cloth, linen, and silk.

In the words of the six men from the *Fancy* sentenced to hang in London in October 1696, crewmen received anything from £300 to £1,000, depending on their position on the ship and role in the heist on the *Gunsway*. Henry Avery took a double cut as commander, but that may not even be half the truth. Did the pirate king really keep word of the jewels the granddaughter of the Mughal emperor gave him in secret for his future pleasure?

A note tacked onto the end of the letter written by Henry Avery from Falmouth in December 1700 seems to lay bare how the captain did not go to the trouble of becoming the world's most wanted man for loose change. Alongside his official cut, Avery secreted away a private bounty. This was his ultimate payback for the despicable way England treated him—stealing his family estate, robbing his inheritance, and cheating him of a salary and adventure in Spanish La Coruna.

The pirate king's sparkling fortune included wooden chests, two by one feet long, crammed with large rubies, sapphires, emeralds, and diamonds. Under the floorboards of his cabin aboard the *Fancy*, Avery stowed and spirited to London 120 gold ingots and 3,000 pieces of eight.[2] The haul was more than enough to wipe his identity and vanish. Henry Avery, his children, and his children's children would never have to work again.

When taken together, all the clues—the coded nature of his letter of 1700, the thread running through most historical accounts, and Daniel Defoe's bizarre apology for piracy in the *Review*—point in one direction: Henry Avery cashed in part of his treasure for a royal pardon.

How much of his stash was then left, who can say? The authorities were undoubtedly convinced either Avery, or some of his crewmen, took out the insurance policy of burying some of their loot away for a rainy day before they split up. And the Mughal emperor's treasure was thought to be hidden in Cornwall—the pirates' plunder returned home to the West Country, the land where many of the *Fancy*'s crewmen were born and their families had lived for generations.

Henry Avery's Loot (Letter, December 27, 1700)

1. Chest Seadarwood Two foot long and one Square, in itt pretious stone in Gerdler & Brassletto, and large Rubyes, Sapphirs, Emeralds, Topaces & Diamonds, & Jewells all sett with pretiouse stones and severall sorts and couloures, theire vallue unknowne.

2. The second Chest almost the same size and make as ye first stufft of some pieces of the right Indean Brockados.

      120 ingotts of Gold

      40 thick flatt peeces of Gould as large as a round Tobacco

          box wth. Variouse Carreters on some of them

      25 Barrs of Gould some 4 & 5 Inches long.

3. The 3d has 3000 peeces of eight besids Bullion not wayed itt being cramed in with the Peeces of Brockadores.

Secretary of State James Vernon took the stories seriously. Since 1693, John Tyzack had been granted a seven-year royal warrant to search and salvage shipwrecks within thirty miles of Sable Island off the coast of Nova Scotia, "the graveyard of the Atlantic." One fifth of any treasure would go to the Crown. With his strong contacts, Tyzack next turned the focus of his treasure hunting to England, "praying his Majesty's grant of one third part of such monyes and goods, as he shall discover to have belonged to the pirates that were executed for Avery's piracy, which are conceal'd from the Crown."[3] The Lord Commissioners of the Treasury gave the treasure hunter the green light as long as he bore the costs of the risky venture.

Tyzack found nothing but sand. Ever hopeful, in 1701 Vernon ordered the justices of Cornwall to continue the hunt. Word of strange goings-on had reached the ears of George St. Loe, commissioner of the Royal Navy in Plymouth, where Henry Avery spent his influential childhood. After St. Loe wrote to the king, Vernon advised that

> the king has been acquainted with your letter of 4th inst., concerning treasure said to be hid by some of the pirates of Every's crew in Cornwall. You are to search for the treasure according to the information that is given you, and the persons who contribute to the discovery shall be rewarded.[4]

Quick to reply, St. Loe promised to "enquire after the persons you mention, and if I can get any light that may be of use to you in the discovery of the treasure supposed to be hid on the coast of Cornwall I will transmit it to you."[5]

The search for Avery's missing millions soon turned to a cave east of the Lizard in Cornwall. There lay "certain chests of treasure, containing jewels, gold ornaments, diamonds, ingots, bars and coins of gold, of untold value." A catalogue of the booty, allegedly written down by Captain Avery himself, was supposed to have been bought by Cornelius Ffurssen, who "in the year 1702, obtained a grant from George, Prince of Denmark, to search for the treasure at any point between Helford haven and the Loe Pool."[6] Prince George was Queen Anne of England's husband and Lord High Admiral who owned the rights to shipwrecked and salvaged goods.

Ffurssen sold his treasure map down the line to hunter after hunter for decades. Several expeditions tried their luck in the Lizard, ending in 1779 with John Knill, former collector of customs in St Ives and later the town's mayor. Then in October 1781 a descendant of the pirate king told a meeting in St Ives that Avery had died a pauper in Barnstaple. No treasure ever existed, the family claimed.[7]

Was this yet another smoke screen? Did both Henry Avery and his treasure fool the world? To this day, local legend is convinced that somewhere out there, under the wind-swept sand dunes of Cornwall, a great Mughal emperor's riches may be hidden just waiting to be dug up.

These days, buried pirate treasure is seen as an unfashionable made-up myth. Pirates spent their plunder fast rather than thinking about long-term investments. At times, though, sea bandits really did bury loot. In 1932 a poor fishermen working long hours to feed his family chanced upon five gold bars on the southern shore of New Providence, the Bahamas, where Henry Avery the pirate king landed in April 1696 and where Blackbeard and the Flying Gang lived in the 1710s. At first, the fisherman refused to tell the British colonial authorities—still there since the 1670s—where the gold was buried. They locked him up until he saw sense. In the end, the finder gave up the fight and was rewarded with one third of what was thought to be pirate treasure. The rest went to the British imperial government.

A strange detail makes the idea of buried pirate loot sound odd: the gold was found under a wild plum tree and rocks incised with Freemasonry symbols.[8] What did pirates have to do with God-fearing, do-gooder Freemasons? The Freemasons believed in the divine right of kings and many were pro-Catholic Jacobites who fled England in 1715. Pirates, too, shared legitimate grievances against the British government.[9] So the idea of pirates, buried treasure, and Freemasons is far from incredible. When it comes to the strange or surprising, pirates often bucked the trend. Henry Avery more than most.

Epilogue

At the time, Henry Avery and Daniel Defoe thought forcing through the union between England and Scotland in May 1707 was the crowning glory of their lives as spies. There would be no quiet retirement on a Crown pension, however. The union did not bring unity. If anything, the Catholic threat got worse.

No sooner was Defoe slipping back to his wheeling and dealing, from horse trading to partnering with a Scottish weaver to make Act of Union commemorative tablecloths, than the Old Pretender—James Francis Edward Stuart, son of King James II—planned an invasion in 1708. Defoe warned his handlers about the looming French attack that "endangered not the Union only, but bid fair for overturning the whole frame of the present establishment in church and state, tearing up the very foundation of our constitution, I mean the Revolution, and restoring, not only tyranny and arbitrary government, but even popery it self."[1]

The raiders reached the coast of Scotland in March 1708. Thanks to Defoe and Avery's intelligence, they hit a brick wall at the mouth of the Firth of Forth: the English fleet primed to fire. James's homecoming party was spoiled. Scotland remained a powder keg for years to come. The spies were still shuttling between Edinburgh and London in 1713, shutting down the enemy's propaganda machine like the *Flying Post*, which promised its Scottish readers that "the papists Are Arming and Prepareing for a Generall Massacre."[2]

In spite of the fallout from the Act of Union, Daniel Defoe felt like the national hero he always dreamed of being. Only his past never allowed him a peaceful bow. In April 1713 he was back in prison. This time his political enemies were out to silence him.[3] Henry Avery, in his new guise, was free to ride and sail and became the less silent partner while Defoe's movements were shackled. Avery infiltrated Catholic groups sympathetic to the Scottish cause and scheming about the next invasion.

Robert Harley was next to go. When the political winds of change blew hard through England's political corridors in 1714, the spy handler was elbowed out into exile and a retired life as a country gent.[4] Defoe and Avery were left treading water and found themselves working for the next succession of rulers. Defoe, attacked as a "Fellow who has prostituted his Pen in the vilest manner to all Partys, and to all Persons,"[5] would do whatever it took to survive, as the Dissenter always had.

Avery may well have been sent overseas to northern France to replicate his intelligence setup in Falmouth, where he perhaps operated as a double agent. A Mr. Ivery cropped up in Dunkirk in January 1717 delivering a reverend father's letter and box to James Maghee, a Jacobite spy. The letter promised that a source will "instruct you of abundance of affairs . . . he will open your eyes very much. You must never let his name be known to any body."[6]

In June the following year, a spy sent a letter to John Churchill, 1st Duke of Marlborough, an expert in "keeping secret correspondence, and getting intelligence of the enemies motions and designs,"[7] which explained how "Mr. Avery has got another letter from his correspondents, who are extremely pressing to know how their project was received by the king [George I of England] and seem willing to prove their sincerity by sending money to him."[8] Churchill and his wife, Sarah, companion to Queen Anne, enjoyed positions of the highest power in Britain's royal circle.

In these years, Avery was living in Calais, hopping back and forth across the Narrow Seas. Another letter addressed to Marlborough explained in July 1718 that Mr. Evrie, as he was also known, "was subsisted [formerly] by the Queen. He is a Church of England man and very well esteemed by the Nonjuring Clergy, and I always heard he had the reputation of an honest man."[9]

By now Henry Avery was playing both sides of the fence. No one other than his royal handlers could be sure where his allegiances lay. The pirate king was using the smoke-screen tactics Daniel Defoe and Archbishop Thomas Tenison had taught him years before. Later, Lord Marlborough was warned mysteriously that "though the king has agents everywhere, you know some men won't trust themselves with any sent to them, but rather trust those they know, so that may very well be Avery's case and after all where can the trick be . . . I am sure you'll see clearly that Avery's behaviour is most upright."[10]

Finally, in November 1718 Marlborough learnt that "severall fellow on t'other side of the water were entertained as faithful friends to the [king's] cause, who were in fact the veriest rascals. He mentioned Mr. Avery particularly . . . a great man entrusted in matters of the greatest moment, without whom nothing is transacted of the highest concern . . . You will be amazed when you hear his name . . . when you come to my friend, he'll communicate such strange things as you'll conclude to be of the greatest consequence."[11] No one would believe the life of adventure, escape, and reinvention that Henry Avery had experienced.

Reading between the lines, was Daniel Defoe the "great man" pulling strings behind the scenes? Or had the bubble burst? Had Henry Avery's true identity been outed? Soon after, Avery vanished once more, fleeing to Italy. This time for good. The pirate king who escaped the hangman's noose was never seen or heard of again.

Henry Avery finally may have been gone for good, but his legacy grew down the decades and centuries. The astonishing heist he pulled off on the high seas changed the pirate landscape forever. Where New

Providence in the Bahamas was a sleepy backwater of misfits when Avery arrived on the deck of the *Fancy* in April 1696 in the guise of Henry Bridgeman, he proved its perfect criminal potential. At the height of the Flying Gang's reign of terror, the island was home to five thousand sea rogues.[12]

The who's who of the greatest pirate princes the world would ever celebrate—Benjamin Hornigold, Edward "Blackbeard" Thatch, Henry Jennings, John "Calico Jack" Rackham, Charles Vane, Mary Read, Anne Bonny, "Black Sam" Bellamy, Stede Bonnet, Olivier "the Buzzard" Levasseur, Paulsgrave Williams, and Edward England—made Nassau their home. They all dreamed of "doing a Henry," pulling off the big shakedown, escaping, and spending their loot with their heads intact. Almost none succeeded.

Most of the great sea bandits met grisly endings. Sam Bellamy sank on the *Whydah* off Cape Cod in 1717.[13] Blackbeard's head was severed in battle with the Royal Navy off Ocracoke Island, North Carolina, in November 1718.[14] Stede Bonnet was hanged in Charleston, South Carolina, a month later;[15] Jack Rackham swung in Port Royal in 1720, Charles Vane at Gallows Point in Port Royal in 1721; and Mary Read died of fever in jail the same year.[16] In 1721 the Americas' toughest pirate hunter, Governor Woodes Rogers of New Providence, was able to write home to London with the message *Expulsis Piratis, Restituta Commercia* (Piracy Expelled, Commerce Restored).[17] The golden age of piracy was over.

The inspiration of Henry Avery the pirate king haunted sailors' dreams. In the summer of 1722, the *Fancy* was terrorizing the seas once more. At the helm was Edward "Ned" Low of Boston by way of London, one of the most evil pirates ever born. Once, off Grenada in the West Indies, he had seized a Portuguese ship. The captain threw one thousand moidore gold coins into the ocean rather than surrender them to a pirate.

Ned Low reacted savagely and "slashed off the poor man's lips with his cutlass and had them broiled before the galley fire and then compelled the Portuguese mate to eat them while hot from the fire."[18] The captain and crew were then murdered. No greater monster ever infested the seas than Ned Low in the second coming of the *Fancy*. Low may have named his vessel in homage of the pirate king's flagship, but he failed to "do a Henry." Eventually, fate caught up with him when the French hanged him in Martinique in 1724.[19]

Henry Avery was no such lowlife. A complicated, misunderstood character, he believed in fair play and decency. The compass of his moral code was shattered when his parents died in his youth and his governor stole his inheritance and got away with the crime scot-free. Something cracked inside Avery's heart. He would take his vengeance on their world. When wealthy men in high places decided to shaft the Protestant British crew of Sir James Houblon's Spanish Expedition in La Coruna, Spain, in 1694, Avery clenched his fists and struck.

History has painted the pirate king into a corner as a merciless chancer with no respect for authority or the law. In truth, not only had King William III commanded the Admiralty to protect the one hundred men serving on the *Charles II*, *James*, and *Dove* in the ill-fated expedition[20]— which they failed to do—but Henry Avery was not alone in refusing to be rolled over. The rest of the crews were seething as well. After Avery fled La Coruna on the *Charles II*, Admiral Arturo O'Bruin "treacherously imprisoned" a captain and two officers, "pretending we were about to run away with the ships."[21] Back in London in July 1694, Sir James started worrying about his investment and asked Secretary of State John Trenchard for help in

> quelling mutinies on the ships *James*, Captain Street, the *Dove*, Captain Humphrey, and the *Seventh Son*, Captain Thomas, who will not obey the commands of General Don Aurturo O'Bruin . . . It is feared they will follow the example

of the *Charles*, the crew of which, in May last, seized upon
the said ship, made one Henry Every their commander, and
sailed out of Corruna in the night, leaving notice in writing
of their intention of pirating on the English as well as on
other nations.[22]

So, Henry Avery was far from a lone wolf agitator. All the British
subjects who signed up to the Spanish treasure-hunting scheme were up
in arms. Only Avery was steadfast that no one would make a fool of him
again and took quick action.

In his laser focus, Henry Avery made an unusual pirate king. For sure
he was a man with a steel spirit who would commit outrage and burn a
town if crossed, but he was untypically principled and controlled for
a captain of the golden age of piracy. Avery was no hell-raising psycho-
path like Charles Vane or a self-obsessed dandy like Calico Jack. He was
mentally tough and would have had no time for the flaky millionaire
Stede Bonnet who, despite being "a Gentleman of good Reputation"
and a "Master of a plentiful Fortune" as a plantation owner in Barbados,
suffered from "a Disorder in his Mind."[23] Avery would have had little
patience for the theatrics of Blackbeard, who pretended he had fourteen
wives and would attack enemies looking like the devil, with smoke
drifting off his face from matches lit under his hat, to scare foes into
submission before they had even been boarded.[24] Greed was not part of
his DNA.

Henry Avery was no monster or spineless rapist. The surprisingly just
moral codes that later pirates signed up to—fair votes, no stealing, no
fighting other crewmen, no interfering with women without their consent[25]—sound like the moral version of Henry Avery committed to paper.

Avery did not stoop so low as to callously sew victims' lips together.
He was not intrinsically evil. Nor was he trying to build a new world of
liberty for the underprivileged or fighting class warfare. His whole being
revolved around one obsessive personal goal: retribution. And anyone

who got in his way would be made to pay. Ultimately, Avery would do whatever it took to claw back the fortune stolen by his governor in Cattedown, Plymouth. If that meant enslaving Africans from Madagascar to camouflage the *Fancy*'s true role as a pirate ship or acting with an iron fist when the fellow pirates who had helped him defeat the *Gunsway* tried to cheat him of cash by clipping gold coins, so be it.

Avery preferred playing fair, trying his damnedest not to attack other English ships. But he was a master strategist for formulating plans and a hyper realist. The rape of the *Gunsway*'s women pained him personally, but he hid his disgust for the sake of the long game. The long game meant staying alive above all else. Almost every other pirate prince of the golden age failed to reign in their obsession with chasing ever more filthy cash, adventure, and mayhem. Even Avery's highly talented great friend Daniel Defoe never knew when to quit: in his endless madcap get-rich-quick schemes he flew too close to the sun and never found solace or unfettered happiness.

As soon as Henry Avery seized Emperor Aurangzeb's treasure ship and hit the jackpot, he started planning a way out. There would be no second coming of the pirate king, unlike his partner Thomas Tew, whose repeat daring saw his bowels blown out in the fall of 1695, days before the *Gunsway* was raided. You can bet that Avery eventually made his way back to Plymouth and took vengeance on the family of his old, long-deceased governor, Bartholomew Knowles. Revenge was a dish best served brutally cold.

Avery had gone to extremes to fight for his beliefs and now he was the most wanted man on the planet. Circumstance and chance brought together one of the first great spy rings when Henry Avery and Daniel Defoe joined forces around the fall of 1696. The idea sounds incredible, something out of the novel *Robinson Crusoe*, but the letter discovered by Zélide Cowan in 1978 changes everything we thought we knew about the pirate king's fate. Until now, all the world knew was that Henry Avery vanished in the summer of 1696, and became a ghost. The reason why the pirate was never heard of again, or tracked down and captured, was because of the royal protection he bought and the service he pledged to the Crown. Henry Avery, turned by Daniel Defoe, became the pirate who came in from the cold to serve a line of monarchs: King William III, Queen Anne, and King George I.

The idea that Daniel Defoe, the man who wrote the world's first novel in *Robinson Crusoe*, and later *Moll Flanders*, *Colonel Jack*, and *Roxana*, was first and foremost a spy also sounds utterly unbelievable. But this was his true calling. Historical letters rarely survive in numbers, if at all. No correspondence describes Defoe's early years: King William III's correspondence has not survived the passage of time. Defoe burned a pile of his writing when he was imprisoned for the terribly judged *Shortest Way with the Dissenters* in 1702. The writer's secret life as a spy for king and country is seen almost exclusively in the chance existence of the letters of Robert Harley, 1st Earl of Oxford, and his runner.

Defoe pushed the limits of counterinsurgency, invented practices still used today, and was respected as a master spy. He was a one-man complete secret service. And none of it would have been possible without Henry Avery, the thinking hardman, risk-taker, and enforcer by his side. Both had their personal reasons to keep Britain free of French rule and Roman Catholicism and were willing to do whatever it took to fight for freedom. The world of espionage was becoming modern. Spies and informers were everywhere, from military camps to coffeehouses. Secret letters were written in code, cypher, and invisible ink drafted in urine. As Defoe realized:

> This is an age of plot and deceit, of contradiction and paradox, and the nation can hardly know her friends from her ene- mies, men swearing to the government, and wishing it over- turned, abjuring the Pretender, yet earnestly endeavouring to bring him in, eating the Queen's bread and cursing the donor, owning the Succession, and wishing the successors at the

Devil, making the marriage, UNION, yet endeavouring the divorce, fawning upon the Toleration, yet railing at the liberty; it is very hard indeed under all these masks to see the true countenance of any man . . . the whole town seems to look one way and now another.[26]

As large as the pirates of the Caribbean and the golden age of piracy loom in our imagination today, their wave of mayhem did not last long. Henry Avery ripped up the high seas in 1695 and by 1721 it was all over. Or was it? Avery, Blackbeard, and the Flying Gang found eternal fame because of the colorful, often exaggerated shenanigans played out in the bestselling *A General History of the Pyrates*. The public lapped up their adventures in 1724 and have ever since.

Even after Woodes Rogers threw the might of England at Blackbeard and New Providence and brought them to heel, pirates still terrorized the seas. Between January 1819 and January 1820, for instance, a schooner from Bermuda was robbed of forty pieces of gold. The American ship the *Louisa* plundered numerous cargoes of various nationalities and divided the spoils in the Cape Verde Islands off West Africa. When one of the pirates shot a man on an American ship, he claimed his crew were "at war with all nations."[27]

In the same year, a German ship from Hamburg was robbed of $50,000 of property off the Florida Keys. When the supercargo in charge of the consignments was threatened with being hanged, he jumped into the sea. The brig the *Rising Sun* was boarded off the Florida Reef by a pirate sloop, which robbed the passengers of clothing, gold watches, and everything of value. Pirates from Philadelphia plundered the *Neptune* of Liverpool of $30,000 in coins off Tortuga.

In the same waters sailed by Henry Avery, Blackbeard, and the Flying Gang, $1,200 was looted from the brig *Mercury* of Boston sailing for Exuma, the Bahamas. The pirate's captain threatened to hang the crew if they refused to give up their hidden money, and hoisted one poor soul up from the deck, with a rope around his neck, to make his point.

And in New Providence, 101 years after Woodes Rogers very publicly hanged nine pirates in front of Fort Nassau on December 12, 1718, including a prize fighter and William Cunningham, a gunner with Blackbeard,[28] Jean Luis Dupois was convicted of piracy and murder on the high seas and hanged on the same shore. Dupois had seized the *Saucy Jack* under British colors that February. It was minding its own business, heading from Mayarí, Cuba, for St. Thomas with a cargo of tobacco. The Spanish pilot, Eugenio Nuaez, was accompanied by his wife, a handsome young woman about seventeen years old. Dupois's crew "committed the most inhuman brutalities" on the woman in sight of her husband,[29] and "After the most brutal and diabolical abuse of this unfortunate creature, they slung the husband overboard, and having shot him, cut the body adrift."[30]

Piracy was in rude health in the Caribbean and Americas a century after Woodes Rogers announced *Expulsis Piratis, Restituta Commercia*: that he had kicked out the pirates and restored commerce and the rule of law. Dupois sounds like an even meaner rogue than Blackbeard and the Flying Gang. Unlike Avery and his crew, Dupois did not sail under the strict code of behavior pirates followed.[31] And no one has ever heard about him. There was no talented wordsmith around to commit his horrors to a nineteenth-century version of Captain Charles Johnson's *A General History of the Pyrates*.

The colorful cast that made it into the blockbuster's pages enjoyed richer afterlives than their misadventures deserved. Except for one man. The sea dog who received the honor of being the first story told in Captain Johnson's book: Henry Avery. The pirate king's double life as a plunderer of treasure and spy on His Majesties Secret Service is as strange and surprising as anything the imagination of Daniel Defoe could invent.

You need great luck or a cunning genius to become a pirate and escape with your life. And researchers need immense fortune to discover a rare treasure of a letter misfiled in a remote archive that lifts the lid on the greatest sea bandit of the golden age of piracy. Over four pages written in code, the afterlife of Henry Avery snaps into focus, a stunning revelation. The man who made a "great a Noise in the World" is silent no more.

Acknowledgments

U nlocking Henry Avery's secret mind, and the writing of *The Pirate King*, would have been impossible without the sharp eye of Zélide Cowan who "discovered" the "Avery the Pirate" letter in 1978. To her the glory. The research about Avery possibly cropping up spying in northern France in 1717 and 1718 comes from Zélide's unpublished research notes.

Great thanks to Dame Liz Forgan for her enthusiastic support of this project from its inception to end and for offering valuable feedback on the manuscript.

Special thanks to Joceyln Grant, Senior Outreach and Learning Manager at the National Records of Scotland, for sharing information about the "Avery the Pirate" letter in the Records' archives and to her and her colleagues for thoughts about Professor John Bruce's involvement in its survival.

For various feedback and ideas about the code used in the "Henry the Avery" letter, sincere appreciation goes to Craig Bauer of York College of Pennsylvania, Nichola Seager of Keele University, and Katherine Ellison of Illinois State University. Shailendra Bhandare, Curator of South Asian and Far Eastern coins and paper money at the Ashmolean Museum in Oxford, generously brought clarity to the question of the value of the loot plundered by the pirate king from the *Gunsway* in 1695 and what it might equate to in the modern day. The late Elias Kupfermann shared sources about the survival of correspondence written and received by Daniel Defoe.

Many long hours have been enjoyed talking all things pirates and Avery with television producer and anthropologist Jason Williams, especially concerning why Avery turned his flagship the *Fancy* into a slaver in the spring of 1696, and where the enslaved people came from and their fate.

Michael P. Pateman, Director of the Bahamas Maritime Museum, shared nuggets of his wide knowledge with us. James Jenney of In Search of Shipwrecks extremely generously shared historical sources about the continuation of piracy in the Caribbean, and on New Providence, in the early nineteenth century.

Great appreciation to Sir Tim Smit for his interest in this project and finding this book a home. And for most kindly sharing photos: to Cindy Stavely, Executive Director, and Matt Frick, Curator, of the St. Augustine Pirate & Treasure Museum, as well as Baldwin's of London.

This book has benefitted greatly from the vision and incredible energy of Jessica Case and Pegasus Books, who are a delight to collaborate with and stand for everything authors might hope for from a publisher. Ally Purcell, Victoria Wenzel, and Maria Fernandez at Pegasus helped craft this book into superb shape; and the hawk-eyed excellence of Jessica Bax, Mary O'Mara, and Melody Englud pounced on gremlins to smooth the pages. Meghan Jusczak continues to coordinate publicity and marketing with endless belief, energy, and passion. Sincere appreciation to the whole Pegasus team for giving *The Pirate King* wings.

Sean Kingsley thanks Madeleine and Andrew Kingsley for their ever-constant enthusiasm and fascination in *The Pirate King* during its writing, and Lexia and Felix Kingsley for living with the pressure and pleasure that the writing involves. All errors are our own.

Further Reading

Allen, Carl, Michael Pateman, James Sinclair, Dan Porter, and Sean Kingsley. *Ocean Marvels of the Bahamas*. Grand Bahama: Allen Exploration, 2023.

Backscheider, Paula R. "Daniel Defoe and Early Modern Intelligence." *Journal of Intelligence and National Security* 11, no. 1 (1996): 1–21.

Bastian, F. *Defoe's Early Life*. London: Macmillan, 1981.

Carpenter, Edward. *Thomas Tenison, Archbishop of Canterbury; His Life and Times*. London: Society for Promoting Christian Knowledge, 1948.

Craton, Michael, and Gail Saunders. *Islanders in the Stream: A History of the Bahamian People*. Vol. 1. Athens: University of Georgia Press, 1999.

Dolin, Eric Jay. *Black Flags, Blue Waters: The Epic History of America's Most Notorious Pirates*. New York: Liveright, 2018.

Fox, E. T. *King of the Pirates. The Swashbuckling Life of Henry Every*. Stroud, UK: History Press, 2008.

Frohock, Richard. "The Early Literary Evolution of the Notorious Pirate Henry Avery." *Humanities* 9, no. 6 (2020), 1–13.

Hanna, Mark G. *Pirate Nests and the Rise of the British Empire, 1570–1740*. Chapel Hill: University of North Carolina Press, 2015.

Kynn, Tyler Joseph. "Pirates and Pilgrims: The Plunder of the *Ganj-i Sawai*, the Hajj, and a Mughal Captain's Perspective." *Journal of the Economic and Social History of the Orient* 64 (2021): 93–122.

Moore, John Robert. "Daniel Defoe: King William's Pamphleteer and Intelligence Agent." *Huntington Library Quarterly* 34, no. 3 (1971): 251–60.

Novak, Maximillian E. *Daniel Defoe: Master of Fictions*. Oxford: Oxford University Press, 2001.

Rediker, Marcus. "Libertalia: The Pirate's Utopia." In *Pirates: Terror on the High Seas—From the Caribbean to the South China Sea*, edited by David Cordingly, 124–39. Atlanta: Turner Publishing Inc., 1996.

Richetti, John. *The Life of Daniel Defoe: A Critical Biography*. Oxford: Blackwell, 2005.

Rogozinski, Jan. *Honor among Thieves: Captain Kidd, Henry Every, and the Pirate Democracy in the Indian Ocean*. Mechanicsburg, PA: Stackpole Books, 2000.

Woodard, Colin. *The Republic of Pirates: Being the True and Surprising Story of the Caribbean Pirates and the Man Who Brought Them Down*. Boston: Houghton Mifflin Harcourt, 2007.

Zacks, Richard. *The Pirate Hunter: The Story of Captain Kidd*. London: Headline Book Publishing, 2002.

Notes

Preface

1   For the 1715 start date of the golden age of piracy, see, for example, Colin
    Woodard, *The Republic of Pirates: Being the True and Surprising Story of the
    Caribbean Pirates and the Man Who Brought Them Down* (Boston: Houghton
    Mifflin Harcourt, 2007), 11: "The Golden Age of Piracy lasted only ten
    years, from 1715 to 1725." For a broader understanding of the start of the
    golden age of piracy in the 1690s, see Eric Jay Dolin, *Black Flags, Blue
    Waters: The Epic History of America's Most Notorious Pirates* (New York:
    Liveright Publishing, 2018), 23; and Mark G. Hanna, *Pirate Nests and the
    Rise of the British Empire, 1570–1740* (Chapel Hill: University of North
    Carolina Press, 2015), 12n20.

2   The pirate king's name was written various ways in seventeenth-century
    documents, most frequently Avery, Every, and, most commonly, Avory in
    1695 and 1696.

3   E. T. Fox, *King of the Pirates. The Swashbuckling Life of Henry Every* (Stroud,
    UK: History Press, 2008), 101.

4   Khafi Khan's contemporary account of the attack of the *Gunsway* in the
    Muntakhab l-lubáb of Kháfí Khán, Selected Records of the Wise and Pure,
    described the *Gunsway* as transporting "fifty-two lakhs of rupees in silver
    and gold"; see H. M. Elliot and John Dowson, *The History of India as Told
    by Its Own Historians: The Muhammadan Period, Vol. VII* (London: Trübner
    & Co., 1877), 350. Shailendra Bhandare, curator of South Asian and Far
    Eastern coins and paper money at the Ashmolean Museum in Oxford,

has clarified that in 1695 a British shilling, composed of 0.925 sterling silver, weighed 6.00 grams. In comparison, the Mughal rupee, composed of 0.990 silver, weighed about 11.33 grams. The rupee's worth can be estimated at around two shillings, perhaps a little more. This equates to about half a million pounds for fifty-two lakhs of rupees. The Bank of England's inflation calculator specifies an equivalent of £1 in 1695 as £167.33 today. Thus, half a million pounds in 1695 would be worth about £87 million today (Shailendra Bhandare, personal communication, June 5, 2023). At current exchange rates, this corresponds to just under $108 million.

5   David Graeber, *Pirate Enlightenment, or the Real Libertalia* (London: Allen Lane, 2023).

6   Woodard, *Republic of Pirates*, 68.

7   Frank Sherry, *Raiders & Rebels: The Golden Age of Piracy* (New York: HarperCollins, 2008), 83.

8   Steven Johnson, *Enemy of All Mankind: A True Story of Piracy, Power and History's First Global Manhunt* (New York: Riverhead Books, 2020), 18.

9   John Howell, *The Life and Adventures of Alexander Selkirk, the Real Robinson Crusoe: A Narrative Founded on Facts* (New York: M. Day & Co., 1841).

10   Douglas R. Burgess Jr., "Piracy in the Public Sphere: The Henry Every Trials and the Battle for Meaning in Seventeenth-Century Print Culture," *Journal of British Studies* 48, no. 4 (2009): 895–96.

11   For payments of £50–£100 to Claude Guilot between 1710 and 1714, see J. A. Downie, "Secret Service Payments to Daniel Defoe, 1710-1714," *Review of English Studies* 30, no. 120 (1979): 437.

12   Charles Johnson, *The Successful Pyrate*, 2nd ed. (London: Bernard Lintott, 1713), 3.

13   Adrian van Broeck, *The Life and Adventures of Capt. John Avery, the Famous English Pirate, (Rais'd from a Cabbin-Boy, to a King) Now in Possession of Madagascar* (London: n.p., 1709), 6.

14   *Some Memoirs Concerning the Famous Pyrate Capt. Avery, with Remarks on St Lawrence, Otherwise Called Madagascar, and the Neighbouring Islands on Which He Now Resides* (Memoirs for the Curious, November 1708), 348.

15   Johnson, *Successful Pyrate*, 4.

16   van Broeck, *Life and Adventures of Capt. John Avery*, 12.

17   Daniel Defoe, *Robinson Crusoe* (New York: Bantam Books, 1991), 140.

Chapter 1: Dusty Treasure

1   National Records of Scotland, Edinburgh, GD152/160: Copy memo-
      randum on "Avery the Pirate" and copy letter (December 27, 1700) by him
      in cipher addressed to "Rev James Richardson at the library over against
      Orenge Street, St Martin's-in-the-Fields, London," with note annexed of
      treasure-filled chests, Papers of the Hamilton-Bruce Family of Grange
      Hill and Falkland, c.1806.
2   W. Foster, "John Brice, Historiographer, 1745–1826," *Scottish Historical
      Review* 9, no. 36 (1912): 366–75.
3   "Bruce, John (?1745–1826), of Grangehill, Fife," in *History of Parliament:
      The House of Commons 1790–1820*, ed. R. G. Thorne (London: Boydell and
      Brewster, 1986).
4   Olivera Jokic, "Commanding Correspondence: Letters and the 'Evidence
      of Experience' in the Letterbook of John Bruce, the East India Company
      Historiographer," *Eighteenth Century* 52, no. 2 (2011): 111.
5   John Bruce, *Annals of the Honorable East-India Company, From Their
      Establishment by the Charter of Queen Elizabeth, 1600, to the Union of the
      London and English East-India Companies, 1707–8, Volume III* (London:
      Black Parry & Kingsbury, 1810), 204.

Chapter 2: Disinherited

1   *Some Memoirs Concerning the Famous Pyrate Capt. Avery, with Remarks on
      St Lawrence, Otherwise Called Madagascar, and the Neighbouring Islands on
      Which He Now Resides* (Memoirs for the Curious, November 1708), 344.
2   Adrian van Broeck, *The Life and Adventures of Capt. John Avery, the Famous
      English Pirate, (Rais'd from a Cabbin-Boy, to a King) Now in Possession of
      Madagascar* (London: n.p., 1709), 3.
3   van Broeck, *Life and Adventures of Capt. John Avery*, 3.
4   R. N. Worth, *History of Plymouth: From the Earliest Period to the Present
      Time* (Plymouth: William Brendon & Son, 1890), 3.
5   Worth, *History of Plymouth*, 10–38.
6   Worth, *History of Plymouth*, 39; Michael Lewis, *The Spanish Armada* (New
      York: Pan, 1960), 63, 79.
7   Worth, *History of Plymouth*, 67.

8   van Broeck, *Life and Adventures of Capt. John Avery*, 3.

9   van Broeck, *Life and Adventures of Capt. John Avery*, 3.

10   van Broeck, *Life and Adventures of Capt. John Avery*, 4.

11   van Broeck, *Life and Adventures of Capt. John Avery*, 3, 4.

12   van Broeck, *Life and Adventures of Capt. John Avery*, 4.

13   van Broeck, *Life and Adventures of Capt. John Avery*, 3.

14   van Broeck, *Life and Adventures of Capt. John Avery*, 5.

15   *Some Memoirs Concerning the Famous Pyrate Capt. Avery*, 347.

16   van Broeck, *Life and Adventures of Capt. John Avery*, 6.

17   John Avery, *The King of Pirates: Being an Account of the Famous Enterprises of Captain Avery, the Mock King of Madagascar* (London: A. Bettesworth, 1719), 1.

18   van Broeck, *Life and Adventures of Capt. John Avery*, 6.

19   Charles Johnson, *A General History of the Pyrates*, 2nd ed. (London: T. Warner, 1724), 46.

20   *Some Memoirs Concerning the Famous Pyrate Capt. Avery*, 348.

21   van Broeck, *Life and Adventures of Capt. John Avery*, 7.

22   van Broeck, *Life and Adventures of Capt. John Avery*, 4.

23   Presumably the Fourth Anglo-Dutch War of 1780–1784, which ended when Henry Avery was twenty-four years old.

24   Charles Johnson, *The Successful Pyrate*, 2nd ed. (London: Bernard Lintott, 1713), 2.

25   Johnson, *Successful Pyrate*, 3.

26   Johnson, *Successful Pyrate*, 4.

Chapter 3: The Outsider

1   Who wrote *A General History of the Pyrates* (1724) remains unproven. Into the 1990s an association with Daniel Defoe seemed set in stone; for example, Joel H. Baer, "'The Complicated Plot of Piracy': Aspects of English Criminal Law and the Image of the Pirate in Defoe," *Eighteenth Century* 23, no. 1 (1982): 6; Manuel Schonhorn, *Daniel Defoe: A General History of the Pyrates* (London: Dover Publications, 1999). More recently, strong evidence has pointed to the London publisher Nathaniel Mist as the work's author; see Arne Bialuschewski, "Daniel Defoe, Nathaniel Mist, and the 'General History of the Pyrates,'" *Papers of the Bibliographical Society of America* 98, no. 1 (2004): 21–38. The Defoe link, however,

remains favored in many circles; see Douglas R. Burgess Jr., "Piracy in the Public Sphere: The Henry Every Trials and the Battle for Meaning in Seventeenth-Century Print Culture," *Journal of British Studies* 48, no. 4 (2009): 887; David Graeber, *Pirate Enlightenment, or the Real Libertalia* (London: Allen Lane, 2023), xxiv. The current authors believe a work of such complexity is most likely to have been researched, compiled, and written by multiple authors, perhaps including both Daniel Defoe and Nathaniel Mist.

2   John Richetti, *The Life of Daniel Defoe: A Critical Biography* (Oxford: Blackwell, 2005), 2.

3   Bonamy Dobrée, "The Writing of Daniel Defoe," *Journal of the Royal Society of Arts* 108, no. 5050 (1960): 729; F. Bastian, *Defoe's Early Life* (London: Macmillan, 1981), 1, 158.

4   Richetti, *Life of Daniel Defoe*, 2, 3.

5   Bastian, *Defoe's Early Life*, 25.

6   Richetti, *Life of Daniel Defoe*, 3.

7   Richetti, *Life of Daniel Defoe*, 2, 4.

8   Bastian, *Defoe's Early Life*, 109.

9   Bastian, *Defoe's Early Life*, 21.

10   Bastian, *Defoe's Early Life*, 9, 10, 20.

11   Bastian, *Defoe's Early Life*, 48.

12   Richetti, *Life of Daniel Defoe*, 5.

13   Bastian, *Defoe's Early Life*, 50.

14   Titus Oates, *A Tragedy Called the Popish Plot Reviv'd Detecting the Secret League between the Late King James and the French King* . . . (London: n.p., 1678).

15   Daniel Defoe, *The Meditations* (London: n.p., 1681), 4.

16   Daniel Defoe, *Memoir of a Cavalier; Or, a Military Journal of the Wars in Germany and the Wars in England. From the Years 1632 to 1648* . . . (London: n.p., 1720), 10–11.

17   Bastian, *Defoe's Early Life*, 63.

Chapter 4: On the Pirate Account

1   Daniel Defoe, *The Life, Adventures and Piracies of the Famous Captain Singleton* (London: n.p., 1720).

2   Adrian van Broeck, *The Life and Adventures of Capt. John Avery, the Famous English Pirate, (Rais'd from a Cabbin-Boy, to a King) Now in Possession of*

Madagascar (London: n.p., 1709), 4; John Biddulph, *The Pirates of Malabar, and An Englishwoman in India Two Hundred Years Ago* (London: Smith, Eldar & Co., 1907), 17; E. T. Fox, *King of the Pirates. The Swashbuckling Life of Henry Every* (Stroud, UK: History Press, 2008), 19.

3   van Broeck, *Life and Adventures of Capt. John Avery*, 4.

4   van Broeck, *Life and Adventures of Capt. John Avery*, 6.

5   The narrative of Captain Redhand is from John Avery, *The King of Pirates: Being an Account of the Famous Enterprises of Captain Avery, the Mock King of Madagascar* (London: A. Bettesworth, 1719).

6   Avery, *King of Pirates*, 6.

7   Avery, *King of Pirates*, 5.

8   Avery, *King of Pirates*, 13, 16, 20, 21. There is no reason to believe that the figures for the Spanish prize seized near Santo Domingo are anything but fictionalized exaggeration.

9   William John Hardy, *Calendar of State Papers: Domestic Series, of the Reign of William and Mary, 1693* (London: HM Stationery Office, 1903), 164.

10   Fabio López Lázaro, "Labour Disputes, Ethnic Quarrels and Early Modern Piracy: A Mixed Hispano-Anglo-Dutch Squadron and the Causes of Captain Every's 1694 Mutiny," *International Journal of Maritime History* 22, no. 2 (2010): 76, 80.

11   Lázaro, "Labour Disputes," 81.

12   Lázaro, "Labour Disputes," 84.

13   Lázaro, "Labour Disputes," 84.

14   Lázaro, "Labour Disputes," 88, 89.

15   Lázaro, "Labour Disputes," 89.

16   Lázaro, "Labour Disputes," 89.

17   Lázaro, "Labour Disputes," 91, 92.

18   Hardy, *Calendar of State Papers: Domestic Series, 1693*, 286.

19   Lázaro, "Labour Disputes," 94, 95.

20   Péter Illik, "The Fall of the Spanish Armada: Historiography, Identity and Reception," *West Bohemian Historical Review* 8 (2018): 2.

21   Lázaro, "Labour Disputes," 77, 82.

22   Lázaro, "Labour Disputes," 78, 101.

23   Lázaro, "Labour Disputes," 96.

24   Lázaro, "Labour Disputes," 99, 103.

25   Avery, *King of Pirates*, 3.

26 Charles Johnson, *A General History of the Pyrates*, 2nd ed. (London: T. Warner, 1724), 47; *The Voluntary Confession & Discovery of William Philips Concerning the Ship Charles*, British Library, London, IOR/H/36.

27 Joel Baer, "'Captain John Avery' and the Anatomy of a Mutiny," *Eighteenth-Century Life* 18 (1994): 13.

28 Johnson, *General History of the Pyrates*, 47.

29 Johnson, *General History of the Pyrates*, 48.

30 Johnson, *General History of the Pyrates*, 48.

31 *The Tryals of Joseph Dawson, Edward Forseith, William May, William Bishop, James Lewis, and John Sparkes: For Several Piracies and Robberies by Them Committed in the Company of EVERY the Grand Pirate, Near the Coasts of the East-Indies; and Several Other Places on the Seas* (London: John Everingham, 1696).

32 *Tryals of Joseph Dawson, Edward Forseith, William May, William Bishop, James Lewis, and John Sparkes*, 10.

33 *A Copy of Verses Composed by Captain Henry Every, Lately Gone to Sea to Seek His Fortune* (London: Theophilus Lewis, 1694).

Chapter 5: True-Bred Merchants

1 John Richetti, *The Life of Daniel Defoe: A Critical Biography* (Oxford: Blackwell, 2005), 6.

2 F. Bastian, *Defoe's Early Life* (London: Macmillan, 1981), 92.

3 Daniel Defoe, *A Review of the State of the English Nation, Vol. III* (London: n.p., 1706), 6–7.

4 Bastian, *Defoe's Early Life*, 89.

5 George Harris Healey, *The Letters of Daniel Defoe* (Oxford, Clarendon Press, 1955), 16: Daniel Defoe to Robert Harley, June 1704.

6 Bastian, *Defoe's Early Life*, 20, 90.

7 Bastian, *Defoe's Early Life*, 91, 149.

8 Bastian, *Defoe's Early Life*, 94, 125.

9 Bastian, *Defoe's Early Life*, 101, 102.

10 Bastian, *Defoe's Early Life*, 160.

11 Bastian, *Defoe's Early Life* 163.

12 Daniel Defoe, *The Life and Strange Surprizing Adventures of Robinson Crusoe, of York, Mariner . . .* (London: n.p., 1719), 27.

13 Daniel Defoe, *A Review of the State of the English Nation, Vol. V* (London: n.p., 1709), 454.

14   Daniel Defoe, *An Essay Upon Projects* (London: Cassell & Company, 1887), 16.

15   James R. Sutherland, "Some Early Troubles of Daniel Defoe," *Review of English Studies* 9, no. 35 (1933): 284–85.

16   Bastian, *Defoe's Early Life*, 168.

17   Bastian, *Defoe's Early Life*, 167.

18   Daniel Defoe, *A Tour Thro' the Whole Island of Great Britain* (London: n.p., 1778), 370.

19   Sutherland, "Some Early Troubles of Daniel Defoe," 284, 285.

20   Bastian, *Defoe's Early Life*, 170.

21   Daniel Defoe, *Caledonia: &c. A Poem in Honour of Scotland, and the Scots Nation* (Edinburgh: Andrew Anderson, 1706).

22   Bastian, *Defoe's Early Life*, 178, 179.

23   Bastian, *Defoe's Early Life*, 182.

24   Bastian, *Defoe's Early Life*, 183.

25   Daniel Defoe, *The Compleat English Tradesman, Vol. II* (London: Charles Rivington, 1727), 58.

26   For Avery's mother, see Adrian van Broeck, *The Life and Adventures of Capt. John Avery, the Famous English Pirate, (Rais'd from a Cabbin-Boy, to a King) Now in Possession of Madagascar* (London: n.p., 1709), 3.

Chapter 6: Red Sea Riches

1   Kevin P. McDonald, *Pirates, Merchants, Settlers, and Slaves. Colonial America and the Indo-Atlantic World* (Berkeley: University of California Press, 2015), 81–98.

2   *A Copy of Verses Composed by Captain Henry Every, Lately Gone to Sea to Seek His Fortune* (London: Theophilus Lewis, 1694), 1694.

3   Clement Downing, *A Compendious History of the Indian Wars: With an Account of the Rise, Progress, Strength, and Forces of Angria the Pirate* (London: T. Cooper, 1737), 63.

4   The itinerary of the *Fancy* between La Coruna, Madagascar, and the Red Sea is drawn from *The Tryals of Joseph Dawson, Edward Forseith, William May, William Bishop, James Lewis, and John Sparkes: For Several Piracies and Robberies by Them Committed in the Company of EVERY the Grand Pirate, Near the Coasts of the East-Indies; and Several Other Places on the Seas* (London: John Everingham, 1696).

5   *Copy of Verses Composed by Captain Henry Every.*

6   *Tryals of Joseph Dawson, Edward Forseith, William May, William Bishop, James Lewis, and John Sparkes*, 20.

7   William John Hardy, *Calendar of State Papers: Domestic Series, of the Reign of William III, July 1–Dec. 31 1695* (London: HM Stationery Office, 1908), 334.

8   Marcus Rediker, "Libertalia: The Pirate's Utopia," in *Pirates: Terror on the High Seas—From the Caribbean to the South China Sea*, ed. David Cordingly (Atlanta: Turner Publishing Inc., 1996), 152.

9   Charles Johnson, *A History of the Pyrates, Vol. II* (London: T. Woodward, 1724), 104.

10   Kevin McDonald, "'A Man of Courage and Activity': Thomas Tew and Pirate Settlements of the Indo-Atlantic Trade World, 1645–1730," University of California, Berkeley, UC World History Workshop, 2005, 11.

11   McDonald, "Man of Courage and Activity," 11.

12   "Examination of Samuel Perkins of Ipswich in New England, August 25, 1698," National Archives, Kew, CO 323/2/388.

13   Arne Bialuschewski, "Pirates, Slavers, and the Indigenous Population in Madagascar, *c.* 1690–1715," *International Journal of African Historical Studies* 38 no. 3 (2005), 406.

14   McDonald, "Man of Courage and Activity," 15.

15   Rediker, "Libertalia," 152.

16   *Madagascar; Or, Robert Drury's Journal, during Fifteen Years' Captivity on that Island* (London: T. W. Meadows, 1729), 298.

17   Johnson, *General History of the Pyrates*, 58.

18   Libertalia first appears as an idea in the account of Captain Mission in Johnson, *A History of the Pyrates, Vol. II*. See also Rediker, "Libertalia," and Sean Kingsley, "Pirate Kings of Libertalia," *Wreckwatch*, 3–4 (2020): 59–65.

19   McDonald, "Man of Courage and Activity," 12.

20   Charles Grey, *Pirates of the Eastern Seas (1618–1723)* (London: Sampson Low, Marston & Co. Ltd., 1933), 54, 55.

21   Deposition of Adam Baldridge, May 5, 1699, in John Franklin Jameson, *Privateering and Piracy in the Colonial Period: Illustrative Documents* (New York: Macmillan, 1923), 180.

22   *Madagascar; Or, Robert Drury's Journal*, 111.

23   Johnson, *General History of the Pyrates*, 61.

24   McDonald, "Man of Courage and Activity," 13.

25   McDonald, "Man of Courage and Activity," 13.

26   McDonald, "Man of Courage and Activity," 13–14.

27   Johnson, *A History of the Pyrates, Vol. II*, 104.

28   Bialuschewski, "Pirates, Slavers, and the Indigenous Population in Madagascar," 408.

29   Frederick H. Hanselmann, *Captain Kidd's Lost Ship: The Wreck of the Quedagh Merchant* (Gainesville: University Press of Florida, 2019), 27.

30   Rediker, "Libertalia," 144.

31   Audrey Truschke, *Aurangzeb: The Life and Legacy of India's Most Controversial King* (Stanford, CA: Stanford University Press, 2017), 110.

32   Hanselmann, *Captain Kidd's Lost Ship*, 27.

33   Atiya Khan, "Indo-Persian Trade during Mughal Rule: Some New Insights," *International Journal of Social Science and Economic Research* 4, no. 7 (2019): 4931.

34   Chloe Wigston Smith, "'Callico Madams': Servants, Consumption, and the Calico Crisis," *Eighteenth-Century Life* 31 no. 2 (2007): 31–32.

35   John F. Richards, *The New Cambridge History of India: The Mughal Empire* (Cambridge: Cambridge University Press, 1995), 198.

36   Richards, *New Cambridge History of India*, 198.

37   Peter T. Leeson, "The Invisible Hook: the Law and Economics of Pirate Tolerance," *New York University Journal of Law & Liberty* 4 (2009): 153.

38   Lord Bellomont to Lords of the Admiralty, Boston, September 7, 1699, in Cecil Headlam, *Calendar of State Papers Colonial, America and West Indies: Volume 17, 1699 and Addenda 1621–1698* (London: His Majesty's Stationary Office, 1908), 769.

39   Michael Naylor Pearson, *Pious Passengers: The Hajj in Earlier Times* (Dhaka: University Press Limited, 1994), 58.

40   Johnson, *General History of the Pyrates*, 51.

41   *The Travels of Sig. Pietro della Valle, a Noble Roman, into East-India and Arabia Deserta in which, the Several Countries . . . are Faithfully Described, in Familiar Letters to his Friend Signior Mario Schipano . . .* (London: J. Macock, 1665), 210.

42   Wolseley Haig, *The Cambridge History of India, Volume IV: The Mughul Period* (Cambridge: Cambridge University Press, 1937), 316.

Chapter 7: Bottomless Plunder

1   *The Narrative of Phillip Middleton, a Youth Belonging to the Ship Charles Alias Fancy, 4 August 1696*, British Library, London, IOR/H/36.

2   *Capt. Henry Avery of the Fancy to all English Commanders, February 28, 1695*, British Library, London, IOR/E/3/50 f 354.

3   *Extract of a Clause in the Generall Letter from Bombay Dated May 28, 1695*, National Archives, Kew, PC 1/46/2.

4   *The Examination of John Dann of Rochester Mariner Taken the 3rd of August 1696*, National Archives, Kew, CO 323/2/250.

5   *The Tryals of Joseph Dawson, Edward Forseith, William May, William Bishop, James Lewis, and John Sparkes: For Several Piracies and Robberies by Them Committed in the Company of EVERY the Grand Pirate, Near the Coasts of the East-Indies; and Several Other Places on the Seas* (London: John Everingham, 1696).

6   *The Voluntary Confession & Discovery of William Philips Concerning the Ship Charles*, British Library, London, IOR/H/36.

7   *Tryals of Joseph Dawson, Edward Forseith, William May, William Bishop, James Lewis, and John Sparkes*.

8   Alexander Hamilton, *A New Account of the East-Indies, Volume I* (Edinburgh: John Mosman, 1739), 22.

9   *Voluntary Confession & Discovery of William Philips*.

10 *Examination of John Dann*; James H. Thomas, "Merchants and Maritime Marauders: The East India Company and the Problem of Piracy in the Eighteenth Century," *Great Circle* 36, no. 1 (2014): 88; Srinivas Reddy, "Disrupting Mughal Imperialism: Piracy and Plunder on the Indian Ocean," *Asian Review of World Histories* 8 (2020): 136.

11 Reddy, "Disrupting Mughal Imperialism," 134.

12 *Narrative of Phillip Middleton*.

13 André Raymond, "A Divided Sea: The Cairo Coffee Trade in the Red Sea Area during the Seventeenth and Eighteenth Centuries," in *Modernity and Culture: From the Mediterranean to the Indian Ocean*, ed. Leila Tarazi Fawaz and C. A. Bayly (New York: Columbia University Press, 2002), 48.

14 C. G. Brouwer, *Al-Mukha: The Transoceanic Trade of a Yemeni Staple Town as Mapped by Merchants of the VOC (1614–1640)* (Amsterdam: D'Fluyte Rarob Press, 2006), 38.

15 C. G Brouwer, "Al-Mukhā as a Coffee Port in the Early Decades of the Seventeenth Century According to Dutch Sources," in *Le commerce du café avant*

l'ère des plantations colonials, ed. Michel Tuchschere (Cairo: Institut Français d'Archéologie Orientale, Cahier des Annals Islamologiques, 2001), 272, 283.

16   *Voluntary Confession & Discovery of William Philips.*

17   Douglas R. Burgess, "Trial and Error: Piracy Trials in England and Its Colonies, 1696–1723," in *The Golden Age of Piracy: The Rise, Fall, and Enduring Popularity of Pirates*, ed. David Head (Athens: University of Georgia Press), 78.

18   *Voluntary Confession & Discovery of William Philips.*

19   John Avery, *The King of Pirates: Being an Account of the Famous Enterprises of Captain Avery, the Mock King of Madagascar* (London: A. Bettesworth, 1719), 56.

20   *Voluntary Confession & Discovery of William Philips.*

21   *Tryals of Joseph Dawson, Edward Forseith, William May, William Bishop, James Lewis, and John Sparkes.*

22   Thomas, "Merchants and Maritime Marauders," 88.

23   Monika Sharma, "Idea of Money for Merchants of Gujarat in Sixteenth–Seventeenth Centuries," *IOSR Journal Of Humanities And Social Science* 19, no. 5 (2014): 16, 18, 19.

24   Hamilton, *New Account of the East-Indies*, 147.

25   *Voluntary Confession & Discovery of William Philips.*

26   *Tryals of Joseph Dawson, Edward Forseith, William May, William Bishop, James Lewis, and John Sparkes.*

27   Windjammer, "The Pirate King," from the album *Awaken* (2022).

28   Charles Johnson, *A General History of the Pyrates*, 2nd ed. (London: T. Warner, 1724).

29   Avery, *King of Pirates*, 56.

30   Joel H. Baer, ed., *British Piracy in the Golden Age: History and Interpretation, 1660–1730*, vol. 2 (London: Pickering & Chatto, 2007), 109.

31   Tyler Joseph Kynn, "Pirates and Pilgrims: The Plunder of the *Ganj-i Sawai*, the Hajj, and a Mughal Captain's Perspective," *Journal of the Economic and Social History of the Orient* 64 (2021): 111.

32   The *Muntakhab l-lubáb of Kháfí Khán*, in H. M. Elliot and John Dowson, *The History of India as Told by Its Own Historians: The Muhammadan Period, Vol. VII* (London: Trübner & Co., 1877), 350.

33   Avery, *King of Pirates*, 56.

34   Elliot and Dowson, *History of India as Told by Its Own Historians*, 350.

35   *Voluntary Confession & Discovery of William Philips.*

36   Avery, *King of Pirates*, 57.

37   Elliot and Dowson, *History of India as Told by Its Own Historians*, 350.

38   Kynn, "Pirates and Pilgrims," 110.

39   Kynn, "Pirates and Pilgrims," 114.

40   Ashin Das Gupta, "Gujarati Merchants and the Red Sea Trade, 1700–1725," in *The Age of Partnership. Europeans in Asia before Dominion*, ed. Blair B. Kling and M. N. Pearson (Honolulu: University of Hawaii Press, 1979), 125, 128.

41   Gupta, "Gujarati Merchants and the Red Sea Trade," 126–28.

42   Kynn, "Pirates and Pilgrims," 109.

43   D. Pant, *The Commercial Policy of the Moguls* (Bombay: D. B. Taraporevala Sons and Co., 1930), 100.

44   Patrick Olivelle, ed., *Dharmasūtras: The Law Codes of Āpastamba, Gautama, Baudhāyana and Vasistha* (Oxford: Oxford University Press, 1999), 2.1.39.

45   Johnson, *General History of the Pyrates*, 57.

46   Charles Johnson, *The Successful Pyrate*, 2nd ed. (London: Bernard Lintott, 1713), 6.

47   Elliot and Dowson, *History of India as Told by Its Own Historians*, 350.

48   *Tryals of Joseph Dawson, Edward Forseith, William May, William Bishop, James Lewis, and John Sparkes.*

49   Adrian van Broeck, *The Life and Adventures of Capt. John Avery, the Famous English Pirate, (Rais'd from a Cabbin-Boy, to a King) Now in Possession of Madagascar* (London: n.p., 1709), 8.

50   Charles Grey, *Pirates of the Eastern Seas (1618–1723)* (London: Sampson Low, Marston & Co. Ltd., 1933), 162; Jan Rogozinski, *Honor among Thieves: Captain Kidd, Henry Every, and the Pirate Democracy in the Indian Ocean* (Mechanicsburg, PA: Stackpole Books, 2000), 87.

51   Thomas, "Merchants and Maritime Marauders," 88.

52   *Tryals of Joseph Dawson, Edward Forseith, William May, William Bishop, James Lewis, and John Sparkes.*

53   Charles Johnson, *A History of the Pyrates, Vol. II* (London: T. Woodward, 1724), 109.

54   *Examination of John Dann.*

55   *Examination of John Dann.*

56   Johnson, *General History of the Pyrates*, 53.

57   *Voluntary Confession & Discovery of William Philips.*

58   *Narrative of Phillip Middleton.*

59   Avery, *King of Pirates*, 62.

60   *Villany Rewarded; Or, the Pirates Last Farewel to the World: Who was Executed at Execution Dock, on Wednesday the 25th of November, 1696. Being of Every's Crew. Together with Their Free Confession of their Most Horrid Crimes* (London: Charles Barnet, 1696).

Chapter 8: Raping the Gunsway

1   Tyler Joseph Kynn, "Pirates and Pilgrims: The Plunder of the *Ganj-i Sawai*, the Hajj, and a Mughal Captain's Perspective," *Journal of the Economic and Social History of the Orient* 64 (2021): 109.

2   John Avery, *The King of Pirates: Being an Account of the Famous Enterprises of Captain Avery, the Mock King of Madagascar* (London: A. Bettesworth, 1719), iii.

3   *A Narrative of Mr Henry Watson Who Was Taken by the Pyrates 15th August 1696*, National Archives, Kew, CO 323/2/90.

4   Avery, *King of Pirates*, 57.

5   Avery, *King of Pirates*, 57.

6   Robert Snead to Sir John Houblon, September 20, 1697, in *Calendar of State Papers Colonial, America and West Indies: Volume 15, 1696–1697*, ed. J. W. Fortescue (London: HM Stationery Office, 1904), 614.

7   Charles Johnson, *The Successful Pyrate*, 2nd ed. (London: Bernard Lintott, 1713), 10.

8   Avery, *King of Pirates*, 8.

9   Adrian van Broeck, *The Life and Adventures of Capt. John Avery, the Famous English Pirate, (Rais'd from a Cabbin-Boy, to a King) Now in Possession of Madagascar* (London: n.p., 1709), 274.

10   Avery, *King of Pirates*, 58.

11   Avery, *King of Pirates*, 59.

12   Avery, *King of Pirates*, 61.

13   Avery, *King of Pirates*, 61.

14   Avery, *King of Pirates*, 59.

15   H. M. Elliot and John Dowson, *The History of India as Told by Its Own Historians: The Muhammadan Period, Vol. VII* (London: Trübner & Co., 1877), 350–51.

16   Avery, *King of Pirates*, 58.

17   William John Hardy, *Calendar of State Papers: Domestic Series, of the Reign of William III, 1 January–31 December 1696* (London: HM Stationery Office, 1913), 332.

18   *The Voluntary Confession & Discovery of William Philips Concerning the Ship Charles*, British Library, London, IOR/H/36.

19   van Broeck, *Life and Adventures of Capt. John Avery*, 8.

20   Charles Johnson, *The Successful Pyrate*, 2nd ed. (London: Bernard Lintott, 1713), 7.

Chapter 9: Strong Men of Nassau

1   John Graves, *A Memorial: Or, A short Account of the Bahama-Islands; Of their Situation, Product, Conveniency of Trading with the Spaniards. . . .* (London: n.p., 1708), 5.

2   John Oldmixon, *The British Empire in America, Containing the History of the Discovery, Settlement, Progress and Present State of all the British Colonies on the Continent and Islands of America* (London: John Nicholson, 1708), 356.

3   Michael Craton and Gail Saunders, *Islanders in the Stream: A History of the Bahamian People*, vol. 1 (Athens: University of Georgia Press, 1999), 82.

4   Carl Allen, Michael Pateman, James Sinclair, Dan Porter, and Sean Kingsley, *Ocean Marvels of the Bahamas* (Grand Bahama: Allen Exploration, 2023), 61–88.

5   Harcourt Malcom, *Bahamas: Historical Memorandum Relating to Forts in New Providence* (Nassau: New Providence, 1913), 2; David Fictum, "'The Strongest Man Carries the Day': Life in New Providence, 1716–1717," *Colonies, Ships, and Pirates* (blog), July 26, 2015, https://csphistorical.com/2015/07/26/the-strongest-man-carries-the-day-life-in-new-providence-1716-1717/.

6   Cecil Headlam, *Calendar of State Papers Colonial, America and West Indies: Volume 23, 1706–1708* (London: HM Stationary Office, 1916): Capt. Chadwell, of the *Flying-Horse* sloop, to Robt. Holden, October 3, 1707.

7   Malcom, *Bahamas*, 1.

8   Anna MacAlpine, "Weather the Storm: Female Pirates, Sexual Diversity and the Reconstruction of Women's History" (Master's thesis, University of Calgary, 2016), 21.

9   Cecil Headlam, ed., *Calendar of State Papers Colonial, America and West Indies: Volume 23, 1706-1708* (London, 1916): October 3, 1707.

10   *Capt. Henry Avery of the Fancy to all English Commanders, February 28, 1695*, British Library, London, IOR/E/3/50 f 354.

11   Craton and Saunders, *Islanders in the Stream*, 100.

12   Cecil Headlam, *Calendar of State Papers Colonial, America and West Indies: Volume 17, 1699 and Addenda 1621–1698* (London: HM Stationery Office, 1908): April 24, 1699, Whitehall, complaint of Dutch ambassador.

13   Cecil Headlam, *Calendar of State Papers Colonial, America and West Indies: Volume 18, 1700* (London: HM Stationery Office, 1910): Edward Randolph to the Council of Trade and Plantations, New Providence, March 25, 1700.

14   Headlam, *Calendar of State Papers Colonial, America and West Indies: Volume 17*: Governor the Earl of Bellomont to the Council of Trade and Plantations, Boston, August 28, 1699.

15   *The Voluntary Confession & Discovery of William Philips Concerning the Ship Charles*, British Library, London, IOR/H/36.

16   For the elephant teeth cargo and Avery name change to Bridgeman, see *The Examination of John Dann of Rochester Mariner Taken the 3rd of August 1696*, National Archives, Kew, CO 323/2/250; *The Narrative of Phillip Middleton, a Youth Belonging to the Ship Charles Alias Fancy, 4 August 1696*, British Library, London, IOR/H/36; Colin Woodard, *The Republic of Pirates: Being the True and Surprising Story of the Caribbean Pirates and the Man Who Brought Them Down* (Boston: Houghton Mifflin Harcourt, 2007), 34, 37. The most accurate figure for the elephant tusk cargo seemingly is from *The Case of Nicholas Trott the Elder Esq: Late Governor of the Bahama Islands Relating to the Ship Charles als Fancey Henry Every als Bridgman Comander, wth: 46 Guns Mounted That Came into the Port of Providence*, British Library, London, Sloane MS 2902.

17   *Voluntary Confession & Discovery of William Philips*.

18   Michael Craton, *A History of the Bahamas* (Waterloo, Ontario: San Salvador Press, 1986), 89.

19   Craton, *History of the Bahamas*, 81.

20   Frederick H. Hanselmann, *Captain Kidd's Lost Ship: The Wreck of the Quedagh Merchant* (Gainesville: University Press of Florida, 2019), 60–94.

21   Richard Zacks, *The Pirate Hunter: The Story of Captain Kidd* (London: Headline Book Publishing: 2002), 8.

Chapter 10: World's End

1   John Richetti, *The Life of Daniel Defoe: A Critical Biography* (Oxford: Blackwell, 2005), 9.

2   F. Bastian, *Defoe's Early Life* (London: Macmillan, 1981), 178.

3   James R. Sutherland, "Some Early Troubles of Daniel Defoe," *Review of English Studies* 9, no. 35 (1933): 284; Bastian, *Defoe's Early Life*, 167.

4   Theodore F. M. Newton, "The Civet-Cats of Newington Green: New Light on Defoe," *Review of English Studies* 13, no. 49 (1937): 10–19.

5   Richetti, *Life of Daniel Defoe*, 16.

6   John P. Kenyon, *The Popish Plot* (Harmondsworth: Penguin, 1974).

7   Peter Earle, *Monmouth's Rebels: The Road to Sedgemoor, 1685* (London: Weidenfeld & Nicolson, 1977).

8   Bastian, *Defoe's Early Life*, 116.

9   Daniel Defoe, *A Review of the State of the British Nation, 1710–1711, Vol. VII* (London: n.p., 1710), 308.

10   Maximillian E. Novak, *Daniel Defoe: Master of Fictions* (Oxford: Oxford University Press, 2001), 114.

11   George Harris Healey, *The Letters of Daniel Defoe* (Oxford, Clarendon Press, 1955), 16: Daniel Defoe to Robert Harley, June 1704.

12   Bastian, *Defoe's Early Life*, 190.

13   Sutherland, "Some Early Troubles of Daniel Defoe," 287.

14   Daniel Defoe, *Giving Alms No Charity, and Employing the Poor: A Grievance to the Nation* (London: n.p. 1704), 27.

15   An association between the World's End tavern and Daniel Defoe is purely speculative.

16   Bastian, *Defoe's Early Life*, 194.

17   *The Tryals of Joseph Dawson, Edward Forseith, William May, William Bishop, James Lewis, and John Sparkes: For Several Piracies and Robberies by Them Committed in the Company of EVERY the Grand Pirate, Near the Coasts of the East-Indies; and Several Other Places on the Seas* (London: John Everingham, 1696).

18   John Avery, *King of Pirates: Being an Account of the Famous Enterprises of Captain Avery, the Mock King of Madagascar* (London: A. Bettesworth, 1719), iv.

19   John Robert Moore, "Daniel Defoe: King William's Pamphleteer and Intelligence Agent," *Huntington Library Quarterly* 34 no. 3 (1971): 254.

Chapter 11: India in Chains

1   Philip J. Stern, "'A Politie of Civill & Military Power': Political Thought
     and the Late Seventeenth-Century Foundations of the East India Com-
     pany-State," *Journal of British Studies* 47, no. 2 (2008): 253.

2   Unless otherwise stated, the following association with Samuel Annesley
     comes from Arnold Wright, *Annesley of Surat and His Times: The True
     Story of the Mythical Wesley Fortune* (London: Andrew Melrose Ltd.,
     1918).

3   Wright, *Annesley of Surat and His Times*, 158.

4   Wright, *Annesley of Surat and His Times*, 166.

5   Wright, *Annesley of Surat and His Times*, 170.

6   Wright, *Annesley of Surat and His Times*, 167.

7   Ruby Maloni, "Piracy in Indian Ocean Waters in the Seventeenth Cen-
     tury," *Proceedings of the Indian History Congress* 52 (1991): 413.

8   H. M. Elliot and John Dowson, *The History of India as Told by Its Own
     Historians: The Muhammadan Period, Vol. VII* (London: Trübner & Co.,
     1877), 354.

9   National Archives, Kew, PC 1/46/2, October 12, 1695.

10   John Biddulph, *The Pirates of Malabar and an Englishwoman in India Two
     Hundred Years Ago* (London: Smith, Elder & Co., 1907), 3.

11   Biddulph, *Pirates of Malabar and an Englishwoman in India*, 3–5.

12   Biddulph, *Pirates of Malabar and an Englishwoman in India*, 5–6.

13   Biddulph, *Pirates of Malabar and an Englishwoman in India*, 8.

14   John Clark Marshman, *The History of India from the Earliest Period to
     the Close of Lord Dalhousie's Administration* (London: Longmans, Green,
     Reeder & Dyer, 1867), 211.

15   Peter Carleton Craft, "Warfare, Trade, and 'Indians' in British Literature,
     1652–1711," Doctoral thesis, University of Illinois at Urbana-Champaign,
     2010, 8.

16   Biddulph, *Pirates of Malabar and an Englishwoman in India*, 11.

17   John Ovington, *A Voyage to Suratt in the Year 1689 Giving a Large Account
     of that City and its Inhabitants and of the English Factory There . . .* (London:
     Jacob Tonson, 1696), 103.

18   Biddulph, *Pirates of Malabar and an Englishwoman in India*, 13.

19   Biddulph, *Pirates of Malabar and an Englishwoman in India*, 15.

20   Aditi Govil, "Mughal Perception of English Piracy—Khafi Khan's Account of the Plunder of 'Ganj-i Sawai': and the Negotiations at Bombay, 1694," *Proceedings of the Indian History Congress* 61, no. 1 (2000–2001): 409.

21   Angus Konstam, *Pirates: The Complete History from 1300 BC to the Present Day* (Lanham, MD: Rowman & Littlefield, 2011), 253–54.

22   J. W. Fortescue, ed., *Calendar of State Papers Colonial, America and West Indies: Volume 15, 1696–1697* (London: HM Stationery Office, 1904): February 19, 1697.

23   National Archives, Kew, CO 323/2/238.

24   Wright, *Annesley of Surat and His Times*, 176.

25   Wright, *Annesley of Surat and His Times*, 177–78.

26   J. W. Fortescue, ed., *Calendar of State Papers Colonial, America and West Indies: Volume 16, 1697–1698* (London: HM Stationery Office, 1905), 473.

27   Philip Ranlet, "A Safe Haven for Witches? Colonial New York's Politics and Relations with New England in the 1690s," *New York History* 90, no. 1–2 (2009): 37–57.

28   Fortescue, *Calendar of State Papers Colonial, America and West Indies, Volume 16*, 472.

29   Fortescue, *Calendar of State Papers Colonial, America and West Indies, Volume 16*, 473: Governor the Earl of Bellomont to Council of Trade and Plantations, New York, May 8, 1698.

30   Fortescue, *Calendar of State Papers Colonial, America and West Indies, Volume 16*, 473: Deposition of Samuel Burgess, May 3, 1698.

31   Fortescue, *Calendar of State Papers Colonial, America and West Indies, Volume 16*, 473.

32   Fortescue, *Calendar of State Papers Colonial, America and West Indies, Volume 16*, 323: Extract of Letters Sent the East India Company from Severall Parts of India . . . Received 14 February 1697.

33   Cornelius Neale Dalton, *The Real Captain Kidd: A Vindication* (New York: Duffield & Co., 1911), 30, 240, 241.

34   Grant Tapsell, "Immortal Seven (Act 1688)," *Oxford Dictionary of National Biography* (Oxford: Oxford University Press, 2007).

35   Henry St. Clair, *The United States Criminal Calendar or an Awful Warning to the Youth of America* (Boston: Charles Gaylord, 1850), 30.

36   Frederick H. Hanselmann, *Captain Kidd's Lost Ship: The Wreck of the Quedagh Merchant* (Gainesville: University Press of Florida, 2019), 76, 77.

37   *Proclamation for Apprehending Pirate Every*, July 17, 1696, British Library, London, IOR/H/36; William John Hardy, *Calendar of State Papers: Domestic Series, of the Reign of William and Mary, 1693* (London: HM Stationery Office, 1903), 277.

38   *The Companyes Declaration for Apprehending Every & His Ship*, July 22, 1696, British Library, London, IOR/H/36.

39   *By the Lords Justices of England: A Proclamation*, August 10, 1696, British Library, London, IOR/H/36.

40   Wright, *Annesley of Surat and His Times*, 213.

41   Govil, "Mughal Perception of English Piracy," 410.

42   East India House, August 20, 1696, British Library, London, IOR/H/36.

43   *Narrative of Pyracies Committed in India*, British Library, London, IOR/H/36, 291.

44   Bombay, December 15, 1696, National Archives, Kew, CO 323/2/722.

45   *Narrative of Pyracies Committed in India*.

46   *Narrative of Pyracies Committed in India*.

47   *Petition from Governors of Company of Merchants of London Trading to the East Indies*, February 26, 1697, British Library, London, IOR/H/36.

48   Wright, *Annesley of Surat and His Times*, 225.

49   Wright, *Annesley of Surat and His Times*, 317.

Chapter 12: Manhunt

1   *The Voluntary Confession & Discovery of William Philips Concerning the Ship Charles*, British Library, London, IOR/H/36.

2   *The Narrative of Phillip Middleton, a Youth Belonging to the Ship Charles Alias Fancy, 4 August 1696*, British Library, London, IOR/H/36.

3   William Phillipp and Edward Savill, Dublin, August 15, 1696, National Archives, Kew, CO 323/2/238.

4   Mark G. Hanna, *Pirate Nests and the Rise of the British Empire, 1570–1740* (Chapel Hill: University of North Carolina Press, 2015), 190.

5   *Memorial of the East India Company about Captain Every*, National Archives, Kew, PC 1/46/2.

6   Providence, April 16, 1696, National Archives, Kew, PC 1/46/2.

7   New Providence, March 30, 1696, National Archives, Kew, PC 1/46/2.

8   National Archives, Kew, PC 1/46/2.

9   National Archives, Kew, PC 1/46/2.

10   *The Case of Nicholas Trott the Elder Esq: Late Governor of the Bahama Islands
     Relating to the Ship Charles als Fancey Henry Every als Bridgman Comander,
     wth: 46 Guns Mounted That Came into the Port of Providence*, British Library,
     London, Sloane MS 2902.

11   *Case of Nicholas Trott the Elder.*

12   *Case of Nicholas Trott the Elder.*

13   *Case of Nicholas Trott the Elder.*

14   Memorial to their Excellencies the Lords Justices, August 6, 1696, by Sir
     Alex Rigby & Wynne Houblon, National Archives, Kew, PC 1/46/2.

15   Extract of Letter from my Lord Justice Porter, Dublin, August 2, 1696,
     National Archives, Kew, PC 1/46/2.

16   Nicholas Trott, Providence, April 16, 1696, National Archives, Kew, PC
     1/46/2.

17   New Providence, To Sir James Houblon & the Rest of the Owners, British
     Library, London, Sloane MS 2902.

18   Cecil Headlam, *Calendar of State Papers Colonial, America and West Indies:
     Volume 17, 1699 and Addenda 1621–1698* (London: HM Stationary Office,
     1908): Earl of Bellomont, August 28, 1699.

19   Headlam, *Calendar of State Papers Colonial, America and West Indies: Volume
     17, 1699*: Earl of Bellomont, August 28, 1699.

20   National Archives, Kew, CSP Colonial, 1696–97: 1001, May 6, 1697;
     1055, June 7, 1697; 1130, July 1, 1697.

21   *Narrative of Captain Robert Sneed, Province of Pennsylvania re Governor
     Markham*, National Archives, Kew, CO 323/2/326.

22   *Narrative of Captain Robert Sneed*, National Archives, Kew, CO
     323/2/326.

23   *Narrative of Captain Robert Sneed*, National Archives, Kew, CO
     323/2/326.

24   Extract of Letters Sent the East India Company from Severall Parts of
     India, Bombay, April 28, 1697, British Library, London, E/3/92: 323.

25   Letters to the Fort & Bombay. Our Lieut. General Presidents Councill
     of Fort St George, May 14, 1697, British Library, London, E/3/92: 588.

26   Extract of the Surratt General to the Company Dated the 6th February
     1697, National Archives, Kew, CO 323/2/232.

27 Extract of Letters Sent from the East India Company from Severall Parts of India in Their Overland Packet Received the 14th February 1697, National Archives, Kew, CO 323/2/246.

28 The Surratt General to the Company, by Another Letter from Bombay Dated 9th February 1697, National Archives, Kew, CO 323/2/232.

Chapter 13: Defending the Crown

1 F. Bastian, *Defoe's Early Life* (London: Macmillan, 1981), 128.

2 Bastian, *Defoe's Early Life*, 139.

3 John Richetti, *The Life of Daniel Defoe: A Critical Biography* (Oxford: Blackwell, 2005), 11.

4 Kevin Clancy, "Presidential Address: The Silver Crisis of the 1690s," *British Numismatic Journal* 88 (2018): 139.

5 Clancy, "Presidential Address," 139.

6 Maximillian E. Novak, *Daniel Defoe: Master of Fictions* (Oxford: Oxford University Press, 2001), 133.

7 Novak, *Daniel Defoe*, 134–35.

8 *Reflections Upon the Late Horrid Conspiracy Contrived by Some of the French Court to Murther His Majesty in Flanders* (London: Richard Baldwin, 1692), 1.

9 *An Appeal to Honour and Justice: Tho' it be of his Worst Enemies. By Daniel De Foe. Being a True Account of his Conduct in Publick Affairs* (London: J. Baker, 1715), 5–6.

10 Bastian, *Defoe's Early Life*, 188.

11 Novak, *Daniel Defoe*, 113, 116.

12 Daniel Defoe, *A Tour Through the Whole Island of Great Britain* (Letchworth: Aldine Press, 1962), 124.

13 Bastian, *Defoe's Early Life*, 184, 186.

14 The attempt on King William III's life described here is based on Thomas Percival, *A True and Exact Account of the Rise, Progress and Contrivance of the Horrid Plot and Conspiracy Against the Life of . . . King William the Third, etc.* (London: Published by Authority, 1697), 13–15, 29, 32, 33, 36, 45–46.

15 Percival, *A True and Exact Account*, 37–38.

16 Matthew Smith, *Memoirs of Secret Service* (London: A. Baldwin, 1699), XII, 117.

17   John Robert Moore, "Daniel Defoe: King William's Pamphleteer and Intelligence Agent," *Huntington Library Quarterly* 34, no. 3 (1971): 252.

18   Moore, "Daniel Defoe," 254.

19   Richetti, *Life of Daniel Defoe*, 12.

20   Novak, *Daniel Defoe*, 125.

21   Bastian, *Defoe's Early Life*, 212–13.

22   William John Hardy, *Calendar of State Papers: Domestic Series, of the Reign of William III, 1 January–31 December 1697* (London: HM Stationery Office, 1927), 438.

23   Bastian, *Defoe's Early Life*, 214.

24   Bastian, *Defoe's Early Life*, 220.

Chapter 14: Vanishing Act

1   Margarette Lincoln, *British Pirates and Society 1680–1730* (New York: Routledge, 2016), 33.

2   Unless otherwise stated, the details of the hearing of Avery's crew are drawn from *The Tryals of Joseph Dawson, Edward Forseith, William May, William Bishop, James Lewis, and John Sparkes: For Several Piracies and Robberies by Them Committed in the Company of EVERY the Grand Pirate, Near the Coasts of the East-Indies; and Several Other Places on the Seas* (London: John Everingham, 1696).

3   Douglas R. Burgess Jr., "Piracy in the Public Sphere: The Henry Every Trials and the Battle for Meaning in Seventeenth-Century Print Culture," *Journal of British Studies* 48 (2009): 898.

4   *Tryals of Joseph Dawson, Edward Forseith, William May, William Bishop, James Lewis, and John Sparkes*, 8.

5   Charles Johnson, *A General History of the Pyrates*, 2nd ed. (London: T. Warner, 1724), 45.

6   John Dann, *Mr Bridgman's Accomplice: Long Ben's Coxwain, 1660–1722* (Peterborough, UK: Fastprint Publishing, 2019), 15.

7   William John Hardy, *Calendar of State Papers: Domestic Series, of the Reign of William III, 1 January–31 December 1696* (London: HM Stationery Office, 1913), 364.

8   Hardy, *Calendar of State Papers: Domestic Series, 1696*, 364.

9   Sir John Dutton Colt to W. Trumbell, July 22, 1696, Bristol, Downshire Mss Cat. P.680–81.

10   *The Narrative of Phillip Middleton, a Youth Belonging to the Ship Charles alias Fancy, 4 August 1696*, National Archives, British Library, London, IOR/H/36.

11   *Narrative of Phillip Middleton.*

12   *The Examination of John Dann of Rochester Mariner Taken the 3rd of August 1696*, National Archives, Kew, CO 323/2/250; Hardy, *Calendar of State Papers: Domestic Series, 1696*, 319–20.

13   *An Abstract of Letters Relating to the Sloop Isaac*, National Archives, Kew, ADM 106/487.

14   *Narrative of Phillip Middleton*, 1696.

15   The account of the landing of Thomas Hollingsworth's sloop, the *Isaac*, in western Ireland comes from the National Archives, Kew, PC 1/46/2 (11. 1696 / 79.893.1–4): *An Abstract of Letters Relating to the Sloop Isaac of Providence whereof Captain Thomas Hollandsworth Commander.*

16   *An Abstract of Letters Relating to the Sloop Isaac*, the National Archives, Kew, PC 1/46/2.

17   *An Abstract of Letters Relating to the Sloop Isaac*, the National Archives, Kew, PC 1/46/2.

18   *An Abstract of Letters Relating to the Sloop Isaac*, the National Archives, Kew, PC 1/46/2.

19   *An Abstract of Letters Relating to the Sloop Isaac*, the National Archives, Kew, PC 1/46/2.

20   *An Abstract of Letters Relating to the Sloop Isaac*, the National Archives, Kew, PC 1/46/2.

21   *An Abstract of Letters Relating to the Sloop Isaac*, the National Archives, Kew, PC 1/46/2.

22   Sir John Dutton Colt to Sir William Trumball, July 22, 1696, Bristol, Downshire Mss Cat. P.680–81.

23   Sir John Dutton Colt to Sir William Trumball, July 22, 1696, Bristol, Downshire Mss Cat. P.680–81.

24   *Tryals of Joseph Dawson, Edward Forseith, William May, William Bishop, James Lewis, and John Sparkes.*

25   Burgess, "Piracy in the Public Sphere," 901. The below hearing of Avery's crew of the *Fancy* continues from *Tryals of Joseph Dawson, Edward Forseith, William May, William Bishop, James Lewis, and John Sparkes.* See Joel

H. Baer, ed., *British Piracy in the Golden Age: History and Interpretation, 1660–1730*, vol. 2 (London: Pickering & Chatto, 2007), 111.

26   *Tryals of Joseph Dawson, Edward Forseith, William May, William Bishop, James Lewis, and John Sparkes*, 4.

27   *Tryals of Joseph Dawson, Edward Forseith, William May, William Bishop, James Lewis, and John Sparkes*, 4.

28   *Tryals of Joseph Dawson, Edward Forseith, William May, William Bishop, James Lewis, and John Sparkes*, 28.

29   John Stow, "The Suburbs Without the Walls," in *A Survey of London. Reprinted From the Text of 1603*, ed. C. L. Kingsford (Oxford, n.p., 1908), 69–91.

30   Samantha Frénée, "Pirates and Gallows at Execution Dock: Nautical Justice in Early Modern England," in *Actes du Colloque: les Fourches Patibulaires du Moyen Âge à l'Époque Moderne. Approche Interdisciplinaire*, *vol. 5*, ed. Martine Charageat and Mathieu Vivas (2015). [Published online: https://journals.openedition.org/criminocorpus/3080.]

31   William John Hardy, *Calendar of State Papers: Domestic Series, of the Reign of William III, 1 January–31 December 1697* (London: HM Stationery Office, 1927), 4, 28.

32   Hardy, *Calendar of State Papers: Domestic Series, 1697*, 23, 44.

33   Edward Bateson, *Calendar of State Papers: Domestic Series, of the Reign of William III, 1 January 1699–31 March 1700* (London: HM Stationery Office, 1937), 198.

34   *Our Lieut. General Presidents Councill of Fort St George London*, December 8, 1696, British Library, London, E/3/92.

35   *The Voluntary Confession & Discovery of William Philips Concerning the Ship Charles*, British Library, London, IOR/H/36; Hardy, *Calendar of State Papers: Domestic Series, 1696*, 300–331.

36   London, August 27, 1696, to Fort St George, British Library, London, E/3/92, 262.

37   London, April 23, 1696, to Our President & Councill at Surratt, British Library, London, E/3/92, 262.

38   P. Coode, W. Glynn & T. Malby to Sir W. Trumball, Downshire Mss Cat., February 17, 1697, London, 139.

39   Hardy, *Calendar of State Papers: Domestic Series, 1696*, 445.

40 Edward Bateson, *Calendar of State Papers: Domestic Series, of the Reign of William III, 1 January–31 December 1698* (London: HM Stationery Office, 1933), 36, 404.

41 Bateson, *Calendar of State Papers: Domestic Series, 1699–1700*, 11.

42 Narcissus Luttrell, *A Brief Historical Relation of State Affairs from September 1668 to April 1714*, vol. 4 (Oxford: Oxford University Press, 1857), 663.

43 Memorandum to the "Avery the Pirate," National Records of Scotland, Edinburgh, GD152/160.

44 A. Rumble and C. Dimmer, eds., *Calendar of State Papers: Domestic Series, of the Reign of Anne, Volume III, May 1704–October 1705* (London: Boydell Press, 2005), 3.

45 Margarette Lincoln, "Henry Every and the Creation of the Pirate Myth in Early Modern Britain," in *The Golden Age of Piracy. The Rise, Fall, and Enduring Popularity of Pirates*, ed. David Head (Athens: University of Georgia Press, 2018), 171.

46 J. W. Fortescue, ed., *Calendar of State Papers Colonial, America and West Indies: Volume 16, 1697–1698* (London: HM Stationery Office, 1905): November 24, 1697.

47 *The Laws of Jamaica Passed by the Assembly, and Confirmed by His Majesty in Council, Feb. 23. 1683* (London: Printed by H. Hills for Charles Harper, 1683).

48 Petition of John Dann, National Archives, Kew, PC 2/77.

49 CSP Treasury (1697-8), December 21, 1696, Out Letters (Gen) XV, 176.

50 Hardy, *Calendar of State Papers: Domestic Series, 1696*, 358.

51 Treasury Minute Book XII, 164: 401.

52 *Charges on the Pyrates Account*, British Library, London, E/3/92.

53 Johan Berglund Björk, "The Discipline of the Seas: Piracy and Polity, 1688" (Master's thesis, University of Gothenburg, 2020), 20n70.

54 Proclamation about Pirates in the East Indies, Kensington, December 8, 1698, National Archives, Kew, PC 2/77.

Chapter 15: His Majesty's Secret Service

1 Susan E. Gay, *Old Falmouth: The Story of the Town from the Days of the Killigrews to the Earliest Part of the 19th Century* (London: Headley Bros., 1903), 33.

2   Lucy Toulmin Smith, *The Itinerary of John Leland in or About the Years 1535–1543* (London: George Bell & Sons, 1910), 321.

3   Daniel Defoe, *A Tour Thro' The Whole Island of Great Britain, Divided into Circuits or Journeys* vol. 1 (London: n.p., 1742), 345.

4   Daniel Lysons and Samuel Lysons, "Parishes: Falmouth—Fowey," in *Magna Britannia: Volume 3, Cornwall* (London: T Cadell and W Davies, 1814), 99–112.

5   Lysons and Lysons, "Parishes: Falmouth," 99–112.

6   Richard Carew, *A Survey of Cornwall and an Epistle Concerning the Excellencies of the English Tongue* (London: n.p., 1603), 151.

7   Gay, *Old Falmouth*, 40.

8   Gay, *Old Falmouth*, 42.

9   Cathryn Jean Pearce, "'So Barbarous a Practice': Cornish Wrecking *ca.* 1700–1860, and Its Survival as Popular Myth" (PhD diss., University of Greenwich, 2007), 218.

10   Gay, *Old Falmouth*, 114.

11   Lysons and Lysons, "Parishes: Falmouth," 99–112.

12   National Records of Scotland, Edinburgh, GD152/160: Copy memorandum on "Avery the Pirate" and copy letter (December 27, 1700) by him in cipher addressed to "Rev James Richardson at the library over against Orenge Street, St Martin's-in-the-Fields, London," with note annexed of treasure-filled chests, Papers of the Hamilton-Bruce Family of Grange Hill and Falkland, c.1806.

13   Copy memorandum on "Avery the Pirate," National Records of Scotland, Edinburgh, GD152/160.

14   The code used in the "Avery the Pirate" letter of December 1700 does not match any seen by the authors in the British Library, London, such as those used by the Duke of Marlborough in 1706–1711 (Add MS 61151). Daniel Defoe's code book dated to October 1710 in the British Library starts with the number 52 (BL Add. MS. 70314, section 7); the "Avery the Pirate" letter's code mostly range between two and twenty-nine. It also has no master code book parallel amongst known diplomatic codes of the period: see http://cryptiana.web.fc2.com/code/glorious.htm. Or among John Falconer's *Cryptomenysis Patefacta* (1685): see Katherine Ellison, *Secret Writing in the Long Eighteenth Century: Theories and Practices of Cryptology*

(Cambridge: Cambridge University Press, 2022), 34–35, 65–66. Almost all extant examples post-date the letter in question.

15 John Richetti, *The Life of Daniel Defoe: A Critical Biography* (Oxford: Blackwel, 2005), 219.

16 John Tutchin, *The Foreigners. Part I a Poem* (London: A. Baldwin, 1700), 10.

17 Daniel Defoe, *The True-Born Englishman. A Satyr by Daniel Defoe* (Leeds: Alice Mann, 1836).

18 *The True-Born Englishman*, 15.

19 See F. Bastian, *Defoe's Early Life* (London: Macmillan, 1981), 225–26, for Defoe's possible trip to the Netherlands in summer or autumn 1701.

20 Bastian, *Defoe's Early Life*, 226–27.

21 Daniel Defoe, *A True Collection of the Writings of the Author of the True-Born Englishman* (London: n.p., 1703), 362.

22 Letter of Defoe to Harley in John Robert Moore, "Daniel Defoe: King William's Pamphleteer and Intelligence Agent," *Huntington Library Quarterly* 34, no. 3 (1971): 254.

23 *The True-Born-Hugonot: Or, Daniel de Foe. A Satyr* (London: n.p., 1703).

24 *By the King: A Proclamation for the Suppression of Coffee-Houses* (London: John Bill and Christopher Barker, 1675).

25 Maximillian E. Novak, *Daniel Defoe: Master of Fictions* (Oxford: Oxford University Press, 2001), 227.

26 Section 7, Cypher, October 20, 1710, British Library, London, BL Add. MS. 70314.

27 Paula R. Backscheider, "Daniel Defoe and Early Modern Intelligence," *Journal of Intelligence and National Security* 11, no.1 (1996): 5.

28 Backscheider, "Daniel Defoe and Early Modern Intelligence," 9.

29 Alan Marshall, "Robert Harley as Secretary of State and his Intelligence Work: 1702–1708," *History: The Journal of the Historical Association* (2023): 5.

30 Backscheider, "Daniel Defoe and Early Modern Intelligence," 15.

31 Bastian, *Defoe's Early Life*, 266.

32 George Harris Healey, ed., *The Letters of Daniel Defoe* (Oxford: Clarendon Press, 1955), 16.

33 Richetti, *The Life of Daniel Defoe*, 16.

34 Bastian, *Defoe's Early Life*, 99, 222.

35 Bastian, *Defoe's Early Life*, 222–23.

36 Bastian, *Defoe's Early Life*, 223.

37 Edward Bateson, *Calendar of State Papers: Domestic Series, of the Reign of William III, 1 April 1700–8* (London: HM Stationery Office, 1937), 178.

38 Bateson, *Calendar of State Papers: Domestic Series, 1700–8*, 155.

39 Bateson, *Calendar of State Papers: Domestic Series, 1700–8*, 185, 186.

40 John Beck, *The Falmouth Post Office Packet Service 1689–1850* (Exeter, UK: South West Maritime History Society, 2009), 2.

41 Bateson, *Calendar of State Papers: Domestic Series, 1700–8*, 173.

42 This quote was actually given by Captain Cranbey but is used here as artistic license: Thomas Slade to Mr. Tregeagle, MP, Falmouth, March 31, 1700, in Bateson, *Calendar of State Papers: Domestic Series, 1700–8*, 284.

43 Bateson, *Calendar of State Papers: Domestic Series, 1700–8*, 308.

44 Bastian, *Defoe's Early Life*, 242.

45 *The Apparent Danger of an Invasion, Briefly Represented in a Letter to a Minister of State. By a Kentish Gentleman* (London: A. Baldwin, 1701), 4.

46 Bateson, *Calendar of State Papers: Domestic Series, 1700–8*, 178.

47 Bateson, *Calendar of State Papers: Domestic Series, 1700–8*, 179.

48 King's proclamation, March 6, 1701, Kensington, in Bateson, *Calendar of State Papers: Domestic Series, 1700–8*, 245.

49 November 21, 1700, Whitehall, James Vernon to Postmasters-general, in Bateson, *Calendar of State Papers: Domestic Series, 1700–8*, 150.

Chapter 16: Spy Factory

1 *Strype's Survey of London, Volume II* (London: n.p., 1720), 73.

2 John Forster, *The Life of Jonathan Swift. Volume I, 1667–1711* (London: John Murray, 1875), 180.

3 Peter Hoare, "Archbishop Tenison's Library in St Martin's-in-the-Fields: The Building and its History," *London Topographical Record* 29 (2006): 128.

4 George H. Gater and F. R. Hiorns, *Survey of London: Volume 20, St. Martin-in-The-Fields, Part III: Trafalgar Square and Neighbourhood* (London: London County Council and the Committee for the Survey of the Memorials of Greater London, 1940), 112–14.

5 John Timbs, *Curiosities of London: Exhibiting the Most Rare and Remarkable Objects of Interest in the Metropolis* (London: Longman, Green, Reader, & Dyer, 1855), 463.

6 See the watercolor painting by Thomas Hosmer Shepherd, 1850.

7   Timbs, *Curiosities of London*, 463.

8   Edward Carpenter, *Thomas Tenison, Archbishop of Canterbury: His Life and Times* (London: Church Historical Society, 1948), 68.

9   Carpenter, *Thomas Tenison, Archbishop of Canterbury*, 69.

10   J. Raithby, ed., *Statutes of the Realm: Volume 7, 1695-1701*, (1820), 586-87.

11   Carpenter, *Thomas Tenison, Archbishop of Canterbury*, 70, 74.

12   Carpenter, *Thomas Tenison, Archbishop of Canterbury*, 76.

13   Carpenter, *Thomas Tenison, Archbishop of Canterbury*, 69.

14   Carpenter, *Thomas Tenison, Archbishop of Canterbury*, 69.

15   George Harris Healey, *The Letters of Daniel Defoe* (Oxford: Clarendon Press, 1955), 27: Daniel Defoe to Robert Harley, August 1704.

16   David Onnekink, *The Anglo-Dutch Favourite: The Careers of Hans Willem Bentinck, 1st Earl of Portland (1649–1709)* (London: Routledge, 2016), 153.

17   Onnekink, *Anglo-Dutch Favourite*, 15, 41, 153.

18   Tobias Smollett, *A Complete History of England* (London: James Rivington and James Fletcher, 1759), 375.

19   Louis Crompton, *Homosexuality and Civilization* (Cambridge, MA: Harvard University Press, 2006), 405, 408, 409, 410.

20   John Martin, *Beyond Belief: The Real Life of Daniel Defoe* (Pembroke Dock: Accent Press, 2006), 102.

21   Fred Sommer, "Anthony Blunt and Guy Burgess, Gay Spies," *Journal of Homosexuality* 29, no. 4 (1995): 273–94.

22   Gater and Hiorns, *Survey of London*, 109–11.

Chapter 17: State of the Union

1   F. Bastian, *Defoe's Early Life* (London: Macmillan, 1981), 251.

2   Pat Rogers, "Defoe in the Fleet Prison," *Review of English Studies* 22 (1971): 451–55.

3   Daniel Defoe, *The Shortest Way with the Dissenters; Or, Proposals for the Establishment of the Church* (London: n.p., 1702).

4   John Richetti, *The Life of Daniel Defoe: A Critical Biography* (Oxford: Blackwell, 2005), 21.

5   Richetti, *Life of Daniel Defoe*, 22.

6   George Harris Healey, *The Letters of Daniel Defoe* (Oxford: Clarendon Press, 1955), 1–2: To Daniel Finch, Earl of Nottingham, January 9, 1702.

7   Richetti, *Life of Daniel Defoe*, 23.

8   Richetti, *Life of Daniel Defoe*, 23.

9   Daniel Defoe, *The Fortunes and Misfortunes of the Famous Moll Flanders, &c* (London: W. Chetwood, 1722), 337.

10   Richetti, *Life of Daniel Defoe*, 26.

11   Richetti, *Life of Daniel Defoe*, 26.

12   Paula R. Backscheider, "Daniel Defoe and Early Modern Intelligence," *Journal of Intelligence and National Security* 11, no. 1 (1996): 4.

13   Richetti, *Life of Daniel Defoe*, 114.

14   Backscheider, "Daniel Defoe and Early Modern Intelligence," 6.

15   Richetti, *Life of Daniel Defoe*, 114.

16   The pass of freedom of movement from Lord Harley was a "Certificate as from the Office, that being Travailling on my Lawfull Occasions I may not be stopt by any Malitious persons on the Road—or which may be worse—Search't": Healey, *The Letters of Daniel Defoe*, 34: Daniel Defoe to Robert Harley, June 1705.

17   Richetti, *Life of Daniel Defoe*, 114.

18   Healey, *The Letters of Daniel Defoe*, 55: Robert Harley to Daniel Defoe, October 1706.

19   Healey, *The Letters of Daniel Defoe*, 68: Daniel Defoe to Robert Harley, November 26, 1706.

20   Backscheider, "Daniel Defoe and Early Modern Intelligence," 7.

21   Healey, *The Letters of Daniel Defoe*, 66: Daniel Defoe to Robert Harley, November 22, 1706; Ann McKim, *Defoe in Scotland: A Spy Among Us* (Dalkeith: Scottish Cultural Press, 2006).

22   Backscheider, "Daniel Defoe and Early Modern Intelligence," 7, 8.

23   Backscheider, "Daniel Defoe and Early Modern Intelligence," 15.

24   Richetti, *Life of Daniel Defoe*, 119.

25   Backscheider, "Daniel Defoe and Early Modern Intelligence," 8.

26   Backscheider, "Daniel Defoe and Early Modern Intelligence," 8.

27   Healey, *The Letters of Daniel Defoe*, 99: Daniel Defoe to Robert Harley, March 18, 1707.

28   Richetti, *Life of Daniel Defoe*, 118.

29   Healey, *The Letters of Daniel Defoe*, 56: Daniel Defoe to Robert Harley, October 24, 1706.

30   Richetti, *Life of Daniel Defoe*, 120.

31   Healey, *The Letters of Daniel Defoe*, 81: Defoe to Robert Harley, December 27, 1706.

32   John Gay, *Trivia; Or, the Art of Walking the Streets of London* (London: n.p., 1716), book 2, lines 221–26.

33   Richetti, *Life of Daniel Defoe*, 24.

34   Richetti, *Life of Daniel Defoe*, 337.

35   *A Hymn to the Pillory* (London: n.p., 1708), 5-6.

36   Bastian, *Defoe's Early Life*, 298.

Chapter 18: Smoke Screens

1   Neil Rennie, *Treasure Neverland: Real and Imaginary Pirates* (Oxford: Oxford University Press, 2013), 30; Frederick Burwick and Manushag N. Powell, *British Pirates in Print and Performance* (New York: Palgrave Macmillan, 2015), 30.

2   Charles Johnson, *The Successful Pyrate*, 2nd ed. (London: Bernard Lintott, 1713), 9–10.

3   Johnson, *The Successful Pyrate*, 61, 62.

4   John Timbs, *Club Life of London; with Anecdotes of the Clubs, Coffee-Houses and Taverns of the Metropolis during the 17th, 18th, and 19th Centuries, Volume II* (London: John Camden Hotten, 1871), 64–72.

5   Joseph Hatton, *Club-Land, London and Provincial* (London: J. S. Virtue & Co., 1890), 8.

6   Extract of Letter from my Lord Justice Porter, Dublin, August 2, 1696, National Archives, Kew, PC 1/46/2.

7   Adrian van Broeck, *The Life and Adventures of Capt. John Avery, the Famous English Pirate, (Rais'd from a Cabbin-Boy, to a King) Now in Possession of Madagascar* (London: n.p., 1709), 6.

8   For an overview of the various historical works published about Avery, see Richard Frohock, "The Early Literary Evolution of the Notorious Pirate Henry Avery," *Humanities* 9, no. 6 (2020): 3.

9   *Some Memoirs Concerning the Famous Pyrate Capt. Avery, with Remarks on St Lawrence, Otherwise Called Madagascar, and the Neighbouring Islands on Which He Now Resides* (Memoirs for the Curious, November 1708), 350.

10   *Some Memoirs Concerning the Famous Pyrate Capt. Avery*, 344–53.

11   van Broeck, *Life and Adventures of Capt. John Avery*, 10.

12   van Broeck, *Life and Adventures of Capt. John Avery*, 12.

13   van Broeck, *Life and Adventures of Capt. John Avery*, 12.

14   van Broeck, *Life and Adventures of Capt. John Avery*, 12.

15   van Broeck, *Life and Adventures of Capt. John Avery*, 12.

16   van Broeck, *Life and Adventures of Capt. John Avery*, 14.

17   van Broeck, *Life and Adventures of Capt. John Avery*, 6.

18   van Broeck, *Life and Adventures of Capt. John Avery*, 14.

19   Margarette Lincoln, "Henry Every and the Creation of the Pirate Myth in Early Modern Britain," in *The Golden Age of Piracy. The Rise, Fall, and Enduring Popularity of Pirates*, ed. David Head (Athens: University of Georgia Press, 2018), 173, 177.

20   John Avery, *The King of Pirates: Being an Account of the Famous Enterprises of Captain Avery, the Mock King of Madagascar* (London: A. Bettesworth, 1719), iii.

21   Joshua Grasso, "The Providence of Pirates: Defoe and the 'True-Bred Merchant,'" *Digital Defoe: Studies in Defoe & His Contemporaries* 2, no. 1 (2010): 22–23.

22   Avery, *The King of Pirates*, 1.

23   Avery, *The King of Pirates*, 34.

24   Avery, *The King of Pirates*, 44.

25   Avery, *The King of Pirates*, 74.

26   Avery, *The King of Pirates*, 80, 93.

27   Charles Johnson, *A General History of the Pyrates*, 2 (London: T. Warner, 1724), 45.

28   Johnson, *General History of the Pyrates*, 55–56.

29   Whitehall, February 28, 1697, National Archives, Kew, CO 323/2/574.

30   Abstract of Papers Relating to Piracy in the East Indies, National Archives, Kew, CO 323/2/274; Fortescue, Volume 16, 226–27.

31   Daniel Defoe, *A Review of the State of the British Union, Vol. IV, No. 107, October 16, 1707*, 549.

32   Defoe, *A Review of the State of the British Union, Vol. IV, No. 108, October 18, 1707*, 552, 554.

33   Manuel R. Schonhorn, "Defoe's Pirates: A New Source," *Review of English Studies* 14, no. 56 (1963): 387; Grasso, "Providence of Pirates," 25.

Chapter 19: Hunting Treasure

1   William John Hardy, *Calendar of State Papers: Domestic Series, of the Reign of William III, 1 January–31 December 1696* (London: HM Stationery Office, 1913), 319–20.

2   Another nineteenth-century account of Henry Avery's treasure appears in a letter in the Kresen Kernow Archive, Redruth, Cornwall, J/2277. The letter claims the treasure was buried near the Lizard. The text is written in a different hand than the Avery the Pirate letter of 1700 and not in code. It seems likely that the author of the suspicious Kresen Kernow document saw the list thought to have been discovered by Professor John Bruce and created a forgery.

3   National Archives, Kew, PC 2/77, February 17, 1697.

4   E. Bateson, ed., *Calendar of State Papers. Domestic Series of the Reign of William III, 1 April 1700-8 March, 1702* (London: His Majesty's Stationery Office, 1937), 216: Whitehall, February 7, 1701.

5   Bateson, *Calendar of State Papers, of William III, 1*, 231: Whitehall, February 22, 1701.

6   *Notice of John Knill of Gray's Inn, 1733–1811* (London: n.p., 1871), 10.

7   *Notice of John Knill*, 9; Sabine Baring-Gould, *Cornish Characters and Strange Events* (New York: John Lane, 1909), 171–73.

8   "Fisherman Finds Pirate Treasure," *Boston Herald*, February 23, 1932; "Pirate Gold in the Bahamas," *Milwaukee Journal*, March 7, 1932.

9   Andrew Barker, "Treasure without Glitter: The *Whydah* Gally," *Wreckwatch* 9, no. 19 (Winter 2021–2022): 84–85.

Epilogue

1   Daniel De Foe, *The History of the Union between England and Scotland* (London: John Stockdale, 1786), 2.

2   John Richetti, *The Life of Daniel Defoe: A Critical Biography* (Oxford: Blackwell, 2005), 140.

3   Brian Fitzgerald, *Daniel Defoe: A Study in Conflict* (Chicago: Henry Regnery Co., 1955), 171, 173.

4   Angus McInnes, "The Political Ideas of Robert Harley," *History* 50, no. 170 (1965): 310.

5   Tsim Keirn, "Daniel Defoe and the Royal African Company," *Historical Research* 61, no. 145 (1988): 246.

6   James Maghee to Captain John Ogilvie, Stuart vol. 5, 1717.

7   Matthias Pohlig, "The Uses and Utility of Intelligence: The Case of the British Government during the War of the Spanish Succession," *Journal of Intelligence History* 21, no. 3 (2022): 289–305.

8   Stuart vol. 6, 568.

9   Stuart vol. 7, 13.

10   Stuart vol. 8, 13.

11   Stuart vol. 8, 568.

12   Marcus Rediker, "Libertalia: The Pirate's Utopia," in *Pirates: Terror on the High Seas—From the Caribbean to the South China Sea*, ed. David Cordingly (Atlanta: Turner Publishing Inc., 1996), 128.

13   Barry Clifford and Kenneth J. Kinkor, *Real Pirates: The Untold Story of the Whydah from Slave Ship to Pirate Ship* (Washington, DC: National Geographic), 2007.

14   David D. Moore, "Captain Edward Thatch: A Brief Analysis of the Primary Source Documents Concerning the Notorious Blackbeard," *North Carolina Historical Review* 95, no. 2 (2018): 184–85.

15   Jeremy Moss, *The Life and Tryals of the Gentleman Pirate, Major Stede Bonnet* (Virginia Beach, VA: Koehler Books, 2020), 174.

16   Charles Johnson, *A General History of the Pyrates*, 2 (London: T. Warner, 1724), 149, 156, 165.

17   Carl Allen, Michael Pateman, James Sinclair, Dan Porter, and Sean Kingsley, *Ocean Marvels of the Bahamas* (Grand Bahama: Allen Exploration, 2023), 100.

18   George Francis Dow and John Henry Edmonds, *The Pirates of the New England Coast, 1630–1730* (New York: Dover Publications, 1996), 201.

19   Robert Francis Seybolt, Jonathan Barlow, and Nicholas Simons, "Captured by Pirates: Two Diaries of 1724–1725," *New England Quarterly* 2, no. 4 (1929): 659.

20   William John Hardy, *Calendar of State Papers: Domestic Series, of the Reign of William and Mary, 1693* (London: HM Stationery Office, 1903), 44.

21   William John Hardy, *Calendar of State Papers: Domestic Series, of the Reign of William and Mary, 1694–1695* (London: HM Stationery Office, 1906), 226.

22   Hardy, *Calendar of State Papers: Domestic Series, 1694–1695*, 226.

23   Moss, *Life and Tryals of the Gentleman Pirate, Major Stede Bonnet*, 7.

24   Moore, "Captain Edward Thatch," 151–52.

25   Edward Theophilus Fox, "'Piratical Schemes and Contracts': Pirate Articles and Their Society, 1660–1730" (PhD diss., University of Exeter, 2013), 324–25.

26   Laura A. Curtis, *The Elusive Daniel Defoe* (Old Woking, UK: Unwin Brothers Ltd., 1984), 113.

27   "List of Piracies; Taken from the *Boston Daily Advertiser*, since January 1, 1819," *Naval Intelligencer*, January 1, 1820.

28   Cindy Vallar, *Woodes Rogers Circumnavigator, Privateer, Author, & Governor* (2021): http://www.cindyvallar.com/WoodesRogers.html.

29   *Boston Daily Advertiser*, August 16, 1819.

30   *Royal Gazette*, April 10, 1819.

31   Fox, "Piratical Schemes and Contracts," 306–26.

Index